SOCIAL POLICY REVIEW 18

Analysis and debate in social policy, 2006

Edited by Linda Bauld, Karen Clarke and
Tony Maltby

First published in Great Britain in June 2006 by

The Policy Press
University of Bristol
Fourth Floor, Beacon House
Queen's Road
Bristol BS8 1QU

Tel +44 (0)117 331 4054
Fax +44 (0)117 331 4093
e-mail tpp-info@bristol.ac.uk
www.policypress.org.uk

British Library Cataloguing in Publication Data
A catalogue record for this book is available from the British Library.

Library of Congress Cataloging-in-Publication Data
A catalog record for this book has been requested.

ISBN-10 1 86134 843 6 paperback
ISBN-13 978 1 86134 843 2 paperback
ISBN-10 1 86134 844 4 hardcover
ISBN-13 978 1 86134 844 9 hardcover

The right of Linda Bauld, Karen Clarke and Tony Maltby to be identified as editors of this work has been asserted by them in accordance with the 1988 Copyright, Designs and Patents Act.

The statements and opinions contained within this publication are solely those of the editors and contributors and not of The University of Bristol or The Policy Press. The University of Bristol and The Policy Press disclaim responsibility for any injury to persons or property resulting from any material published in this publication.

The Policy Press works to counter discrimination on grounds of gender, race, disability, age and sexuality.

Cover design by Qube Design Associates, Bristol.
Front cover: view of The Great Court, British Museum kindly supplied by Luca Pellanda (www.FluidDesignLab.com).
Printed and bound in Great Britain by MPG Books, Bodmin.

Contents

Part 3: Ageing and employment

List of figures and tables

Figures

Tables

List of contributors

Mel Ainscow is Professor of Education in the University of Manchester, UK (www.education.manchester.ac.uk/academicstaff furtherinfomation,16371,en.htm).

Linda Bauld is a senior lecturer in public policy in the Department of Urban Studies, University of Gl;asgow, UK (www.gla.ac.uk/ departments/urbanstudies/staff/bauldl.html).

Tania Burchardt is a senior research fellow in the ESRC Research Centre for Analysis of Social Exclusion, London School of Economics and Political Science, UK (http://sticerd.lse.ac.uk/case/).

Elaine Cameron is a senior lecturer in the Centre for Applied Social Research, University of Wolverhampton, UK.

Karen Clarke is a senior lecturer in social policy in the School of Social Sciences, University of Manchester, UK (www.socialsciences.manchester.ac.uk/politics/about/staff_profiles/ Karen_Clarke.htm).

David Craig is a senior lecturer in the Department of Sociology, University of Auckland, New Zealand (www.arts.auckland.ac.nz/staff/ index.cfm?S=STAFF_dcra009).

Robert A. Cummins is a Professor of Psychology in the School of Psychology, Deakin University, Melbourne, Australia (www.deakin.edu.au/hbs/psychology/ staffprofiles.php?username=cummins).

Paul Dornan is Head of Policy and Research at the Child Poverty Action Group (www.cpag.org.uk).

Alan Dyson is Professor of Education in the School of Education, University of Manchester, UK (www.education.manchester.ac.uk/ academicstaff/furtherinformation,47102,en.htm).

Caroline Glendinning is Professor of Social Policy in the Social Policy Research Unit, University of York, UK (www.york.ac.uk/inst/spru/profiles/cg.htm).

Patrick Grattan is Chief Executive of The Age and Employment Network (TAEN) (www.taen.org.uk).

Kirstin Kerr is a research associate in the Centre for Equity in Education, School of Education, University of Manchester, UK (www.manchester.ac.uk/academicstaff).

Anna L.D. Lau is an assistant professor in the Department of Rehabilitation Sciences, Hong Kong Polytechnic University (www.rs.polyu.edu.hk/personnel/OT/annalau.htm).

Ruth McDonald is a research fellow at the National Primary Care Research and Development Centre, University of Manchester, UK (www.npcrdc.man.ac.uk/staffDetail.cfm?ID=88).

John Macnicol is Visiting Professor in Social Policy at the London School of Economics and Political Science.

Tony Maltby is a senior lecturer in social policy at the Institute of Applied Social Studies, University of Birmingham, UK (www.spsw.bham.ac.uk/members/Staff.asp?stID=33).

Jonathan Mathers is the deputy director of the Health Impact Assessment Research Unit in the Department of Public Health and Epidemiology at the University of Birmingham, UK (www.phintranet.bham.ac.uk/directory/homepage.htm?id=49).

Robin Means is the Associate Dean for Research and International Developments in the Faculty of Health and Social Care at the University of the West of England, Bristol, UK (www.uwe.ac.uk/hsc/index.asp?pageid=734).

Janet Newman is Professor of Social Policy in the Faculty of Social Sciences, The Open University, UK (www.open.ac.uk/socialsciences/staff/jnewman/).

Jayne Parry is a senior lecturer and director of the Health Impact Assessment Research Unit at the University of Birmingham, UK (www.phintranet.bham.ac.uk/directory/homepage.htm?id=46).

Chris Phillipson is Professor of Applied Social Sciences and Social Gerontology in the School of Criminology, Education, Sociology and Social Work at Keele University, UK (www.keele.ac.uk/depts/so/staff/chris_phillipson.htm).

Kerry Platman is a senior research associate in the Faculty of Social and Political Sciences, University of Cambridge, UK (www.sps.cam.ac.uk/stafflist/kplatman.html).

Deborah Quilgars is a senior research fellow in the Centre for Housing Policy, University of York, UK (www.york.ac.uk/inst/chp/Staff/quilgars.htm).

Mark Stephens is Assistant Director and Professor of European Housing in the Centre for Housing Policy, University of York, UK (www.york.ac.uk/inst/chp/Staff/stephens.htm).

Philip Taylor is a senior research associate and Executive Director of the Cambridge Interdisciplinary Research Centre on Ageing at the University of Cambridge, UK (www.sps.cam.ac.uk/stafflist/ptaylor_profile.html).

Elizabeth Vidler is a research fellow in the Faculty of Social Sciences, The Open University, UK.

Introduction

Linda Bauld, Karen Clarke and Tony Maltby

This is the third *Social Policy Review* (*SPR*) to follow the new structure initially introduced in *SPR 16*. It includes three sections. Part 1 provides a review of key policy developments during 2005 in the main areas of UK social policy: education, health, housing, the personal social services and social security. Part 2 draws on current research in social policy, including chapters that use empirical findings to explore key policy issues or challenges. Part 3 explores a contemporary policy theme selected by the *SPR* editors.

This year, Part 2 examines the broad theme of health and well-being, in particular different ways of defining, measuring and applying concepts of health and well-being. The chapters themselves are drawn from a selection of presentations at the Social Policy Association conference held at the University of Bath in June 2005.

Part 3 of *SPR 18* examines the theme of employment and later life. This is a particularly fast-changing area of social policy in the UK and beyond. The collection of chapters in Part 3 provides a key contemporary resource for researchers interested in this area of policy.

Part I

Karen Clarke edited Part 1 of *SPR 18*. It examines the main developments in social policy in relation to five key areas of welfare provision in 2005. A number of common themes emerge from these chapters that characterise the Labour government in its third term in office. The first is the centrality of individual choice as the means for accessing and shaping services across health, housing, social care and education. Choice is significant in government policy not only as the means for enabling market mechanisms to bring about an improvement in the quality and diversity of services, but also as a way of promoting a particular conception of active and responsible citizenship, and encouraging the virtues of independence and autonomy. The centrality of the individual citizen-consumer has been accompanied by a gradual transformation in the role of local authorities from their traditional role as service providers, through their role in the 1990s as purchasers of services on behalf of service users, to a more strategic managerial role with responsibility for assessing likely needs and ensuring that provision from a variety of sources is available to meet those needs, in a way that leaves the specific choice of service to the individual. Developments in 2005 look likely to further change the role of individual service departments into one of providing guidance and support to individuals (such as parents, carers, disabled adults and older people) about how to exercise the increasing degree of choice and responsibility that policies have accorded them. The emphasis on individual choice and market mechanisms carries the danger of raising public expectations about service entitlement. In both health and social care, the role of professionals in assessing need and acting as gatekeepers to services that are limited by resources will continue to sit uneasily alongside the active, empowered citizen-consumer.

Chapter One by Caroline Glendinning and Robin Means examines policy developments in 2005 in social care for adults and older people, focusing on three key policy documents covering disabled people, adult social care and older people. The policies proposed seek to promote active citizenship, social inclusion, independence, an improved quality of life and enhanced well-being. Services relevant to these aims are envisaged as extending more broadly than those that have traditionally been considered the province of social care provision, including resources such as leisure, transport and housing support. In the case of older people, social care is conceived as having preventative aims and therefore seeks to include people with much lower levels of dependency than hitherto. A major new development in 2005 has been the introduction on a pilot basis of individual budgets. These are intended to address the past failures of social services departments to deliver fully user-centred services by giving service users the means to choose the services they want using a budget based on the value of their total service entitlement. Pilot individual budget schemes have been introduced in 13 local authority areas in England. While there is evidence from the experience of direct payments that giving service users direct financial control over the services they receive produces benefits in terms of well-being and quality of life, Glendinning and Means identify a number of important problems in using individual consumer choice in quasi-markets as the means for ensuring equitable and appropriate social care provision. They also identify some important unresolved issues about the relationship between the direction of policy in relation to social care and current developments in the health service.

In Chapter Two, Ruth McDonald discusses developments in health policy. Her chapter makes clear that individual choice has a number of different roles to play in healthcare. The introduction of patient choice combined with payment by results further extends the use of market mechanisms as the means for achieving quality, responsiveness and efficiency in hospital care. Paradoxically, however, payment by results, which is a means of trying to contain costs, also creates incentives for individual hospitals to increase their activity, particularly those that can deliver procedures at less than the price that has been fixed, and thereby retain the surplus that they make. The containment of demand reintroduces the professional through the gatekeeping role of general practitioners (GPs) who control access to hospital care. Here the introduction of practice-based commissioning is intended to act as a mechanism for controlling demand for secondary care. This is combined with the provision of an increasing range of services in primary care settings, so that services are visible and delivered as close to the patient as possible. However, McDonald argues that this is again likely to increase demand for services from those with less severe conditions and increase costs because of the loss of the economies of scale. Furthermore, these developments may run counter to the government's goal of reducing health inequalities.

The second way in which individual choice has a part to play within health care is through the individual citizen taking responsibility for his or her health and well-being by choosing to live a healthy lifestyle. The implication of the Wanless Reports and of the Expert Patient Programme is that healthy living and the management of chronic sickness lie in the hands of the informed individual who is to take responsibility for making appropriate choices to ensure their health, with the role of the state being limited to the provision of information and intervention where citizens cannot be trusted (for example, in the introduction of a ban on smoking in public places). It remains to be seen whether the role of central government can be confined to regulation of service provision managed by a combination of reorganised primary care trusts and strategic health authorities, commissioning services from a range of providers, including the private sector, and with the management of patient demand regulated by GPs operating within practice-level budgets.

In their chapter on education policy (Chapter Three), Alan Dyson, Kirstin Kerr and Mel Ainscow argue that the Labour government has reached a pivotal point in its third term, in relation to its two long-standing objectives of raising educational performance, while also reducing social class differences in attainment. Evidence on progress towards these objectives in 2005 was mixed, with some indications that measurement of pupil performance in terms of test and examination results had produced some perverse effects and that social inequalities in educational outcomes had increased rather than decreased. They argue that the 2005 Schools White Paper proposed two somewhat contradictory mechanisms for attaining the objective of excellence and equity. On the one hand, there is the mechanism of parental choice and the reliance, again, on the quasi-market to produce improved educational standards and performance. On this model the autonomous, independent trust school has to compete with other schools for pupils. The role of the local education authority is limited to providing advice to parents to help them exercise choice. On the other hand, there is evidence from initiatives such as the Education Improvement Partnerships of schools being encouraged to cooperate with each other and coordinate provision. The extended schools prospectus, launched in 2005, proposes the development of integrated child and family services based in schools. Here the local education authority may have a more extensive role in coordinating a range of services provided through schools and responding to local community needs. Dyson and colleagues argue that the Schools White Paper presents a challenge for educationalists and others to exploit some of the opportunities and contradictions in the policies proposed and in the process to identify ways of bringing about greater equity in outcomes.

The polarisation of housing tenure between owner-occupation and a residual social housing sector that started with the Thatcher government's Right to Buy policy has continued unchecked under the three Labour administrations. Mark Stephens and Deborah Quilgars (Chapter Four) argue that Labour lacks a coherent strategy in relation to housing policy, and that government policy in relation to social housing, home ownership and homelessness is marked by a degree of contradiction and incoherence. In social housing, as in other areas of social welfare, the role of the local authority has become that of strategic management rather than provision. The choice agenda has been pursued through the piloting of reform to Housing Benefit, in the form of the Local Housing Allowance, which offers a standard payment fixed according to family circumstances and local rents. The idea is that this offers claimants a 'choice' in terms of the quality and quantity of housing they consume (although, in practice, little choice about the provider). However, Stephens and Quilgars point out that current conditions fail to offer genuine choice for all, both in terms of the range of choice available and the adequacy of income to support choices about quality and quantity. Housing supply remains the most significant factor limiting the achievement of the government's target of increasing home ownership. Increasing house building is being left to the private sector, with some measures introduced to assist those entering the housing market for the first time. However, as the authors point out, without these policies being linked carefully to managing the supply of housing, they run the risk of simply driving house prices up further. The

Supporting People programme introduced by the Labour government has been an important initiative providing support for those who would otherwise have difficulty in maintaining a tenancy, and is therefore a significant way of reducing homelessness. Cuts to the programme budget in 2005, combined with the increasing use of the provisions of the antisocial behaviour legislation to evict tenants or curtail tenancies, highlight contradictions in this area of housing policy between control and support for families or individuals with 'problem' behaviour.

The final chapter in Part One examines developments in social security policy in 2005. Dornan discusses the continuation of the government's primary focus on reducing poverty through paid work, supplemented with means-tested benefits in the form of tax credits. These cover an increasingly wide range of those in low-paid work, following the extension of the working tax credit to those without children. The greatly extended role of Her Majesty's Revenue and Customs (HMRC) in delivering social security in the form of tax credits is identified by Dornan as a significant development in social security policy. It involves extending the department's role to one of distributing income as well as collecting revenue, and in the process dealing with a significantly poorer population with different needs and expectations than the traditional client base of the Inland Revenue. This in turn raises issues about the culture of HMRC and its relationship to clients, which has hitherto been very different from that in the Department for Work and Pensions. The recovery of over-payments of tax credits in 2005 continued to present major problems for poor families, for whom an annual model of income is highly problematic. The substantial role of HMRC in social security is one aspect of a more general development, which is the dispersal of responsibility for social security across a wide range of departments, with different ways of assessing income, adding to the complexities of the social security system for users. The issue of choice, which has been identified as a central theme in other areas of welfare provision, has a place in social security policy in the introduction of policies to promote savings, which is seen by the government as increasing choice and opportunity in the future. The Child Trust Fund, introduced in April 2005, is intended to provide all children born after April 2002 with an asset at the age of 18 that can be used to take up opportunities such as training or education. It can also be seen as seeking to promote particular forms of prudent financial behaviour. Interestingly, however, Dornan reports that in the first six months of the scheme only just over half of the vouchers issued had actually been invested by parents on behalf of their children.

Part 2

Linda Bauld edited Part 2 of *SPR 18*. Each of the chapters in this section was presented at the 2005 Social Policy Association annual conference held at the University of Bath. Within the overall conference theme of 'well-being and social justice', we identified a number of chapters that focused on specific aspects of measuring, conceptualising or understanding health and well-being. The result is a section that includes five varied contributions from authors based in the UK, Australia and New Zealand.

What these five chapters have in common is a focus on locating our understanding of 'good health' in a wider social context. Several chapters outline findings from empirical research that seeks to add to knowledge about how we define health and the role of citizens and communities in promoting or maintaining key aspects of health. There is an emphasis in the latter chapters in this section on understanding the links between health and the broader concept of well-being, and how well-being can be measured and conceptualised in policy terms.

Part 2 begins with a chapter from Janet Newman and Elizabeth Vidler examining issues of choice and consumerism in health care in England. The chapter draws on findings from an Economic and Social Research Council/Arts and Humanities Research Board study to illustrate how primary health care is responding to pressures to develop a more consumerist approach. The study draws on an analysis of policy documents, interviews with senior health service managers, front-line staff and service users in two English towns. The research asks to what extent an image of the modern consumer and the need for a 'modern' health service reflect a pre-existent reality or something new. The authors conclude that, despite adherence to some of the 'traditional' values of the National Health Service, there is evidence of a shift in both language and understanding of the role of patient or service user and that this may represent a changing relationship between patients and providers.

Chapter Seven in Part 2 also draws on empirical evidence regarding professionals and service users' views. Elaine Cameron, Jonathan Mathers and Jayne Parry draw on the results of a Department of Health-funded study to explore understanding of health and well-being from the perspective of community members and professionals. The chapter begins by describing how the literature on concepts of health and illness has broadened in recent years to include a growing focus on positive health and well-being. The authors argue that specific definitions of positive health are, however, difficult to identify. Using findings from the HealthCounts study, they argue that further work is needed to develop theoretical frameworks around positive health. They found that concepts of well-being in themselves were not sufficient unless well specified, and were closely linked with formal or official discourse rather than individual or community views. The authors argue that lay accounts of positive health can help to broaden our understanding of health and its influences as well as improve its measurement, and suggest that further research in this area is needed, particularly at the community level.

Tania Burchardt's chapter (Chapter Eight) on happiness and social policy forms the third chapter in this part. She asks whether happiness is a useful way to conceptualise well-being, and whether its promotion is an appropriate goal for social policy. The chapter draws on a review of literature from a number of disciplines. It begins by introducing the 'economics of happiness' and describes indicators commonly used to measure subjective well-being (SWB). It then reviews empirical findings on the determinants of SWB and their policy implications, suggesting that policy should re-examine some areas or topics that have traditionally been given little attention. Burchardt reflects on the evidence and concludes that promoting SWB or happiness as an explicit policy objective would be mistaken. She argues that happiness as a policy goal is probably inadequate if we consider how opportunities or resources should be distributed in society, particularly if the concern is to examine the role of policy in addressing various forms of inequality.

In Chapter Nine, Robert Cummins and Anna Lau also explore the issue of SWB. In contrast with Burchardt's focus on the relevance of SWB as a possible policy goal, they examine issues of measurement. They review and critique different measures of health and well-being and explain the relevance of a measure of SWB for social policy. The chapter begins by describing how the concepts of mental health and quality of life have evolved within medicine and the social sciences. It then offers a critique of two of the most commonly used measures, Quality Adjusted Life Years and Health-related Quality of Life. Cummins and Lau go on to describe the concept of SWB and its measurement, drawing on their own work as part of the International Wellbeing Group in developing the 'Personal Wellbeing Index' (PWI). They explore the relevance of SWB measurement for social policy and argue that the development of new measures, such as the PWI, can inform policy decisions by providing comparable data about perceived quality of life across different groups in the population and between different communities.

The final chapter in Part 2 returns to a more general conception of well-being by examining the development and implementation of a local 'well-being strategy' in New Zealand. David Craig places well-being within a wider political and social context and illustrates how both the interpretation and application of the concept are shaped by context. In political terms, Craig describes the promotion of well-being in 'third way' New Zealand as part of a move away from conservative, neoliberal ideology towards a more inclusive social democratic approach. This is intended to involve building the capacity of individuals and reconstructing community relations, while retaining market reforms. 'Local' well-being is achieved through partnership, with a range of local and national actors working in collaboration to improve communities.

Craig's chapter focuses on the community well-being strategy of Waitakere City, a suburb of Auckland. He draws on a four-year study examining local partnerships and governance issues in Waitakere, in particular research examining the Waitakere community well-being process. He locates research findings within a broader review of New Zealand's shifts from a Keynesian liberal welfare regime to one influenced by New Institutional Economics and New Public Management, followed by a more recent shift to a 'social development' approach. He provides a critique of this approach and the place of well-being within it, drawing parallels with policy developments in the UK and elsewhere.

Part 3

The final section of this year's *SPR*, edited by Tony Maltby and featuring some of the leading researchers in this field, focuses on an often neglected area of social policy, yet one that will increasingly dominate the contemporary news agenda and that has long-term implications for social policy – employment and later life. All the chapters were completed before January 2006 and can therefore only present a snapshot of what is a very rapidly developing policy area, so inevitably there will be some omissions. For example, as they went to press, the latest welfare reform Green Paper *A New Deal for Welfare: Empowering People to Work* was published, setting out, among other things, the reform of Incapacity Benefits and how the 80 per cent employment rate 'aspiration' would be achieved. Clearly, both are of direct relevance to the range of policy-related issues discussed in this themed section.

Chris Phillipson opens this section with a general review of the pertinent issues and prospects for social and public policy on age and employment. Distilled from his (and Allison Smith's) longer and more detailed review for the Department for Work and Pensions (Phillipson and Smith, 2005), this chapter is an attempt to place this whole section in an appropriate context and provide the non-expert reader some insights into the literature and this debate. He first outlines the current issues around work and retirement, then considers the many social policy initiatives that have acted as drivers to the removal or 'exit' of workers from the labour market: the so-called 'push' and 'pull' factors. He then details how social policy, particularly since 1997, has been encouraging and promoting the exact opposite, the extension to working life. Phillipson presents these trends by unambiguously documenting the growing body of work on this area. A reduction in supply-side shocks, mainly in manufacturing associated with the 1980s, changes to the supply of pensions – particularly the shift from defined benefit to defined contribution (occupational) schemes – combined with the increased shift to state means testing via the Supplementary Pension then Minimum Income Guarantee to the current Pension Credit. Increased poor health is one of the major factors for early exit from the labour force and an increased acknowledgement of age management, of better ergonomic design and better occupational health, in short better 'workability' (see, for example, Ilmarinen and Tuomi, 2004), is seen by many commentators as the way ahead to the sustainability of employment, a point noted by Phillipson in his review.

Like the majority of the contributors to this section, he suggests that the 20th century marked out a period in which the traditional notion of retirement became the norm. This was characterised by payment of a pension from the state and combined with a sudden 'cliff edge' break from the world of employment enshrined via the Beveridge 'retirement condition'. Indeed, the past century should be regarded as the one that created retirement as a phase of the lifecycle and with it the development of a structured dependency (cf the work of Walker, Phillipson, Townsend in Estes et al, 2003).

However, later life in the current century may (looking at present trends) be one with increased quality of life in old age, financially supported through paid work and supplemented with a pension. More importantly it will see a wholesale shift in our current understanding of retirement, of the 'traditional' view. Indeed, since the mid-1980s, this trend has been noted. Since then, the state has been withdrawing from providing pensions, shifting this responsibility to the private sector and focusing its support on means testing. Increasingly, the divide between employment and retirement is not as much the clean break that it previously was. Retirement, at least within the Western European setting, can and should be a period of life now extending to an average 30 years (plus) (Pensions Commission, 2004, Figure 2.8). Ideally, with increasing longevity and better health, it is also a time with better quality of life and one where active ageing

(Walker, 2002) can be fully achieved. As the World Health Organization slogan says, 'Years have been added to life, now we must add life to years'.

John Macnicol's chapter (Chapter Twelve) then offers us an insightful historical analysis of the debate. He first outlines the age legislation linking it to four discernable trends: declining economic activity rates, demographic imperatives post-2020 with the associated increased pension costs, skills shortages and rising life expectancy. This leads him to consider its timing and by outlining the recent history of the legislation, evaluates some of the tensions in the age discrimination debate and what has come to be called ageism set within an historical discourse. Based on US experience of similar age legislation, he argues that the difficulty has often been providing legally verifiable proof. He further suggests that the uniqueness of the British 'welfare state', built up over centuries, has resulted in a contradictory assemblage of both positive and negative age-based discriminatory welfares. He therefore suggests that rather than a problem of discrimination, if viewed historically it has more to do with the economics of supply and demand of labour between different sectors of the economy and regional variations. Thus he concludes by suggesting that the focus of the debate should be on the long-term structural labour market shifts and patterns that have 'de-industrialised older men' (p 264).

In Chapter Thirteen, Kerry Platman and Philip Taylor consider an important yet neglected area within this debate – that of training and lifelong learning. They review the recent efforts to support and promote the wider incorporation of training within the employment sphere, focusing on the range of training providers. Our own recently completed work (Admasachew et al, 2005) has also highlighted the lack of attention most employers give to this area of career development for the 50+ cohort.

The chapter continues with an incisive assessment of the role the age legislation, to be introduced late in 2006, will have on current understandings. As the authors state, 'Ageing societies need to ensure that their oldest workers have the skills and training necessary for them to participate in employment' (p 286).

The final chapter presents a forthright, non-academic perspective on the debate from the position of an influential lobbying organisation. Patrick Grattan was directly involved in advising government on the age legislation to be introduced from October 2006, and his chapter completes the set by recounting the establishment, development and running of the leading pressure group in this area, The Age and Employment Network. He views the rapid growth of interest in this area as largely a positive phenomenon since 1997, and observes the many business gains, particularly for those firms and their employees who have ignored the stereotype. He regards this as a win–win relationship (but for a discussion, see Bloom et al, 2006). The chapter outlines the key campaigning issues for the organisation and in particular raises those salient issues, or as he more vividly puts it, 'tricky issues about making the job market a better place for people in mid- and later working life' (p 302). This indeed is the nub for future development in this policy area. It is not simply a question of better pensions (although vitally important) but, crucially, improving working lives across the lifecourse, making them more fulfilling across generations through the adoption and integration of a preventative approach – the workability approach.

References

Admasachew, L., Ogilvie, M. and Maltby, T. (2005) *The Employability of Workers over 50: Issues of Access, Retention and Progression*, Birmingham: University of Birmingham/Equal/European Social Fund/Forward.

Bloom, N., Kretschmer, T. and van Reenen, J. (2006) *Work–Life Balance, Management Practices and Productivity*, London: Centre for Economic Performance, London School of Economics and Political Science.

Estes, C., Biggs, S. and Phillipson, C. (2003) *Social Theory, Social Policy and Ageing: A Critical Introduction*, Buckingham: Open University Press.

Ilmarinen, J. and Tuomi, K. (2004) 'Past, present and future of work ability', *People and Work Research Reports*, vol 65, pp 1-25.

Pensions Commission, (2004) *Pensions: Challenges and Choices, First Report of the Pensions Commission*, London: The Stationery Office.

Phillipson, C. and Smith, A. (2005) *Extending Working Life: A Review of the Research Literature*, DWP Research Report No 299, London.

Walker, A. (2002) 'A strategy for active ageing', *International Social Security Review*, vol 55, no 1, pp 121-39.

Part I
Key areas of social policy

ONE

Personal social services: developments in adult social care

Caroline Glendinning and Robin Means

Introduction

This chapter discusses proposals published during 2005 that will potentially transform the organisation and delivery of social care services for adults and older people in England. The chapter locates these proposals within broader historical and organisational contexts and analyses their implications – for the 1993 community care 'settlement'; for the role of social care within wider local authority responsibilities; and for the interfaces between social care and health care.

Historical contexts

The main community care measures in the 1990 National Health Service (NHS) and Community Care Act came into force on 1 April 1993. The Act gave local authority social services departments lead responsibility for supporting older people, disabled adults and people with mental health problems and learning disabilities. This responsibility included the assessment of individual and locality-wide needs, and the development of a 'mixed economy' of voluntary and for-profit services – particularly domiciliary services – that would be purchased flexibly by the local authority. Social services departments were also required to work in close collaboration with a wide range of other agencies, including health and housing. This settlement was the outcome of a long-standing debate that had been framed by key policy documents, including *Making a Reality of Community Care* (Audit Commission, 1986), *Community Care: An Agenda for Action* (Griffiths Report, 1988) and the White Paper on *Caring for People: Community Care in the Next Decade and Beyond* (DH, 1989).

The drivers behind this settlement were complex but are widely considered to include three main factors. The first was government frustration at the slowness of moving people with mental health problems and learning disabilities out of long-stay hospitals into the community, a problem often explained in terms of the failure of joint working between health and social services (Means et al, 2002). The second was concern at the mushrooming public expenditure costs of supporting people in independent sector residential and nursing homes through a social security system that conducted no assessment of the need for such care. The 1993 changes therefore gave social services departments responsibility for assessing needs, together with a cash limited budget with which to purchase services in response to eligible needs. 'The primary imperative for the Government [was] to find the least bad option for capping social security payments to private residential care'; hence the changes owed 'more to political expediency than to a vision of 'caring for people'' (Hudson, 1990, p 33). Third, the reforms reflected a wider critique of the postwar welfare state as being unresponsive to the individual needs of service users (Hadley and Hatch, 1981). The response to this critique was to introduce quasi-markets in public services (Le Grand and Bartlett, 1993); in this context, social services care managers were to purchase, from within the new 'mixed economy' of services, individually tailored 'packages' of services according to the assessed needs and preferences of individual service users.

The 1990s saw the gradual undermining of the 1993 settlement, a trend supported by the widespread view that social services departments have failed to rise to the challenge of being the 'lead agency' (DH, 1998). This is despite the fact that social services have been demonstrably effective in developing intensive domiciliary services to enable people with increasingly high support needs to avoid admission to institutional care (Warburton and McCracken, 1999) and in targeting support at those most in need (Bauld et al, 2000). Part of this critique has revolved around the failure of the 1993 reforms to promote user-centred services that foster choice and independence (see, for example, Hardy et al, 1999; Parry-Jones and Soulsby, 2001). However, this criticism is not exclusive to social services. Analysts of the public sector quasi-markets of the 1990s as a whole have pointed to the role of professionals, such as social services care managers and general practitioners (GPs) in the NHS, in making choices on behalf of service users. 'It is consumer choice, the feature anticipated in the legislation and rhetoric of quasi-markets, that appears to have been most compromised. The triangular relationship between end user, purchaser and provider of care limits choice ...' (Roberts et al, 1998, p 25).

In 2005, three policy documents were published (Cabinet Office, 2005; DH, 2005a; HM Government, 2005). These offer a brave new vision of how such choice and empowerment might be delivered. The next section of this chapter outlines these proposals. This is followed by a discussion of their potential challenges and implications. The final two sections discuss the broader implications for, first, the role of social services within the wider local authority; and second, the future of the health and social care interface. The discussion will therefore return to two of the key drivers behind the 1993 changes – the problems of joint working between health and social services and the need to control public expenditure.

The 2005 adult social care proposals

All three documents contain similar strategic and operational proposals for the future of social care for working-age adults and/or older people.

The Cabinet Office Strategy Unit's report *Improving the Life Chances of Disabled People* (Cabinet Office, 2005) is remarkable for its strong anti-discriminatory approach and for the cross-government support that was secured prior to publication and that continues to characterise implementation of its numerous targets and recommendations. The report detailed the disadvantage experienced by disabled adults and children and their families, criticising the fragmentation of assessments and support services; the lack of choice about support options; and the risk that the options that are available increase, rather than reduce, dependency. While direct payments can enhance choice and control for some disabled people, the report recognised that they are not appropriate for everyone and are in any case restricted to purchasing a limited range of social care services.

Instead, the Strategy Unit proposed more personalised responses through the introduction of 'individual budgets'. Modelled on the 'In Control' projects that have been piloted in some areas for people with learning disabilities (www.in-control.org.uk), individual budgets bring together, for any individual, the resources from a number of different services to which they are entitled. Potential funding streams include local authority community care resources, integrated community equipment and housing adaptations budgets, the Independent Living Fund, Access to Work resources from the Department for Work and Pensions, and the Family Fund for disabled children. An individual budget for any one person pools these resources and the total amount is made transparent to the individual who uses the budget to secure a flexible range of different types of support, from a wider range of providers than is currently possible, either through direct payments or conventional social care services.

The individual budget proposal was repeated in the Green Paper from the Department of Health on a future 'vision' for adult social care (DH, 2005a). The Green Paper originated from professional and ministerial concerns about the future of social care services following the transfer of responsibility for children's social services to the Department for Education and Skills and the creation of local integrated children's services. It was published after an extensive period of consultation with service user organisations and other interested groups (Hudson et al, 2004).

The Green Paper argued that publicly funded social care services should focus on achieving the outcomes, across a range of domains, that are important for individual service users. These domains include health, quality of life, participation in the local community, the exercise of choice and control, freedom from discrimination, economic well-being and personal dignity. This range of outcomes is potentially challenging for traditional social care services and reflects a marked shift from a paternalistic model of social care, in which professional expertise plays a major role, to one emphasising active citizenship and independence (Audit Commission, 2004a). The orientation was broadly endorsed in the public feedback to the Green Paper (DH, 2005b). The Green Paper also asserted the centrality of choice to the 'modernisation' of public services and again proposed the piloting of individual budgets as offering 'the real benefits of choice and control of direct payments, without the potential burdens' (DH, 2005a, p 33). The Green Paper spelled out the individual budget proposal in more detail, again emphasising the key feature of making transparent to eligible individuals the total resources, from a range of different budgets, available to them. It suggested that an individual budget could be held by the social services department, a user or a carer; could be used to purchase services outside the range traditionally offered by social services; and could be made available as a cash direct payment or in the form of services up to the value of the individual's total 'entitlement'.

The third document, setting out a UK-wide strategy for an ageing society, was published just before the May 2005 General Election (HM Government, 2005). Again reflecting an underlying shift from a paternalistic to a citizenship discourse, *Opportunity Age* emphasised 'active' ageing and the promotion of well-being and independence in later life. It argued that the services contributing to this objective extend far beyond conventional social care and include measures promoting personal safety inside and outside the home, appropriate housing, accessible public transport and leisure facilities, opportunities for lifelong learning and volunteering, and health promotion. Significantly, promoting well-being and independence was acknowledged to involve some redirection of resources to invest in lower-level support for older people whose needs are not (yet) acute, in the expectation that such measures would be preventive and cost-effective in the longer term. As with the other proposals, *Opportunity Age* emphasised the need for greater choice and control over how personal support is provided and restated the piloting of individual budgets. It suggested that an even wider range of resources could be contributed to an individual budget, including housing-related support currently distributed through the Supporting People programme and possibly resources from other local authority budgets such as leisure and transport (HM Government, 2005, p 52). Again, transparency and user control were emphasised:

> In an individual budget, the resources that the state has allocated to meet an older person's needs are made clear and are held in that person's name – somewhat like a bank account. The client controls this resource and uses it to have choice and control over how and when they want to receive care and support.... (HM Government, 2005, pp 51-2)

There are some differences between the three documents, such as their coverage of younger disabled and/or older people and of England and Wales or the entire UK. However, a number of common themes are restated with remarkable consistency. First, a conceptual model of active citizenship and social inclusion underpins the three documents. This involves a significant broadening of the domains in which publicly funded social care services are expected to have an impact, with a particular emphasis on improving quality of life, independence and well-being. Achieving these outcomes is likely to involve a range of services, including employment, leisure, education, transport and housing, that extend far beyond the boundaries of social care as traditionally defined and understood. Second, the documents propose new opportunities for the users of social care services to exercise choice and control through mechanisms such as individual budgets. Exercising choice and control requires transparency about the level of resources available and therefore the decision-making processes by which these are allocated to individuals. The proposals therefore introduce the notion of entitlement by any individual to their allocated resources for social care. This opens up the possibility of greater horizontal equity in the distribution of resources for adult social care (Glendinning, 2007: forthcoming).

These themes were reflected in the announcements in November 2005 of two sets of pilot projects. First, individual budgets are to be piloted in 13 English local authorities from 2006 for 18-24 months for, variously, older people, people with physical or sensory impairments, learning disabilities and mental health needs. Apart from £2.6 million development support, the pilots are to be cost-neutral. Second, local Partnerships for Older People Projects (POPPs) involve £60 million ring-fenced funding to invest in new services between 2006/07 and 2007/08. Each local project, involving a council with social services responsibility and at least one NHS primary care trust (PCT), will test and evaluate innovative approaches to prevention. Here, 'prevention' has two rather different dimensions: reducing numbers of emergency hospital admissions and delayed discharges involving very frail older people; and demonstrating the role of low-level support in preventing needs for higher intensity or institutional care and improving well-being. Nineteen POPP pilots were announced in November 2005, with a second round to be announced during 2006. (For details of both pilots see www.dh.gov.uk/ PublicationsAndStatistics, accessed 23 November 2005.) Both sets of pilots are subject to national evaluations to provide an evidence base for decisions about their wider roll-out.

Towards choice and empowerment?

As noted above, the 1993 community care settlement was intended to introduce choice and flexibility into adult social care. According to liberal economic theory, choice should promote competition between providers and thus improve quality, efficiency and service responsiveness. Pivotal in the exercise of choice were care managers who assessed needs; determined eligibility for social care services; and purchased and coordinated services on behalf of users. This was based on evidence that devolving control over resources to front-line staff improved flexibility and efficiency in social care (Challis, 2004). However, the reality was rather different and many users actually had very limited choices over the service provider and little input into the timing or content of their services, while some dimensions of choice actually diminished (Hardy et al, 1999). In contrast, research on direct payments, where individuals receive the cash equivalent of services with which to arrange their own support, showed how these could indeed offer increased choice and control, with consequent benefits for well-being and quality of life (Glendinning et al, 2000; Stainton and Boyce, 2004). Individual budgets, and the continued promotion of direct payments as alternatives to services in kind, therefore represent the devolution of purchasing power from third-party care manager purchasers to individual service user purchasers, in the expectation that this will enhance outcomes and well-being.

There are strong arguments for maximising choice over personal and other support. The exercise of choice and control over daily life is a commonly desired outcome of social care services (Vernon and Qureshi, 2000); is central to concepts of independence (Parry et al, 2004); and is argued to be crucial for the mental well-being of adults with extra support needs (Boyle, 2005).

However, devolving purchasing power to service users brings a number of major risks. First, users are likely to be far more restricted than third-party professional purchasers by informational asymmetries (Barnes and Prior, 1995) that weaken their position in negotiations with powerful providers. Second, users may find it difficult to 'exit' from unsatisfactory provision if their needs are particularly specialised or local supply is scarce. Third, choices are easier to make and fulfil by people who have extensive resources on which to draw. Relevant resources include wealth; knowledge of service structures and practices; personal skills in dealing with professionals and managers; and familiarity with decision-making practices in public sector organisations (Lent and Arend, 2004). Users of social care services are especially likely to be disadvantaged – by illness, disability, social exclusion and other problems – in accessing such resources. Without appropriate information and other support (see below), greater choice risks exacerbating the wider social inequalities that universal public services are intended to diminish (Lent and Arend, 2004).

Individual budgets raise particular questions about equity. As noted above, they should make transparent the level of resources available for each eligible individual. However, this transparency will also reveal significant variations in individual resource allocations between localities and service user groups. Variations include both formal and informal differences at the local level in cost ceilings for individual support packages; and the lower levels of funding (and/or tighter eligibility criteria) that commonly characterise older people's services compared with those for younger adults. Moreover, younger adults will be able to contribute resources to their individual budgets from a wider range of funding streams (including Access to Work and the Independent Living Fund) than older people, thus further exacerbating inter-user inequities. Because of the enhanced transparency, the chronic under-funding of services for older people may become a significant political issue (Help the Aged, 2002).

Information, advocacy, brokerage and other support are vital to ensure that those less well equipped to make choices do not lose out to the better informed and articulate (Lent and Arend, 2004). Thus support services, often run by disabled people themselves, have been shown to be crucial in encouraging and supporting the take-up of direct payments

(DH, 2000a). The Green Paper acknowledges that individual budget holders will require help from people knowledgeable about services, both in and beyond the remit of adult social care, to help them access and manage appropriate support (DH, 2005a). Different models, including 'person-centred planning facilitators', care managers, 'navigators' and brokers, may be appropriate for different user groups. Such support should of course also be available to the approximately one third of adult social care service users who pay for the whole of their support from their private assets and/or income (Comas-Herrera et al, 2004), in order to avoid new inequities between publicly and privately funded individual purchasers.

However, these new tasks may not come easily to local authority care managers. First, transferring command over resources from professionals to service users will require major cultural and organisational changes. Already the low take-up of direct payments has been attributed to care manager neutrality or active discouragement (Dawson, 2000; Clark et al, 2004). Second, care manager roles have been increasingly circumscribed by national frameworks, particularly the Single Assessment Process (DH, 2002a) that allows information to be collected from different professionals; and *Fair Access to Care Services* guidance (DH, 2002b) that sets clear eligibility criteria for social care services. New brokerage or 'navigator' roles may not be easily reconciled with the gatekeeping that will continue to determine access to the funding streams included in individual budgets. This suggests that 'arm's-length' or independent brokerage services may be more effective than in-house models, as they would allow more freedom for advocacy activities. Significant questions then arise over the funding and regulation of such organisations.

A third area of concern is the supply of services. Individual budget holders will 'purchase' their support in a quasi-market whose precise parameters are not yet clear, particularly whether it will include local authority services and/or the work of family carers. However, it is likely to include institutional providers (for long-stay and respite care), home care agencies and voluntary and non-profit community services. The non-institutional care market is highly fragmented and dominated by small providers. In March 2005, over 4,000 domiciliary care agencies were registered with the Commission for Social Care Inspection (CSCI, 2005); half of these are sole traders or partnerships, rather than private or limited companies (Netten et al, 2005). Major challenges in recruiting, training and retaining workers are common (Mathew, 2000; Henwood, 2001), while the core business and economic viability of many agencies rests on large contracts from local authority purchasers (Ware et al, 2001).

In such an environment, providers may not easily respond to the very specific demands of newly empowered individual purchasers. Indeed, a shortage of appropriate supply brings rather different equity risks, as it can encourage providers to select their customers rather than vice versa, as has become apparent in relation to 'choice' of popular schools (Lent and Arend, 2004). Changes will also be needed in local authority social services' commissioning activities, which tend to involve traditional rather than innovative services and long-term block contracts, particularly for residential care (Netten et al, 2005). This suggests the risk of increasing tensions between sustaining market stability and fostering innovation and flexibility. It may also be difficult to sustain economies of scale in the face of more individualised purchasing arrangements, higher transaction and other costs to support user choice and higher levels of financial risk on the part of providers. Finally, the implications for informal carers are unclear; it is possible that they will have to play a far greater role in day-to-day service coordination, particularly for people with multiple service needs.

Changing local authorities

At first glance, there are few tensions between these proposals and the changing role of local authorities. Since 1997, the government has promoted a broad vision of public health in which local authorities have a lead role. The 2000 Local Government Act gave local authorities a duty to promote the social, economic and environmental well-being of residents, through partnerships with other agencies and initiatives such as neighbourhood renewal. Moreover, other local authority services such as education and leisure are also expected to contribute to promoting well-being. Local authorities are expected to provide fewer services themselves and instead act as leaders, brokers and coordinators across the local public, voluntary and private sectors.

However, the 1993 community care settlement gave social services rather than local authorities the lead role for community care. It could therefore be inferred that the failure to develop preventative and personalised services flowed from the narrow mindset of social services in particular, rather than from local authorities in general. This raises questions of how well social services can adapt to these new demands and their future role within the corporate local authority.

The challenges are increased by the fact that the social services departments of the 1990s no longer exist (Ivory, 2005), as social services for children become integrated with local education services. This risks the creation of a new 'Berlin Wall', this time between children's and adults' social care services, and potential problems of continuity for young people with social care needs as they move into adulthood. It also significantly reduces the organisational scale and size of budget commanded by social services within the corporate local authority.

The proposed changes in social care are expected to be cost-neutral. Is this setting social services up to fail? The question is not new; in 2000, social services were held responsible for 'blocked' hospital beds through their slowness to arrange discharge support for older patients (DH, 2000b). However, for much of the 1990s, social services departments struggled to develop their new community care responsibilities in the context of severe public expenditure constraints. Although more recently there has been substantial new public sector investment, the NHS has been much more favoured; resources for social care have not even kept pace with increases in need. The latter result partly from demographic changes and partly from changes in other policy areas (particularly the NHS) that have placed additional demands on social services (Help the Aged, 2002). Consequently, social services have become increasingly targeted on the most severely disabled and highest-risk adults, and low-level preventive services have been largely withdrawn (Clark et al, 1998). Moreover, local authorities in general claim to face 'a black hole' in their finances for the period 2006/07 and beyond (LGA, 2005), although the government fiercely contests these figures. Apart from the limited additional resources available to the POPP pilots, it is difficult to see how they will continue to meet demands for the high levels of support required by many older and disabled people while simultaneously investing in new, low-level preventive services (ADSS/LGA, 2003).

Finally, achieving the wider range of outcomes emphasised in the three policy documents requires a broad, cross-local authority approach, with commitment from elected members and senior officers from across the authority as well as partner agencies (particularly the NHS). There is some debate about whether leadership for this strategic approach should come from a service delivery department or have corporate leadership from, say, the chief executive's department or the local strategic partnership. It is far from evident that social services departments are best placed to provide strategic, cross-cutting leadership at the same time as managing day-to-day operational pressures, or to secure the engagement of other departments (Audit Commission, 2004b).

The boundary between health and social care

The 1993 community care settlement emphasised that adults with additional support needs should be supported within a social care paradigm, rather than a medical one that focuses predominantly on illness and impairment (Means et al, 2003). With their emphasis on choice and empowerment, the three policy documents take this approach to the next logical development.

However, the relationship of the proposals to health care and health care reforms is problematic. One difficulty is that the health elements of personal care, including ongoing treatments like physiotherapy, chiropody and counselling that many disabled and older people require, remain outside the scope of both direct payments (Glendinning et al, 2000; Glendinning, 2006) and individual budgets and can be accessed only through GPs and other NHS services. Second, it is hard to see the links between current policies and service developments relating to long-term health care conditions and the social care proposals. In 2005 the Department of Health also published proposals to support the 17.5 million people with long-term health conditions (DH, 2005c). By introducing effective and systematic approaches to care and management, these aimed to reduce emergency inpatient stays by 5% by March 2008 (using 2003/04 as a baseline). These proposals were followed by a National Service Framework (NSF) for people with neurological conditions (DH, 2005d).

It is arguable that these developments were prompted as much by the high costs of acute hospital care as by the need to improve well-being and quality of life among people with long-term illnesses (Hudson, 2005). The three social care policy documents make little reference to these health care developments; this is especially surprising in the case of the adult social care Green Paper and is not consistent with wider aspirations for 'joined-up' policy (NAO, 2003). Indeed, the discourse of the long-term conditions and NSF proposals is strikingly different from that of the three adult social care documents: the former refer to patients, the latter to service users. Although reducing discomfort and stress is acknowledged, the key performance indicator focuses on hospital bed usage and improving quality of life is assumed to come solely from targeted healthcare interventions rather than a broader vision of social inclusion and well-being. At the centre of these targeted interventions is the new community matron, who will 'case manage' those with multiple health care problems. There is a real danger of re-medicalising community care, at least for those with the most complex health care needs.

Finally, the proposed changes in social care will take place during another period of massive reorganisation and upheaval for the NHS that may place significant obstacles in the way of effective joint working. Changes include expanding the number of Foundation Hospitals at 'arm's length' from the rest of the NHS; the growing use of private sector health care providers; a major restructuring of Strategic Health Authorities and PCTs; and the possible divesting of the role of PCTs in service provision.

The government has acknowledged the apparent fragmentation between NHS and social care policy making and therefore proposed a single White Paper on health and social care outside hospitals early in 2006. Many commentators see the outcome being the incorporation of adult social care into the NHS and the removal of all vestiges of a lead agency role for social services (Ivory, 2005; Sale, 2005). Against this, the Secretary of State for Health is on record as saying that social care will not be 'swamped' by the NHS; rather that the White Paper is 'the best chance for a generation to make social care the major player in government programmes to promote well-being' (quoted in *Community Care*, 27 October/2 November, 2005, p 10).

It is hard to avoid the conclusion that there will be further redrawing of the boundary between health and social care services for adults and older people (Glendinning et al, 2005). The form this will take remains unclear, although a closer integration of the two within the same (NHS) organisational framework seems highly likely. This does not necessarily mean that a medical rather than social care paradigm will dominate. The words of the Secretary of State are encouraging in this respect, although they need to be set against the worsening overall financial position of the NHS and the history of health care neglect for those with community care needs.

Conclusion

The future prospects for adult social care are not promising. The organisational structures and responsibilities that were established in 1993 are being eroded. Those organisational structures, and the status of social services within the wider local authority, have already been weakened with the establishment of separate integrated children's services. The continued promotion of direct payments and the piloting of individual budgets involve the devolution of significant service purchasing responsibilities to individual adult users (and, probably, their carers). The new focus on social inclusion and quality of life outcomes and prevention, rather than conventional service inputs, is to be welcomed. However, this is not a role that many social services departments are familiar with, having been preoccupied since 1993 with developing their roles as service commissioners and purchasers and providing community-based services for adults with increasingly complex support needs. Moreover, achieving these outcomes requires the involvement of a wide range of local authority services, plus local voluntary, community and user organisations, and ideally with corporate local authority rather than social services leadership. Having succeeded in developing systems of service allocation that target resources at people needing particularly intensive support to remain at home, social services are now also required to develop low-level preventive services, without additional resources. Finally, NHS policies and performance have exerted considerable direct and indirect influence over adult social care policy and service development throughout the postwar years and this is likely to continue, if not increase. It is hard to avoid the conclusion that the 'lead' role given to social services in 1993 is about to be irrevocably fragmented – 'hollowed out' between the threefold drivers of user empowerment, local authorities' corporate well-being responsibilities and the demands of the NHS.

There is little evidence that the desire among disabled adults and older people for high-quality, well-coordinated support provided by appropriately trained, regulated and remunerated workers has diminished. Moreover, as Clarke et al (2005) pointed out in *Social Policy Review 17*, there are clear limits to how far the users of social care services see themselves as 'consumers', while both older and younger disabled people have vocally resisted the imposition a of medical model of 'care'. It is an act of faith, rather than an example of evidence-based policy, that the new proposals for adult social care will be able to meet the continuing aspirations of service users.

References

ADSS (Association of Directors of Social Services)/LGA (Local Government Association) (2003) *All Our Tomorrows. Inverting the Triangle of Care*, London: ADSS/LGA.

Audit Commission (1986) *Making a Reality of Community Care*, London: HMSO.

Audit Commission (2004a) *Older People – Independence and Well-being. The Challenge for Public Services*, London: Audit Commission/Better Government for Older People.

Audit Commission, (2004b) *Older People. Building a Strategic Approach*, London: Audit Commission/Better Government for Older People.

Barnes, M. and Prior, D. (1995) 'Spoilt for choice? How consumerism can disempower public service users', *Public Money and Management*, July-September, vol 15, no 3, pp 53-8.

Bauld, L., Chesterman, J., Davies, B., Judge, K. and Mangalore, R. (2000) *Caring for Older People: An Assessment of Community Care in the 1990s*, Aldershot: Ashgate.

Boyle, G. (2005) 'The role of autonomy in explaining mental ill-health and depression among older people in long-term care settings', *Ageing and Society*, vol 25, no 5, pp 731-48.

Cabinet Office (2005) *Improving the Life Chances of Disabled People*, London: Cabinet Office Strategy Unit.

Challis, D. (2004) 'Care management in the long-term care of older people', in M. Knapp, D. Challis, J.-L. Fernández and A. Netten (eds) *Long-term Care: Matching Resources and Needs: A Festschrift for Bleddyn Davies*, Aldershot: Ashgate, pp 231-50.

Clark, H., Dyer, S. and Horwood, J. (1998) *'That Bit of Help': The High Value of Low Level Preventive Services for Older People*, Bristol/York: The Policy Press/Joseph Rowntree Foundation.

Clark, H., Gough, H. and Macfarlane, A. (2004) *It Pays Dividends: Direct Payments and Older People*, Bristol/York: The Policy Press/Joseph Rowntree Foundation.

Clarke, J., Smith, N. and Vidler, E. (2005) 'Consumerism and the reform of public services: inequalities and instabilities', in M. Powell, L. Bauld and K. Clarke (eds) *Social Policy Review 17: Analysis and Debate in Social Policy, 2005*, Bristol: The Policy Press, pp 167-82.

Comas-Herrera, A., Wittenberg, R. and Pickard, L. (2004) 'Long-term care for older people in the United Kingdom: structure and challenges', in M. Knapp, D. Challis, J.-L. Fernández and A. Netten (eds) *Long-Term Care: Matching Resources and Needs: A Festschrift for Bleddyn Davies*, Aldershot: Ashgate, pp 17-34.

CSCI (Commission for Social Care Inspection) (2005) *The State of Social Care in England 2005-05*, London: CSCI.

Dawson, C. (2000) *Independent Success. Implementing Direct Payments*, York: Joseph Rowntree Foundation.

DH (Department of Health) (1989) *Caring for People: Community Care in the Next Decade and Beyond*, London: HMSO.

DH (1998) *Modernising Social Services: Promoting Independence, Improving Protection, Raising Standards*, London: DH.

DH (2000a) *An Easy Guide to Direct Payments*, London: DH.

DH (2000b) *The NHS Plan: A Plan for Investment, a Plan for Reform*, London: DH.

DH (2002a) *Guidance on the Single Assessment Process for Older People*, HSC 2002/001/LAC (2002)1, London: DH.

DH (2002b) *Fair Access to Care Services: Guidance on Eligibility Criteria for Adult Social Care*, LAC (2002)13, London: DH.

DH (2005a) *Independence, Well-being and Choice. Our Vision for the Future of Social Care for Adults in England*, Cm 6499, London: DH.

DH (2005b) *Responses to the Consultation on Adult Social Care in England*, London: DH.

DH (2005c) *Supporting People with Long Term Conditions: An NHS and Social Care Model to Support Local Innovation and Integration*, London: DH.

DH (2005d) *The National Service Framework for Long Term (Neurological) Conditions*, London: DH.

Glendinning, C. (2006) 'Direct payments and health', in J. Bornat and J. Leece (eds) *Developments in Direct Payments*, Bristol: The Policy Press, pp 253-68.

Glendinning, C. (2007: forthcoming) 'Developing a sustainable approach to funding long-term care in the UK', *Social Policy and Society*.

Glendinning, C., Hudson, B. and Means, R. (2005) 'Under strain? Exploring the troubled relationship between health and social care', *Public Money and Management*, vol 25, no 4, pp 245-52.

Glendinning, C., Halliwell, S., Jacobs, S., Rummery, K. and Tyrer, J. (2000) *Buying Independence: Using Direct Payments to Integrate Health and Social Services*, Bristol: The Policy Press.

Griffiths Report (1988) *Community Care: An Agenda for Action*, London: HMSO.

Hadley, R. and Hatch, S. (1981) *Social Welfare and the Failure of the State: Centralised Social Services and Participatory Alternatives*, London: Allen & Unwin.

Hardy, B., Young, R. and Wistow, G. (1999) 'Dimensions of choice in the assessment and care management process. The views of older people, carers and care managers', *Health and Social Care in the Community*, vol 7, no 6, pp 483-91.

Help the Aged (2002) *Nothing Personal. Rationing Social Care for Older People*, London: Help the Aged.

Henwood, M. (2001) *Future Imperfect? Report of the Kings Fund Care and Support Enquiry*, London: Kings Fund.

HM Government (2005) *Opportunity Age. Meeting the Challenges of Ageing in the 21st Century*, London: DWP.

Hudson, B. (1990) 'Social policy and the New Right – the strange case of the community care White Paper', *Local Government Studies*, vol 16, no 6, pp 15-34.

Hudson, B. (2005) 'Sea change or quick fix? Policy in long-term conditions in England', *Health and Social Care in the Community*, vol 13, no 4, pp 378-85.

Hudson, B., Dearey, M. and Glendinning, C. (2004) *New Vision for Adult Social Care: Scoping Service Users' Views*, York: Social Policy Research Unit, University of York.

Ivory, M. (2005) 'Knock it down and start again', *Community Care*, 20-26 October, pp 32-3.

Le Grand, J. and Bartlett, W. (eds) (1993) *Quasi-markets and Social Policy*, Basingstoke: Macmillan.

Lent, A. and Arend, N. (2004) *Making Choices. How Can Choice Improve Local Public Services?*, London: New Local Government Network.

LGA (Local Government Association) (2005) *Beyond the Black Hole*, London: LGA.

Mathew, D. (2000) *Who Cares? A Profile of the Independent Sector Home Care Workforce in England*, Carshalton: UK Home Care Association.

Means, R., Morbey, H. and Smith, R. (2002) *From Community Care to Market Care? The Development of Welfare Services for Older People*, Bristol: The Policy Press.

Means, R., Richards, S. and Smith, R. (2003) *Community Care: Policy and Practice* (3rd edn), Basingstoke: Palgrave Macmillan.

NAO (National Audit Office) (2003) *Developing Effective Services for Older People*, London: NAO.

Netten, A., Darton, R., Davey, V., Kendall, J., Knapp, M., Williams, J., Fernández, J.-L. and Forder, J. (2005) *Understanding Public Services and Care Markets, Care Services Enquiry*, London: Kings Fund.

Parry, J., Vergeris, S., Hudson, M., Barnes, H. and Taylor, R. (2004) *Independent Living in Later Life: Research Review Carried Out on Behalf of the Department for Work and Pensions*, Research Report 216, London: Department for Work and Pensions.

Parry-Jones, B. and Soulsby, J. (2001) 'Needs-led assessment: the challenges and the reality', *Health and Social Care in the Community*, vol 9, no 6, pp 414-28.

Roberts, J.A., Le Grand, J. and Bartlett, W. (1998) *Lessons from Experience of Quasi-markets in the 1990s*, in W. Bartlett, J.A. Roberts and J. Le Grand (eds) *A Revolution in Social Policy: Quasi-market Reforms in the 1990s*, Bristol: The Policy Press.

Sale, A.U. (2005) 'For better or for worse', *Community Care*, 25-31 August, pp 30-1.

Stainton, T. and Boyce, S. (2004) '"I have got my life back": users' experience of direct payments', *Disability and Society*, vol 19, no 5, pp 443-54.

Vernon, A. and Qureshi, H. (2000) 'Community care and independence: self-sufficiency or empowerment?', *Critical Social Policy*, vol 20, no 2, pp 255-76.

Warburton, R. and McCracken, J. (1999) 'An evidence-based perspective from the Department of Health on the impact of the 1993 reforms on the care of frail elderly people', in The Royal Commission on Long-term Care, *Community Care and Informal Care*, London: The Stationery Office, part one, vol 3, pp 25-36.

Ware, P., Matesovic, T., Forder, J., Hardy, B., Kendall, J. and Knapp, M. (2001) 'Movement and change: independent sector domiciliary care providers between 1995 and 1999', *Health and Social Care in the Community*, vol 9, no 6, pp 334-40.

TWO

Creating a patient-led NHS: empowering 'consumers' or shrinking the state?

Ruth McDonald

Introduction

Health policy in England in recent years has been described as embodying elements of both *modernisation* and *marketisation*. These processes are intended to achieve a transformation from an 'old' monolithic service into a 'new' National Health Service (NHS), fit for the 21st century, and are to be pursued in part by curbing the monopoly powers of health care providers and 'harnessing the powers of healthcare users as individuals wishing to access good quality healthcare' (Allsop and Baggott, 2004, p 29). Following the Labour Party's re-election in May 2005, while it commenced a third term in office with a much-reduced majority, this did nothing to dampen its commitment to increase patient choice and promote diversity in the provision of care. The Labour government's role has also been described as moving away from management and towards regulation, setting standards and targets, but allowing local discretion as to how these are achieved (Klein, 2005). Whether this move to 'enforced self-regulation' (Hood et al, 2000; Dent, 2005) is perceived as allowing for greater discretion by those working in the NHS is a moot point, as is the extent to which central government is willing to withdraw from hands-on management. However, on the basis of policies announced in 2005, it seems clear that the government is serious in its intention to reform both the way in which care is commissioned and the way it is provided.

In March 2005, prior to the General Election, Nigel Edwards, Director of Policy for the NHS Confederation, addressed a meeting on the subject of 'Payment By Results' (PBR), a tariff-based system for paying hospitals for care provided. The Confederation is the membership body that represents the vast majority of NHS organisations and the audience largely comprised NHS employees (see www.nhsconfed.org). Edwards' suggestion that New Labour politicians think they have 'fixed what's wrong with hospitals' and are now turning their attention to primary care was greeted with laughter by attendees. This perhaps reflects scepticism towards the potential for PBR to 'fix' the problems of secondary care within the NHS, but the shift in focus, towards 'fixing' problems outside of hospitals, is certainly borne out by policy developments in 2005. This chapter largely concerns policy towards health care outside of hospitals, since, with regard to the NHS in England, the government is increasingly turning its attention to care beyond the hospital doors. The chapter focuses wholly on the NHS in England, since devolution in Scotland and Wales has resulted in health policy developments that diverge somewhat from the English model (Greer, 2004). While not dismissing these developments, it is not possible to do justice to them in this short review chapter. The chapter is divided into four sections. The first briefly describes policies intended to 'fix' the hospital sector and offers an explanation for the shift in attention beyond this sector. The second and third sections examine demand and supply-side policies respectively, and the fourth presents concluding remarks.

Modernisation, marketisation and the reform of hospital care

Writing in *Social Policy Review 17*, Rudolf Klein (2005) outlined developments aimed at increasing opportunities for patient choice and public involvement and changes to the supply side of the NHS. These included moves towards a quasi-market driven by choice, the creation of Foundation Trusts and greater use of the independent sector in the provision of care. In large part, these initiatives can be interpreted as addressing perceived deficiencies in hospital care provision. In 2005 the expansion of PBR, a mechanism to change the flow of funds in the system, enabling money to follow patients, took place. The quasi-market reforms of the NHS in the 1990s were characterised by block contracts between purchasers and providers of care, with the result that money did not follow patients and patient flows remained largely as they had been prior to the market reforms (Le Grand et al, 1998). However, under PBR, providers receive a fixed price for each case treated and providers are no longer guaranteed income, but have to compete for patients (DH, 2002). Hospitals will lose resources if they fail to treat patients within target waiting times or if patients choose to go elsewhere for treatment. PBR can thus be seen as facilitating the processes of modernisation and marketisation. Removing the guarantee of income is intended to make providers more responsive to consumer wishes. Payment based on average cost also rewards low-cost providers who may retain any surplus income over and above the cost of providing care and (in theory) forces 'inefficient' (above-average cost) providers to become more efficient and to reduce their costs in the process.

Policies to reform the hospital sector reflect the government's intention that the substantial increases in NHS resources allocated in recent years (Appleby, 2003) should produce real gains in productivity and responsiveness (Revill, 2002). In 2005 government figures showed a drop in both the number of people on hospital waiting lists in England and the number of people waiting longer than six months for treatment. A combination of unprecedented levels of growth monies and the introduction of quasi-market reforms may, as Edwards suggests, be seen by the government as 'fixing' what it perceives to be the problems of hospital care, by improving efficiency and making services more responsive, both in terms of waiting times and services designed around patient preferences. Certainly this is the stated aim of these policies (DH, 2002; HM Treasury, 2004). However, in the context of a shift from management to regulation, they might also be seen as a means of extricating the government from culpability in the event of systems failures. Moving from 'command and control' to regulation may also reflect an acknowledgment of the need to hold to account private providers, who are intended to play an increasing role in care provision and whom the government can neither command nor directly control. Whether the government can merely restrict its role to regulation remains to be seen, particularly if and when the required improvements in the system fail to materialise. And there are a number of reasons, many of which concern the potential for demand to outstrip service provision, why improvements may fall short of expectations.

Recent levels of growth funding in the NHS cannot continue indefinitely, yet the increased costs associated with technological development and workforce expansion required to deliver health services in the 21st century show little sign of diminishing. In 2005 an Audit Commission report into the implementation of guidance produced by the National Institute for Clinical Excellence (NICE) found that implementation 'has not always been timely or comprehensive' (Audit Commission, 2005, p 23). Eighty-five per cent of NHS senior managers surveyed cited affordability as the main barrier to implementation (Audit

Commission, 2005). As growth funding levels off after 2008, the situation is likely to be exacerbated. The PBR tariff-based system that pays providers a fixed price for each patient treated is likely to result in increased expenditure on patient care. This is because, unlike the previous system in which NHS providers were obliged to manage increases in hospital activity with little or no additional resources, increased workload results in additional payment and PBR creates incentives to increase workload in order to increase income. Experience of such systems elsewhere suggests that the outcome is usually to increase costs overall. (For a brief summary of the potential adverse consequences of tariff-based funding systems and evidence from other countries, see Fotaki et al, 2005.)

There is disagreement among commentators over the likely impact of an aging population on the demand for health care in the future (Zweifel et al, 1999), although other factors such as government policies to promote choice and empower patients are likely to increase expectations of the system. Taken together, these factors point to the need to manage both expectations and demand within the NHS. Since general practitioners (GPs) have traditionally acted as gatekeepers controlling access to secondary care and thereby containing costs, they play an important role in managing demand, particularly in the context of PBR and the market in health services. Other policies to manage demand for hospital care concern attempts to shift responsibility for health and well-being on to citizens and to redesign the delivery of care so that the reliance on scarce and expensive hospital beds is diminished.

Attempts at shifting responsibility from the state to its citizens as part of a process of 'empowerment' are not new. While the self-conscious use of labels such as 'modernisation' may be intended to differentiate New Labour policies from those of its Conservative predecessors, the process of 'modernisation' represents the continuation of a set of policies initiated under previous administrations that seeks to transform the NHS from a rigid and failing bureaucracy to a system of entrepreneurial governance that will ensure its survival. (See Currie and Brown, 2003, for an overview of NHS modernisation and Allsop and Baggott, 2004, for a discussion of specific recent policy initiatives intended to 'modernise' the NHS.)

The rhetoric of enterprise, which reflected the shift to the political right in OECD (Organisation for Economic Co-operation and Development) economies towards the end of the 20th century, underpins this approach (Cohen and Musson, 2000), and the discourse of empowerment can be seen as highly consonant with notions of enterprise culture. 'Enterprise' not only denotes the preferred model of institutional organisation and provision of goods and services, but also refers to activities that are seen as denoting enterprising qualities such as initiative, self-reliance and the ability to accept responsibility for oneself and one's actions (du Gay et al, 1996). Individuals are encouraged to see themselves as active citizens exercising choice and autonomy (Dean, 1995) at the same time as accepting responsibility for managing their health and well-being. What is new is the publication of various documents in 2005 bringing together specific proposals to redesign the way care is delivered, to reorganise commissioning and to 'empower' citizens to make health lifestyle choices and 'care for themselves if they become ill' (DH, 2005a, p 14).

Choice and responsibility – shrinking the state?

In June 2004 the Department of Health published the NHS Improvement Plan, which outlined major changes required to move from a centrally directed system to a patient-led system (DH, 2004a). In 2005 proposals to implement the Improvement Plan by redesigning both the way services are delivered (DH, 2005a) and commissioned (DH, 2005b) were published. These proposals, contained in *Creating a Patient-led NHS* and *Commissioning a Patient-led NHS*, respectively (DH, 2005a, 2005b), place heavy emphasis on the pursuit of both choice and voice in healthcare. In 2004 it was announced that the much-heralded Commission for Patient and Public Involvement in Health, established in January 2003 to oversee the new system of patient and public involvement in the NHS, was to be abolished as part of a review of the Department of Health's arm's-length bodies (Gershon, 2004). Despite this, there are mechanisms intended to ensure that patients and the public are involved in the planning and development of health services. For example, NHS Trusts, Primary Care Trusts (PCTs) and Strategic Health Authorities (SHAs) have a statutory duty to make arrangements to involve and consult patients and the public in service planning and operation, and in the development of proposals for change. In addition, local authority councillors have the power to review and scrutinise the planning, provision and operation of local health services.

However, arrangements for collective voice may clash with those providing for individual choice. These tensions are likely to be exacerbated in a PBR system where treatment is funded according to individual patient choice and where hospital departments or hospitals may be forced into extinction if sufficient numbers of patients choose to be treated elsewhere. While PCTs have an obligation to consult the public on hospital closures, the logic of the quasi-market reforms is that providers that are not financially viable will be forced to close despite any collective opposition voiced by the local community or its representatives. This suggests that individual choice is to take precedence over collective voice.

Despite government pronouncements on the virtues of expanding individual choice, such developments can be interpreted as attempting to shift what have traditionally been seen as responsibilities of the state on to other agencies and on to citizens themselves through partnerships and community 'empowerment' initiatives, and increasingly on to 'responsible' citizens as individuals (Newman et al, 2004). One example of this process is the Expert Patient Programme (EPP) (see www.expertpatients.nhs.uk/what.shtml), which is intended to 'empower' patients with chronic diseases (DH, 2001) and which forms part of a move to promote self-care for the management of long-term conditions (DH, 2005c, 2005d). The EPP entails participants undertaking a structured training course, which offers the potential for people 'to take more control over their health by understanding and managing their conditions, leading to an improved quality of life' (www.expertpatients.nhs.uk/what.shtml). By offering an alternative, active patient identity, to which participants are encouraged to aspire, the programme can be seen less as a means of empowerment than a mechanism for shifting responsibility from the state to the patient.

Derek Wanless's (2002) report, *Securing Our Future Health: Taking a Long-Term View*, has been influential in encouraging the government's pursuit of the 'fully engaged' scenario. As the phrase 'fully engaged' suggests, this involves high levels of engagement by citizens in relation to their health. The report estimated the levels of future state funding required for the NHS and identified the extent to which members of the public actively engage in relation to their health as a key cost driver. Full engagement is estimated to produce dramatically improved health status and increased efficiency in resource use. A subsequent Wanless Report dealing with prevention and the wider determinants of health appeared in February 2004. The notion of full engagement, as outlined in the Wanless Reports (2002, 2004), goes beyond self-management for patients with chronic disease. Indeed, the dramatically improved health status assumed to occur under full engagement relies heavily on all citizens, as opposed to the state, taking responsibility for their own health.

Since the most recent Wanless Report was to focus on 'prevention and the wider determinants of health' (2004, p 3), policies arising from the review had the potential to make a huge contribution to reducing inequalities in health in the UK in line with the government's declared aim of improving the health of the poorest fastest (Wanless, 2004). However, a rather narrow definition of 'wider determinants' was used, with the result that factors such as poverty and deprivation were largely ignored.

This reluctance to recognise the influence of the state on population health is reflected in the 2004 Wanless Report, which states that '[i]ndividuals are ultimately responsible for their own and their children's health and it is the aggregate actions of individuals, which will ultimately be responsible for whether or not such an optimistic scenario as "fully engaged" unfolds' (2004, p 4).

The state's role, as outlined by Wanless, is one of 'shifting social norms' to achieve behaviour change in its citizenry, and assisting in the provision of advice about the adverse health consequences of undesirable behaviours in order to facilitate the individual in making informed lifestyle choices. Regulation will be required from time to time, but such state regulation consists of sending signals to the market (increasing alcohol taxation, for example) rather than interfering with the initial endowments of wealth of consumers. Occasionally, when citizens cannot be trusted to police their own health behaviours (Wanless cites the wearing of seatbelts as one such example), then the state might have a legitimate role in intervening. While the EPP represents an attempt at getting patients with chronic disease to police their behaviour and thereby to reduce their dependence (and hence resource requirements) on the state, the implications of Wanless are that this self-surveillance should be extended to cover the whole population.

Events in 2005 suggest that choosing the issues for which direct state intervention is appropriate is not straightforward. On the subject of restricting smoking in public places in England, for example, the decision taken in October 2005 to exempt private members' clubs and pubs that do not serve food from the proposed smoking ban was at odds with the advice of Health Secretary Patricia Hewitt, whose aides had previously described the proposal as unworkable. The much-publicised Cabinet split on the subject suggests that on this issue at least not everybody in government is willing to accept a shift from state as nanny to mentor.

The idea that 'approved' government involvement consists of ensuring that information is available to enable individuals to make better informed choices about their lifestyles and levying taxes to influence potentially unhealthy consumption decisions underpins *Choosing Health? A Consultation on Action to Improve People's Health* (DH, 2004b), *Choosing Health? Making Healthy Choices Easier* (DH, 2004c) and *The Chief Medical Officer's 'Ten Tips for Better Health'* (Donaldson, 2004). All of these understate or neglect entirely the role of wider societal inequalities on health status (McDonald and Scott-Samuel, 2004). The questions on which the public were consulted largely concerned lifestyle choices (hence the title *Choosing Health?*) and the role of government in supporting the exercise of healthier choices by individual citizens. Rather than tackling poverty and income inequalities, *Choosing Health?* focuses on '[R]edressing inequalities in access to information to tackle disadvantage' (DH, 2004c, p 27). Lest citizens should be in any doubt about the government's role in the process, under the section 'Defining roles and responsibilities', the remarks by the Secretary of State for Health that 'the prime responsibility for improving the health of the public does not rest with the NHS nor with government, but with the public themselves' (p 7) are featured prominently. The health consumer in these policy documents is one whose actions appear to be informed less by choice or empowerment than an obligation to behave in ways that reduce demand on the health system. More recently the government launched 'Your health, your care, your say', a consultation on community health and social care services, which asks people three main questions 'how can we help you take care of yourself? how, when and where do you want to get help when you need you need it? what do you need to help you manage your care and make decisions?' (DH, 2005e, p 1). The consultation is framed in rather narrow terms and the online survey that members of the public are invited to complete starts with the statement that 'We are committed to do more to help people take care of their own health'. While the survey does ask about extending access to primary care services, potentially enabling greater choice, the emphasis on self-care suggests that the choice for individuals to decide whether or not they want to be 'empowered' to take greater responsibility for their own health is not one that is on offer.

Reforming primary care

The consultation exercise has implications for the reform of primary care, since the results are intended to inform policy on care outside of hospitals. In 2004 a new contract was introduced for general practice, placing much greater emphasis on the use of direct financial incentives, which reward practices for meeting performance targets (Roland, 2004). In 2005 the first year's contract performance data were published, with practices achieving 91% of the points available to them. While publicly government ministers praised the performance, anecdotal evidence suggests concern among ministers that the high levels of performance, which were well in excess of budgeted allocations, may reflect targets that were insufficiently demanding. Despite these high levels of performance, the proposals contained in *Creating a Patient-led NHS* suggest other changes to the provision of care. While the White Paper published in January 2006, *Our Health, Our Care, Our Say: A New Direction for Community*

Services (DH, 2006), contains more detailed proposals, *Creating a Patient-led NHS* describes a system characterised by the blurring of professional boundaries and in which a much larger volume of services is delivered in primary care settings. This new system will also 'involve freeing up the entrepreneurialism within primary care and developing new types of provider organisations' (DH, 2005a, p 15).

British primary care has been described as being the envy of the world, with its ability to provide relatively low-cost and accessible care while at the same time acting as gatekeeper to more expensive hospital treatments (de Maeseneer et al, 2000). Furthermore, patients tend to be highly satisfied with the services provided by their practices. However, this satisfaction does not always extend to access to primary care. In April 2005, just days before the General Election, Prime Minister Tony Blair appeared baffled when confronted by a member of the audience on the TV programme Question Time, who described the unintended consequences of government targets to guarantee access to a GP within 48 hours. Blair's comments that 'I would be absolutely astonished if you are saying to your GP "I don't need to see you for four days" and he's insisting he sees you in two' (Blair, 2005) may have given the impression of a Prime Minister out of touch with the everyday concerns of ordinary people. The fact that Department of Health officials had publicly acknowledged the problem at least a month earlier did nothing to dispel this impression. Concerns about access to GPs were a recurrent theme in subsequent public consultation exercises (Healthcare Commission, 2005) and in November 2005 Patricia Hewitt declared it no longer acceptable for GP surgeries to be closed in the evenings and at weekends, hinting that if GPs were unwilling to mend their ways, alternative providers would be commissioned to provide patient-friendly care (Carvel, 2005a). The extension of prescribing powers to nurses and pharmacists from spring 2006, announced the same week amid cheers from the nursing and pharmacy community and jeers from the British Medical Association, further reduces the reliance on GPs and creates opportunities for alternative models of care in line with the aims of *Creating a Patient-Led NHS*.

Although many GPs in England are salaried employees, the majority are still independent contractors. *Creating a Patient-led NHS* acknowledges that GPs remain one of the most highly regarded groups in the NHS (DH, 2005a, p 15), yet the government plans major reform intended to change the way GPs and other primary care professionals deliver care. The new contract provides the government with some element of control in terms of incentivising the delivery of key aspects of care. However, the government is increasingly reliant on the cooperation of GPs to deliver its reform programme. *Creating a Patient-led NHS* outlines the potential for 15 million outpatient attendances to be delivered in primary care (the figure currently stands at one million), and emphasises the important role primary care professionals can play by intervening early in the course of a patient's illness (DH, 2005a, p 15). The thrust of redesign is to deliver as much care as possible as close to the patient as possible. Since an increasing emphasis is being placed on individuals taking responsibility for their own health, primary care professionals are likely to be increasingly engaged in facilitating this process and supporting self-care.

Support for self-care is aimed at reducing demand on hospital services. However, the impact of this is uncertain and likely only to be manifest in the medium to long term. Moving services closer to patients is likely to be popular with patients and the provision of clinics in community settings providing access to specialist care might be construed as providing symbolic reassurance to members of the community. In a context where polls suggest that public perceptions of the NHS remain largely immune to reductions in waiting lists, attempts to create visible symbols of a dependable and 'patient-centred' NHS are understandable. However, evidence suggests that moving care closer to patients largely has the effect of increasing demand (see Roland et al, 2005, for a review of the evidence). Given the financial pressures likely to arise from the introduction of PBR, a more immediate means of restricting demand is needed if budgetary limits and waiting list targets are not to be infringed. Practice-Based Commissioning (PBC), or giving general practices financial responsibility for the cost of care provided to their patients, is one means by which GPs may be incentivised to restrict access to secondary care to within allocated budgets. *The NHS Improvement Plan's* announcement that 'from April 2005, GP practices that wish to do so will be given indicative commissioning budgets' (DH, 2004a, p 69) received a lukewarm reception, with few practices rushing to sign up for the scheme. *Creating a Patient-led NHS* acknowledges the importance of PBC in managing the risk of 'supply-induced demand' and suggests that 'PCTs will need to think about how to engage all of their practices to take an active part in commissioning by 2008' (p 22). Although it appears that policy makers were not inclined to leave the thinking to PCTs, as in July 2005, the Department of Health published *Commissioning a Patient-led NHS*, outlining plans to develop commissioning throughout the whole NHS system, bringing forward the deadline for universal coverage of PBC to December 2006.

These plans are also likely to result in a large-scale reconfiguration of PCTs to more closely reflect local authority boundaries, with a consequent reduction in the number of PCTs. PCT reconfigurations are to be completed by October 2006 with SHA changes completed by 2007. In addition, the document outlines changes in function for PCTs and SHAs to create a 'step-change in the way services are commissioned by front-line staff to reflect patient choice' (DH, 2005b, p 1). In its 2005 manifesto, the Labour Party promised to release £250 million a year from 'streamlining measures' and *Commissioning a Patient-led NHS* makes clear that reconfiguration is not merely intended to deliver change, but also savings. SHAs were asked to work with their local health communities (that is, the NHS organisations including GP practices, and voluntary and independent sector bodies involved in the commissioning, development and provision of health services within the SHA boundary) to submit plans for streamlined commissioning arrangements in October 2005 to be assessed against the following criteria:

- secure high-quality, safe services;
- improve health and reduce inequalities;
- improve the engagement of GPs and the roll-out of PBC with demonstrable practice support;
- improve public involvement;
- improve commissioning and effective use of resources;
- manage financial balance and risk;
- improve coordination with social services through greater congruence of PCT and local government boundaries;
- deliver at least 15% reduction in management and administrative costs (DH, 2005b, p 3).

If accepted, the proposals would result in a reduction in the number of SHAs (from 28 to 11) and PCTs. Although the number of PCTs in London (currently 31) remains undecided, the 271 PCTs outside London are likely to form about 100 new PCTs. Heavy emphasis is placed on engaging front-line primary care clinicians and rolling out PBC in order to align local clinical and financial responsibilities. PBC also entails the involvement of practices in the redesign of patient pathways 'to create community based services that are more convenient for patients' (DH, 2005b, p 6). The inclusion of inequalities in the assessment criteria is understandable given the relatively poor performance in this area reported in 2005 (a continuing widening of inequalities as measured by infant mortality and life expectancy at birth) (DH, 2005f). However, attempts to tackle inequalities via improved working with local authorities may be diminished by moving services closer to patients and shifting responsibility for making healthy lifestyle choices on to 'consumers', in the context of managing the financial risk associated with PBR and the implementation of NICE guidance. Experience of providing services closer to patients during the 1990s suggests that the results are often increased costs, due in part to the loss of economies of scale associated with hospital-based provision, a reduction in the severity of disease treated, rather than reaching patients in greatest need, and an increase in patient demand for those services (Roland et al, 2005).

Commissioning a Patient-led NHS made clear the intention for PCTs to become focused on promoting health and commissioning services, with their role in provision to be reduced to a minimum. This, together with references to contestability in the provision of community services, implies that these services will be subject to greater provider competition, and was interpreted in some quarters as signalling the extensive privatisation of health services outside of hospitals. Plans by Thames Valley SHA to contract out the commissioning of primary and community care services in Oxfordshire (Relph, 2005) did nothing to allay these fears. However, in October 2005 Patricia Hewitt announced that district nurses, health visitors and other staff delivering clinical services would continue to be employed by their PCT unless and until the PCT decided otherwise. The following month Hewitt apologised for the anxiety caused in a speech to NHS staff. 'I know that many of you were very unhappy about what we said at the end of July about the future of services that you currently provide through PCTs, and I am very sorry that you have been caused such anxiety. We have listened very carefully to what you and others have said. Clearly we were too prescriptive in *Commissioning a Patient-led NHS* and we have changed that' (Hewitt, 2005). In a subsequent briefing to journalists, Hewitt implied that the White Paper might introduce a competitive market in 'under-doctored' areas, but nowhere else (Carvel, 2005b). One interpretation of this volte face is that it reflects the government's desire to allow local discretion in line with its move towards regulation and away from hands-on management. (It is not clear whether Thames Valley SHA's decision to postpone plans for contracting out is a result of local discretion or direct intervention from above.) An alternative explanation might be that in the aftermath of its first defeat in eight years (on its proposals to give police powers to detain terrorist suspects for up to 90 days), New Labour might be forced to dilute its plans for major reform rather than risk increasing party dissent.

Conclusion

In *The NHS Plan* the government announced its intentions to 'give the people of Britain a health service fit for the 21st century: a health service designed around the patient' (DH, 2000, p 10). The period covered by this review has seen the government consolidating its attempts at reform by attending to the processes and structures by which care is commissioned and provided. In addition to proposals for reconfiguring PCTs, 2005 saw developments aimed at shifting responsibility for care onto individuals as part of proposals to deliver a 'patient-led NHS'. Redesigning services to move care closer to patients can be interpreted as part of this process. In response to public concerns about the service, it may also reflect a desire to provide highly visible and locally responsive models of care, regardless of their impact on health outcomes and equity (Roland et al, 2005).

Writing in *Social Policy Review 17*, Klein (2005) described the government's stance towards the NHS as shifting from management to regulation, as evidenced by falling numbers of civil servants at the Department of Health and a reduction in the number of centrally imposed targets. Despite the declared intention to allow 'scope for local determination of what works best' (DH, 2004d, p 3), the extent to which central government is serious in this intent is uncertain. While the recent intervention of the Health Secretary in the decision by a PCT to deny Herceptin, an expensive anti-cancer drug to patients, is an isolated instance (Meikle, 2005), it does raise questions about the extent to which Department of Health directives leave room for local discretion. Similarly, the extent to which NHS managers feel themselves to be 'empowered' to manage in this new environment of regulation, which (in theory) leaves them free to get on with the job of managing, depends in large part on the nature of the evolving regulatory regime. For example, labelling the implementation of NICE guidance a 'standard' as opposed to a 'target' may do little to help managers exercise local discretion, since such core standards, like targets, are required to be met. Recent events, such as the backtracking on PCT reform, suggest that the government is prepared to allow room for local discretion in some areas. Whether this is an isolated case, or part of a wider trend, only time will tell.

References

Allsop, J. and Baggott, R. (2004) 'The NHS in England: from modernisation to marketisation', in N. Ellison, L. Bauld and M. Powell (eds) *Social Policy Review 16: Analysis and Debate in Social Policy, 2004*, Bristol: The Policy Press, pp 29-44.

Appleby, J. (2003) 'More money for health care in the UK ... more health?', *Journal of Health Services Research and Policy*, vol 8, pp 1-2.

Audit Commission (2005) *Managing the Financial Implications of NICE Guidance*, London: Audit Commission.

Blair, T. (2005) BBC Question Time, 29 April (www.channel4.com/news/factcheck/quote.jsp?id=144, accessed 5 November 2005).

Carvel, J. (2005a) 'GP surgeries must open evenings and weekends, says Hewitt', *The Guardian*, 11 November, p 14.

Carvel, J. (2005b) 'Hewitt's apology to calm NHS nerves over privatisation plans', *The Guardian*, 12 November, p 12.

Cohen, L. and Musson, G. (2000) 'Entrepreneurial identities: reflections from two case studies', *Organization*, vol 7, no 1, pp 31-48.

Currie, G. and Brown, D. (2003) 'A narratalogical approach to understanding processes of organizing in a UK hospital', *Human Relations*, vol 56, no 5, pp 563-86.

Dean, M. (1995) 'Governing the unemployed self in an active society', *Economy and Society*, vol 24, no 4, pp 559-83.

Dent, M. (2005) 'Post-new public management in public sector hospitals? The UK, Germany and Italy', *Policy & Politics*, vol 33, no 4, pp 623-36.

de Maeseneer, J., Hjortdahl, P. and Starfield, B. (2000) 'Fix what's wrong, not what's right, with general practice in Britain', *British Medical Journal*, vol 320, pp 1616-17.

DH (Department of Health) (2000) *The NHS Plan*, London: The Stationery Office.

DH (2001) *The Expert Patient Programme: Approach to Chronic Disease Management in the 21st Century*, London: The Stationery Office.

DH (2002) *Reforming NHS Financial Flows: Introducing Payment by Results*, London: DH.

DH (2004a) *Creating the NHS Improvement Plan*, London: DH.

DH (2004b) *Choosing Health? A Consultation on Action to Improve People's Health*, London: DH.

DH (2004c) *Choosing Health? Making Healthy Choices Easier*, London: DH.

DH (2004d) *National Standards, Local Action*, London: DH.

DH (2005a) *Creating a Patient-led NHS: Delivering the NHS Improvement Plan*, London: DH.

DH (2005b) *Commissioning a Patient-led NHS*, London: DH.

DH (2005c) *Self Care. A Real Choice – Self Care Support: A Practical Option*, London: The Stationery Office.

DH (2005d) *Supporting People with Long Term Conditions. An NHS and Social Care Model to Support Local Innovation and Integration*, London: The Stationery Office.

DH (2005e) 'Your health, your care, your say' (www.dh.gov.uk/ NewsHome/YourHealthYourCareYourSay/YourSayArticle/fs/ en?CONTENT_ID=4118922&chk=XaM1VB, accessed 22 September 2005).

DH (2005f) *Tackling Health Inequalities: Status Report on the Programme for Action*, London: DH.

DH (2006) *Our Health, Our Care, Our Say: A New Direction for Community Services*, London: The Stationery Office.

Donaldson, L. (2004) *The Chief Medical Officer's 'Ten Tips for Better Health'*, London: DH.

du Gay, P., Salaman, G. and Rees, B. (1996) 'The conduct of management and the management of conduct: contemporary managerial discourse and the constitution of the competent manager', *Journal of Management Studies*, vol 33, no 3, pp 263-82.

Fotaki, M., Boyd, A., McDonald, R., Roland, M., Smith, L., Edwards, A. and Elwyn, G. (2005) *Patient Choice and the Organisation and Delivery of Health Services: Scoping Exercise*, London: SDO Publications.

Gershon, P. (2004) *Releasing Resources to the Front Line: Independent Review of Public Sector Efficiency*, July, London: The Stationery Office.

Greer, S. (2004) *Territorial Politics and Health Policy*, Manchester: Manchester University Press.

Healthcare Commission (2005) 'Patients praise GP and dental care. But some say they still struggle to get appointments', 7 September (www.healthcarecommission.org.uk/NewsAndEvents/PressReleases/ PressReleaseDetail/fs/en?CONTENT_ID=4019367&chk=et3ZLb, accessed 25 November 2005).

Hewitt, P. (2005) 'Providing care – inspiring confidence', Speech by the Secretary of State for Health to the Chief Nursing Officer's Conference, 10 November (www.dh.gov.uk/NewsHome/Speeches/SpeechesList/ SpeechesArticle/fs/en?CONTENT_ID=4123198&chk=Hg6uGt, accessed 12 January 2006).

HM Treasury (2004) *Spending Review. New Public Spending Plans 2005-2008*, Cm 6237, London: HM Treasury.

Hood, C., James, O. and Scott, C. (2000) 'Regulation of government: has it increased, is it increasing, should it be diminished?', *Public Administration*, vol 78, no 2, pp 283-304.

Klein, R. (2005) 'Transforming the NHS: the story in 2004', in M. Powell, L. Bauld and K. Clarke (eds) *Social Policy Review 17: Analysis and Debate in Social Policy, 2005*, Bristol: The Policy Press, pp 51-68.

Le Grand, J., Mays, N. and Mulligan, J. (eds) (1998) *Learning from the NHS Internal Market: A Review of the Evidence*, London: Kings Fund.

McDonald, R. and Scott-Samuel, A. (2004) 'Missed opportunities? Wanless and the White Paper', *Public Health News*, 24 May.

Meikle, J. (2005) 'Hewitt steps in as trust refuses Herceptin to cancer patient', *The Guardian*, 9 November.

Newman, J., Barnes, M., Sullivan, H. and Knops, A. (2004) 'Public participation and collaborative governance', *Journal of Social Policy*, vol 33, no 2, pp 203-23.

Relph, N. (2005) 'Commissioning a patient-led NHS', Board Paper 62/05, Thames Valley Strategic Health Authority (www.tvsha.nhs.uk/board-papers-12th-october-2005/Board_paper_62-05_CPLNHS.pdf, accessed 12 January 2006).

Revill, J. (2002) 'Now nurses demand large hike in pay', *The Observer*, 3 November (http://observer.guardian.co.uk/nhs/story/0,1480,825092,00.html, accessed 25 November 2005).

Roland, M. (2004) 'Linking physicians' pay to the quality of care – a major experiment in the United Kingdom', *New England Journal of Medicine*, vol 351, pp 1448-54.

Roland, M., McDonald. R., Sibbald, B., Boyd. A., Fotaki, M., Gravelle, H. and Smith, L. (2005) *Outpatient Services and Primary Care. A Scoping Review of Research into Strategies for Improving Outpatient Effectiveness and Efficiency*, London: SDO Publications.

Wanless, D. (2002) *Securing Our Future Health: Taking a Long-Term View: Final Report*, London: HM Treasury.

Wanless, D. (2004) *Securing Good Health for the Whole Population: Final Report*, London: HM Treasury.

Zweifel, P., Felder, S. and Meiers, M. (1999) 'Ageing of population and health care expenditure: a red herring?', *Health Economics*, vol 8, no 6, pp 485-96.

THREE

A 'pivotal moment'? Education policy in England, 2005

Alan Dyson, Kirstin Kerr and Mel Ainscow

Equity and excellence

At the Labour Party conference in November 2005, Tony Blair famously declared that:

> Every time I've ever introduced a reform in Government, I wish in retrospect I had gone further. (Blair, 2005a)

In his third and final term, Blair, it seems, wants to make the sorts of fundamental and irreversible changes that he believes Margaret Thatcher was able to make, and the public services are the chosen arena for his reforming zeal. It is no surprise, therefore, that education has been a target for further reform in 2005, nor that he described the introduction of this year's Schools White Paper (DfES, 2005a), which embodied many of his radical ambitions, as a 'pivotal moment for education' (Blair, 2005b).

The analogy with the Thatcher governments is illuminating. Whereas the Thatcher reform agenda took time to gather pace – it was not, for instance, until 1988 that the most significant reform of the education service was attempted – the first Blair government hit the ground running with a major White Paper appearing shortly after the 1997 General Election and a relentless succession of White and Green Papers, guidance documents and centrally driven initiatives ever since. By 2005, therefore, the direction of policy was abundantly clear. Drawing on a human capital theory of economic development, the principal role of education was seen as being to develop the skill and knowledge levels of the workforce so that the country could compete in globalised economic markets (Wolf, 2002). This demanded the highest possible levels of educational achievement, and these were to be obtained by pursuing policies previously associated with Conservative administrations – the pursuit of 'standards', the reform of educational structures and practices in the interests of 'effectiveness', the continuing marketisation of the education system and the creation of a culture of performativity (Phillips and Harper-Jones, 2003, p 126). At the same time – and perhaps in distinction to previous administrations – education was also expected to play its part in tackling 'social exclusion' (Blair, 1997; SEU, 2001) by ensuring, among other things, that everyone – not just the highest attainers nor those from the most advantaged backgrounds – was equipped to compete in an ever more demanding labour market. Crucially, neoliberal policies for excellence and more socially democratic policies for equity were not seen as standing in contradiction to one another, but as constituting two sides of the same coin (Brehony and Deem, 2003). Rather than making fundamental choices between these two agendas, therefore, the trick for the New Labour government was to find specific policy initiatives that would enable both to be pursued simultaneously.

Given the well-established nature of New Labour's overall approach and the length of time it had already spent reforming the education system, it is tempting to ask what could be left to do in 2005. Why should this year more than any other constitute a 'pivotal moment' – and, if it did, why had previous reforms failed to achieve the desired results? Blair's answer to these questions seems to be that his government's previous reforms had simply been too timid – in which case, 2005 constitutes a 'pivotal moment' calling for rededicated purpose and renewed effort. However, we want to suggest that some more fundamental processes are at work here and that some underlying tensions in New Labour education policy have begun to make themselves felt. In this sense, 2005 may constitute a 'pivotal moment' of quite a different kind.

Learning what works, and finding what doesn't

The notion of 'what works' is central to New Labour policy making, not least in education (Brehony, 2005). It stems from the conviction that practical and politically achievable policy solutions can be found to what have hitherto been regarded as intractable social problems. In education, one of the most fundamental of these problems is an association between social background and educational achievement that has proved stubbornly resistant to all previous policy interventions. It is, of course, vital both to the human capital model of economic development and to the attempt to overcome social exclusion that this link be broken. 'That is why', as the Secretary of State for Education and Skills, Ruth Kelly, put it:

> I see my department as the department for life chances. And that is why
> I see it as my job to boost social mobility…. Our task is to make sure
> that for everyone involved in learning, excellence and equity become
> and remain reality. (Kelly, 2005)

However, the commitment to 'what works' requires more than warm
words about the principles on which policy should be based. It also
demands evidence about what is and is not working – evidence that
New Labour governments have secured in education by setting up
increasingly sophisticated monitoring systems at institutional, local and
national level. Unfortunately, by 2005 the evidence from these systems
was beginning to suggest that the task of squaring this equity-and-
excellence circle was proving more difficult than the government might
previously have imagined. Kelly was speaking in response to evidence
that social mobility in England might, if anything, be declining rather
than increasing (Blanden et al, 2005). Worse still, her own department's
review of performance data suggested that the link between social
background and educational achievement was proving almost as
stubbornly resistant to New Labour policy as to previous interventions
(DfES, 2005b). Specifically, although schools with the most disadvantaged
intakes were making some progress, it was less evident that they were
closing the gap on their more advantaged counterparts, or that it was the
most disadvantaged pupils in those schools who were producing the
improved results.

This was not the only troubling evidence to appear in 2005. For instance:

- The Statistics Commission (2005) confirmed the long-standing
  suspicions of some researchers (notably, Tymms, 2004) that primary
  school test scores overstated the real rise in pupil attainment under the
  first New Labour government.
- It became clear that the more modest gains in secondary attainments
  were due at least in part to schools switching their lower-attaining
  students onto courses where it seemed to be easier for them to gain
  accreditation than in standard GCSE examinations (Mansell, 2005).
- Despite successive initiatives, truancy figures showed a record rise of
  nearly 10% to their highest recorded level (Garner, 2005a, b).
- Despite the notional choice of schools that families could exercise, it
  became clear during the year that many families – some 70,0000 in all
  – simply did not get their first-choice schools. Although the problem
  was particularly acute in London, even outside of the capital only 85%
  of families were offered their first choice (Baker, 2005).

- At the same time, it was increasingly clear that choice processes were creating local hierarchies of schools and that the apparent success of some schools depended on having a place in the hierarchy that enabled them to weight their intake towards higher-attaining pupils from more resourceful families. The Sutton Trust (2005a), for example, reported that only 3% of pupils in the secondary schools with the highest levels of performance at GCSE were eligible for free school meals. Likewise, although recruitment to city academies was buoyant, it seemed that two thirds of them were recruiting fewer – in some cases, far fewer – pupils who were entitled to free school meals than had the 'failing' schools that they replaced (Taylor, 2005).
- In terms of university admissions, the widening participation agenda advanced vigorously by New Labour governments had some successes (The Sutton Trust, 2005b), but the percentage of state school recruits to universities fell for the first time and the drop-out rate among first-year students increased (Garner, 2005a, b).
- The evaluation of Sure Start, the family support programme aimed among other things at ensuring that young children from disadvantaged backgrounds would be best placed to take advantage of their schooling, reported that it was unable to find any evidence that the £3 billion investment was producing anything but the most modest improvements in outcomes, and that these tended to be associated with the less disadvantaged among its intended beneficiaries (NESS, 2005).

Had the New Labour education project been more modest in its ambitions, setbacks such as these might have been less significant. Squaring the circle of equity and excellence, however, requires a belief that apparently intractable educational problems are in fact solvable and, in particular, that the established link between background and achievement can indeed be broken. Whatever else the evidence indicated, it did not suggest that New Labour policy was bringing about such profound transformations. Clearly, something significantly different was called for, and both the Prime Minister (Blair, 2005b) and the Secretary of State for Education and Skills (Kelly, 2005) argued vigorously that, despite all that had been achieved since 1997, further education reform was essential.

The government's response

While this rededication to reform was clear, however, it was less certain what direction that reform should take. On the one hand, policy makers might interpret the negative feedback they were receiving as an indication of the necessity to 'go further' in a direction of travel already mapped out – the direction of standards and marketisation relentlessly pursued since 1997. On the other hand, they might decide that 'going further' had to mean, in practice, travelling in a different direction, and that what was needed was not simply more of the same, but a more fundamental rethink of how the contradiction between equity and excellence arose in the first place and about what sort of education system might be needed to bring about its reconciliation.

Our contention is that much of education policy making in 2005 can be understood as a contest between these positions. We do not wish to imply that the contest was open, nor that its participants were necessarily fully aware what it was that they were engaged in. Nonetheless, it is, we suggest, the reality of this contest and the uncertain nature of its outcome that makes 2005 a 'pivotal moment'.

Steady as we go?

Many of the year's policy developments can be read as an attempt to pursue the existing direction of travel. Indeed, many of them had been outlined in the previous year's *Five Year Strategy for Children and Learners* (DfES, 2004), which ensured some continuity of policy making between the second and third New Labour terms. Likewise, although a new Education Act was pased in 2005, its provisions were largely about tidying up the existing system and and making it function more efficiently. Hence, it paved the way for the shorter, sharper school inspections, more predictable and manageable three-year school budgets, and school profiles – shorter documents to replace the annual governors' report and parents' meeting.

Other reforms, too, simply intensified existing policy approaches. The continued 'scholarisation' of the early years was a case in point. In November, the government introduced a Childcare Bill that, among other things, would require every registered nursery and childminder to follow a new Early Years Foundation Stage comprising guidance on learning and development from birth to the age of five. The proposal to regulate early learning and development in this way produced a predictable outcry in the press and from early years specialists (Ward, 2005). In fact, it represented an extension of two existing strands of policy – the creation of a more extensive, coherent and accessible pattern of childcare to release parents for paid work, and the regulation and 'improvement' of children's early learning experiences as a means of equipping them with the necessary tools for tackling the school curriculum proper. The 'curriculum for toddlers', therefore, constituted an attempt to find another lever to pull to achieve well-established ends in a context where existing policies were proving less than totally effective.

At the other end of the age range, a series of developments around 14–19 education, further education (FE) college provision and vocational training can also be read as more of the same. The Tomlinson review of the 14–19 curriculum in the previous year (Tomlinson, 2004) invited the government to undertake a radical overhaul of a phase of education that had become a rather ramshackle mixture of traditional 'academic' qualifications and a plethora of more vocationally oriented pathways, with provision divided between schools, sixth-form colleges, FE colleges and others. Tomlinson advocated a single diploma to incorporate both vocational and academic pathways, a reduction in the amount of assessment required of students, and a reorientation towards more imaginative and integrated modes of assessment.

It was clear as soon as the Tomlinson review was published that the government was unhappy with radical proposals that might threaten the traditional pathways to 'academic' excellence, even if retaining these meant perpetuating the academic–vocational divide that has bedevilled secondary and post-secondary education in England for generations. Nonetheless, in February 2005 the government launched its White Paper on 14–19 education and skills (DfES, 2005c), followed shortly by a Skills White Paper (DfES, 2005d) focused on learning in and around the workplace and later in the year by the publication of the Foster review of FE colleges (Foster, 2005) and the Learning and Skills Council's funding plan (LSC, 2005). The rhetoric surrounding these developments was one of fundamental change. The 14–19 White Paper, for instance, articulated a radical ambition:

> ... to transform secondary and postsecondary education so that all young people achieve and continue in learning until at least the age of 18. (DfES, 2005c, p 4)

The avowed aim was to create a system of post-14 provision that was vocationally oriented, where employers had a greater say in shaping provision to their needs (for instance, through 'National Skills Academies'), which offered a coherent ladder of provision and awards up which learners could progress, and which offered incentives and support for learners who were in danger of becoming stuck at the bottom of that ladder. Insofar as this marked a vocationalisation of post-14 provision, it was, of course, entirely in line with the underlying economic orientation of government education policy. The creation of coherent, vocationally oriented pathways is likely to deliver all learners into the labour marketplace with more economically useful and saleable skills – not least those most at risk of social exclusion who may have given up on academic pathways and might otherwise disengage from education entirely.

At the same time, the 14-19 White Paper opted for the preservation of GCSEs and A levels in much their current form, 'as cornerstones of the new system' (DfES, 2005c, p 6), thus stopping some way short of the reforms proposed by Tomlinson. This can, of course, be read as an exercise in *realpolitik* – a concern about media reaction if 'gold standard' examinations were abolished, covered by a rhetoric of transformation. However, it can also be read as a continuing commitment to the proposition that policies for excellence can be pursued in parallel with policies for equity, and that hard choices between fundamentally different agendas are unnecessary.

New directions?

However, not all developments in 2005 built so clearly on long-established policy frameworks. As the inadequacies of current approaches became more apparent, alternative policy directions began to emerge, either through entirely new initiatives or through the acceleration of recent trends.

One policy area in which this was true was around the issue of school autonomy. In 1997, New Labour inherited a school system in which the power of local education authorities (LEAs) had been considerably weakened and schools were encouraged to pursue their own institutional interests in an increasingly autonomous manner. This increase in autonomy was essential for the efficient working of a market in schooling and for holding individual schools to account for the standards of achievement they were able to generate. At first, therefore, New Labour seemed content for schools to act with a high degree of independence, both from their LEAs and from each other, exercising control through national accountability frameworks and through centrally devised programmes and strategies.

However, the model of autonomous, competitive schools was always likely to create a highly fragmented system that would be inefficient in terms of sharing expertise and resources, engendering and disseminating local innovation, or creating units for the delivery of area-based services. Accordingly, in recent years, the government has sponsored a range of initiatives – such as Excellence in Cities partnerships and the Leadership

Incentives Grants initiative – aimed at promoting inter-institutional collaboration. In 2005, this trend was given further impetus by the launch of Education Improvement Partnerships (EIPs), which strengthened the possibilities of institutions working together to develop shared provision for all the children, families and communities in the area they served (DfES, 2005e). While this was not, by any means, a reinvention of the traditional LEA, it was certainly a distinct move towards a vision of locally coordinated provision.

Moreover, although EIPs at the time of their introduction constituted no more than an enabling mechanism, they may, in the context of a 'new localism' (Aspden and Birch, 2005) across much government policy, signal a more fundamental change. The prospectus, for instance, outlined a model of the location of EIPs in the policy arena that placed them at the centre of interactions between 'national priorities', 'local authority strategy', 'local community needs' and 'schools leading reform' (DfES, 2005e, Foreword). This was significant in the shifting of partnerships to centre stage and in the introduction of 'local community needs' as a factor shaping provision. Both implied a very different model of governance from the linear and hierarchical command structure that had been developed in education since 1988, and from the attempts by the first New Labour government to standardise practice through the National Strategies.

It is no coincidence that part of the rationale for EIPs was that they would be better able than individual schools to respond to the *Every Child Matters* agenda (DfES, 2003a). Here, too, we saw a recently emerged strategy given further impetus by a new development in 2005 – this time, aspects of the Childcare Bill dealing with school provision, and the launch of an extended schools prospectus (DfES, 2005f). *Every Child Matters* was concerned with the development of integrated child and family services, working to generate shared outcomes. In its original form, the emphasis was very much on the reconfiguration of services at local authority level, with a few exemplary 'full service extended schools' (DfES, 2003b, 2003c) becoming heavily involved in areas of disadvantage. What was significant about the 2005 developments was that they envisaged the involvement of *all* schools to differing extents in delivering child, family and community services. This again was very different from the deliberately narrow focus on driving up standards of attainment that was promoted as the sole concern of schools during the first New Labour term.

This is not to say that there was any wholesale change of direction in 2005; insofar as new directions emerged at all, they did so tentatively and alongside established policy frameworks. Nonetheless, it seems to us that there is something distinctive about the model of collaboratively minded institutions, working with each other and with a range of other providers to deliver a wide range of services to children, families and communities – something that would have been inconceivable within the more narrowly conceived and centrally controlled models of 1997, or, for that matter, of 2001.

The Schools White Paper

Of all the developments in 2005, the one that attracted most political and public attention was the publication of the Schools White Paper, *Higher Standards, Better Schools for All* (DfES, 2005a). Here, above all, we see the tensions in government strategy between an intensification of existing policy directions and the tentative emergence of new directions.

The most high-profile of the White Paper's proposals was for the establishment of self-governing 'trust schools' involving external partners and able, among other things, to control their own admissions. However, this was supplemented by a whole raft of other proposals – for the establishment of parent councils to monitor parents' interests in these schools, the further extension of the academies programme, the provision of better information for parents in choosing schools and of extended free transport for children from poorer families, support for parents to set up their own schools, an increased emphasis on one-to-one tuition and on setting and streaming, the easing of restrictions on the expansion of 'successful' schools, and the reformulation of the local authority's role as commissioner of provision and champion for parents. On the face of it, these proposals appeared to amount to radical reform of the school system. Certainly, this was the impression created by the rationale for change offered by the Prime Minister (DfES, 2005a, Foreword), who cast the White Paper as part of a great tradition of educational reform. For Blair, the history of education in England since the Second World War was one of parents – not least, middle-class parents – driving successive reforms of the system so that it more nearly met their needs. Just as comprehensive schools overcame some of the problems of the tripartite system, so further improvements had been brought about by the New Labour reforms that had 're-energised' the comprehensive system. However, while parental choice had played a major part in driving up school standards, there were not yet enough 'good' schools in urban areas, and families who could not deploy financial resources to increase the range of choices were most disadvantaged by this state of affairs – hence the need for one more effort.

This is, of course, a very conservative (with both a large and a small 'c') rationale, insofar as it picks up the 'choice and diversity' approach developed by Conservative governments in the 1980s and 1990s (DfE, 1992), and pursued by New Labour governments since 1997. To this extent, the White Paper's proposals for a diversification of school type, an increased role for parental choice and a reduction in the direct management responsibilities of local authorities, were radical only in the sense that they constituted a significant further move in a well-established policy direction. The trust schools themselves were simply a further development in the long line of quasi-independent schools that began with the City Technology Colleges of the 1980s. Significantly, both opponents and proponents of the White Paper presented it in these terms. Will Hutton, an advocate of the government's approach, for instance, saw it as squaring the excellence and equity circle by extending the benefits of the marketised, standards-driven system to parts of the population that had previously been denied them. 'In reality', he argued,

> ... the White Paper democratises the choices that the middle classes already enjoy and the structures they prefer. (Hutton, 2005)

Even Estelle Morris, a former Secretary of State for Education who emerged as the focus for parliamentary opposition to the government's proposals, commented:

> I'm not sure it's as radical as it was trailed.... (quoted in White, 2005)

Significantly, however, Morris made a distinction between the White Paper's headline proposals, which constituted more of the same, and other, less trumpeted proposals, which she felt were more likely to make a genuine difference (Morris, 2005). The most interesting parts, she suggested, were not the ones to do with choice and diversity, but a series of proposals designed to encourage schools to collaborate with each other – in line, of course, with the developments we have noted above. Nor, we might add, were these the only aspects of the White Paper that strengthened the emerging new directions of policy. The proposals to extend parental involvement and control, to recast local authorities as parents' advocates and to involve external partners in the governance of schools may, in practice, achieve little beyond strengthening the influence of middle-class families and corporate business in the education system. However, they opened up the possibility – to put it no more strongly – of diverse kinds of locally controlled schools, responsive to local communities and priorities, emerging in at least some places. In this respect, it is notable that the initial reaction from commercial and other organisations already involved in running schools was cautious (Shaw et al, 2005), but that there was some anecdotal evidence to suggest that other types of organisations with a more local focus – such as housing associations, universities or genuinely local businesses – were more enthusiastic.

This tension between old and new policy directions was perhaps most obvious in the White Paper's proposals with regard to parental choice of schools. The principle that families should be able to express a preference for particular schools was certainly nothing new, and the proposed strengthening of the mechanisms supporting choice for less advantaged families was, as Hutton (2005) argued, no more than a democratisation of established processes. However, the White Paper's proposals promised to create a new landscape within which choice could be exercised. Although in principle, 'choice and diversity' (DfE, 1992) have always gone together, in practice, real diversity of provision has remained limited and families have had to choose (within sometimes severe constraints) between similar kinds of schools doing broadly similar things. Not surprisingly, local hierarchies have emerged as some schools have been perceived as more successful than others (Riddell, 2005). However, the establishment of trust schools, the extension of academies, the possibilities for federations and the more direct involvement of parents promised to create a situation of more genuine diversity in which different kinds of schools, differently governed and resourced, would be trying to do different kinds of things. In these circumstances, 'choice' might – in principle at least – come to mean something quite different from the scramble for a place at the top of the school hierarchy that it has so often meant in recent years.

A pivotal moment?

Among her many comments on the White Paper, Morris drew attention to what she saw as its inherently contradictory nature:

> The Schools White Paper must be one of the most contradictory documents ever produced by government. Its advance publicity was all about choice, consumer power and freedom. But the content has a strong commitment to social justice and a powerful analysis of how education can help to deliver it. The big question, of course, is whether one can be used to achieve the other.... (Morris, 2005)

This question brings us back to the theme of this chapter – the relationship between 'excellence and equity' in New Labour policy and, specifically, the New Labour project of reconciling essentially Thatcherite policies with a concern for social justice.

Like Morris, other commentators have identified what Brehony (2005) calls the 'irresolvable contradiction' underlying New Labour education policy. In their contribution to *Social Policy Review 17*, for instance, Hulme and Hulme (2005) point to:

> The tensions and contradictions evident in a platform of education reform
> that is couched in the language of social inclusion, yet extends the market
> in education and regulates this through ever more intrusive instruments
> of 'governmentality'. (Hulme and Hulme, 2005, p 33)

They go on to show how this underlying contradiction creates a motor for continual policy development, and argue that this takes the form of the 'reconstitution of tried and tested policy responses' (p 33). To a very large extent, it seems to us, this analysis still holds good for developments in 2005 where a rhetoric of radical innovation has, as we have seen, often camouflaged what is essentially 'more of the same'.

However, we have also tried to suggest that something different has now become apparent. As the New Labour education project has moved into a third term, as early signs of success have given way to much more mixed feedback, and as the renewed commitment to reform has prioritised the need for deep and lasting impacts, new policy formations have, we believe, begun to emerge. We make no claim that these formations are necessarily coherent, well thought through or likely to promote greater educational equity. Nonetheless, we detect an emerging reconfiguration of the relationship between national government, local government, local communities and educational institutions, a redefinition of the role of schools, and the creation of a new landscape of choice that which, we believe, have been inconceivable in 1997. It is in this sense that we agree with Tony Blair that 2005 may indeed mark a 'pivotal moment' in education policy.

There are, it seems to us, important implications of this analysis. It leads us to see policy as restless and dynamic. The apparent certainties of New Labour education policy are much more fragile than they appear, and the future may in fact turn out to be highly unpredictable. If, therefore, the contradictions embodied in policy prevent any straightforward development towards greater social justice, they may also have considerable generative potential and may open up new spaces for educational practice.

With that in mind, it seems to us that there is an important task for educators and researchers who see themselves as committed to the development of a more equitable education system. In addition to identifying the contradictions and impasses in policy, we have also, we suggest, to identify the spaces that are now opening up and to find ways of colonising those spaces. We have, in particular, to respond to the challenge thrown down by Will Hutton in his defence of the Schools White Paper. Its proposals may, he acknowledges, be an uneasy compromise between what we have here called excellence and equity. 'But', he continues,

> ... anybody with a better idea of how we can break out of where we actually are, please come forward. (Hutton, 2005)

While one may disagree with Hutton's analysis of the White Paper, and with the terms in which this challenge is posed, it is, we believe, one that we ignore at our peril.

References

Aspden, J. and Birch, D. (2005) *New Localism – Citizen Engagement, Neighbourhoods and Public Services: Evidence From Local Government,* London: Office of the Deputy Prime Minister.

Baker, M. (2005) 'Which is the fairest path of all?', *Times Educational Supplement,* 21 October, p 19.

Blair, T. (1997) 'Bringing Britain together', Speech by the Prime Minister, the Rt Hon Tony Blair MP, Stockwell Park School, South London, 8 December, London: Social Exclusion Unit (www.socialexclusionunit.gov.uk/downloaddoc.asp?id=61, accessed 16 December 2005).

Blair, T. (2005a) 'We are the change-makers', London: Labour Party (www.labour.org.uk index.php?id=news2005&ux_news[id]= ac05tb&cHash=d8353c3d74, accessed 25 November 2005).

Blair, T. (2005b) 'PM reflects on "pivotal moment" for education', London: 10 Downing Street (www.numberten.gov.uk/output/Page8357.asp, accessed 25 November 2005).

Blanden, J., Gregg, P. and Machin, S. (2005) *Intergenerational Mobility in Europe and North America,* London: Centre for Economic Performance, London School of Economics and Political Science, for The Sutton Trust.

Brehony, K.J. (2005) 'Primary schooling under New Labour: the irresolvable contradiction of excellence and enjoyment', *Oxford Review of Education*, vol 31, no 1, pp 29-46.

Brehony, K.J. and Deem, R. (2003) 'Education policy', in N. Ellison and C. Pierson (eds) *Developments in British Social Policy 2*, Basingstoke: Palgrave Macmillan, pp 177-93.

DfE (Department for Education) (1992) *Choice and Diversity: A New Framework for Schools*, London: HMSO.

DfES (Department for Education and Skills) (2003a) *Every Child Matters*, Cm 5860, London: The Stationery Office.

DfES (2003b) *Full Service Extended Schools: Requirements and Specifications*, London: DfES.

DfES (2003c) *Full Service Extended Schools Planning Documents*, London: DfES.

DfES (2004) *Five Year Strategy for Children and Learners*, London: The Stationery Office.

DfES (2005a) *Higher Standards, Better Schools for All: More Choice for Parents and Pupils*, Cm 6677, London: The Stationery Office.

DfES (2005b) *Has the Social Class Gap Narrowed in Primary Schools?*, A background note to accompany the talk by the Rt Hon Ruth Kelly MP, Secretary of State for Education and Skills, 26 July, London: DfES.

DfES (2005c) *14-19 Education and Skills*, Cm 6476, London: The Stationery Office.

DfES (2005d) *Skills: Getting On in Business, Getting On at Work*, Cm 6483-1, London: The Stationery Office.

DfES(2005e) *Education Improvement Partnerships: Local Collaboration for School Improvement and Better Service Delivery*, London: DfES.

DfES (2005f) *Extended Schools: Access to Opportunities and Services for All. A Prospectus*, London: DfES.

Foster, S.A. (2005) *Realising the Potential*, London: DfES.

Garner, R. (2005a) 'A tough nut to crack – why Blair is failing at his main subject', *The Independent*, 22 September (http://education.independent.co.uk/news/article314255.ece, accessed 16 December 2005).

Garner, R. (2005b) 'Education, education, education: a triple blow for the government', *The Independent*, 22 September (http://education.independent.co.uk/news/article314258.ece, accessed 16 December 2005).

Hulme, R. and Hulme, M. (2005) 'New Labour's education policy: innovation or reinvention?', in M. Powell, L. Bauld and K. Clarke (eds) *Social Policy Review 17: Analysis and Debate in Social Policy, 2005*, Bristol: The Policy Press, pp 33-49.

Hutton, W. (2005) 'At last our schools have been set free', *The Observer*, 30 October, p 30.

Kelly, R. (2005) 'Education and social progress', 26 July, London: DfES (www.dfes.gov.uk/speeches/speech.cfm?SpeechID=242, accessed 4 August 2005).

Learning and Skills Council (LSC) (2005) *Priorities for Success: Funding for Learning and Skills 2006-2008*, Coventry: LSC.

Mansell, W. (2005) 'Provisional scores distort GCSE picture', *TES*, 21 October, p 2.

Morris, E. (2005) 'A contradiction in terms', *The Guardian*, Education Guardian, 22 November, p 4.

NESS (National Evaluation of Sure Start) (2005) *National Evaluation Report: Early Impacts of Sure Start Local Programmes on Children and Families*, Research Report NESS/2005/FR/013, London: DfES.

Phillips, R. and Harper-Jones, G. (2003) 'Whatever next? Education policy and New Labour: the first four years, 1997-2001', *British Educational Research Journal*, vol 29, no 1, pp 125-32.

Riddell, R. (2005) 'Government policy, stratification and urban schools: a commentary on the five-year strategy for children and learners', *Journal of Education Policy*, vol 20, no 2, pp 237-41.

SEU (Social Exclusion Unit) (2001) *Preventing Social Exclusion*, London: SEU.

Shaw, M., Slater, J. and Meghji, S. (2005) 'Firms say no to trust schools', *TES*, 25 November, p 1.

Statistics Commission (2005) *Measuring Standards in English Primary Schools*, Statistics Commission Report No 23, London: Statistics Commission.

Sutton Trust, The (2005a) *Rates of Eligibility for Free School Meals at the Top State Schools*, London: The Sutton Trust.

Sutton Trust, The (2005b) *State School Admissions to our Leading Universities. An Update to the Missing 3000*, London: The Sutton Trust.

Taylor, M. (2005) 'Are city academies really helping the poorest children?', *The Guardian*, 31 October, pp 8-9.

Tomlinson, M. (chair) (2004) *14-19 Curriculum and Qualifications Reform: Final Report of the Working Group on 14-19 Reform*, London: DfES.

Tymms, P. (2004) 'Are standards rising in English primary schools?', *British Educational Research Journal*, vol 30, no 4, pp 477-94.

Ward, L. (2005) 'Toddler curriculum criticised by European education expert', *The Guardian*, 15 November, p 13.

White, M. (2005) 'Reaction', *The Guardian*, 26 October, p 13.

Wolf, A. (2002) *Does Education Matter? Myths about Education and Economic Growth*, London: Penguin Books.

FOUR

Strategic pragmatism? The state of British housing policy

Mark Stephens and Deborah Quilgars

Introduction

In January 2005 the government published the findings of an independent evaluation of English housing policy over the period 1975-2000 (Stephens et al, 2005). This was the first attempt to examine housing policy in this way since the 1977 review (DoE, 1977), and it provides the framework in this chapter for examining current policy developments.

The evaluation found that while many individual policy instruments were successful within their own terms, they often had unexpected and undesirable spillover effects. Sometimes spillover effects took the form of unacknowledged but unavoidable trade-offs between competing objectives. Policies were most successful when they followed the grain of social and economic change and least successful when they did not. Moreover, housing policies interact with related policies and institutions, notably social security and labour markets, to shape the nature of the housing system.

By the late 1990s, housing policy mimicked social security policy. The shift away from the use of social rented housing for general needs purposes mirrored the move away from universal benefits to those that were highly targeted through means testing. The two policies met with the emergence of Housing Benefit as by far the largest single financial subsidy for housing. Meanwhile the growth of home ownership, much of it due to the Right to Buy policy, was accompanied by mortgage market deregulation that not only expanded access to finance, but increased the liquidity of housing as an asset by making equity withdrawal relatively straightforward. Social and economic changes led to the decline in the nuclear family, the increase in household types at risk of poverty, the large rise in poverty and income inequality, and the polarisation of the labour market between two-earner and no-earner households. These were mirrored in acute tenure polarisation that often translated into spatial polarisation (Stephens et al, 2003).

The evaluation also demonstrated how the governance of housing policy has changed over the past three decades since the mid 1970s. The importance of the department with formal responsibility for housing (the Department of the Environment and its successors and now the Office of the Deputy Prime Minister, ODPM) diminished as the emphasis in subsidies shifted away from supply-side and towards Housing Benefit, which, in the 1980s, became the sole preserve of the department with responsibility for social security (now the Department for Work and Pensions). The Treasury's importance also grew, partly as a result of its growing influence over so-called 'spending departments', but crucially from the late 1980s as the importance of the housing market in economic management became apparent. Deregulation of the mortgage market made house prices more sensitive to interest rates, while in turn housing values had an important impact on consumption levels. Since 1997, the responsibility for interest rate setting has been passed to the Bank of England's Monetary Policy Committee (MPC), so adding another arm of government to those already with an interest in housing policy. Unsurprisingly, the dispersal of policy responsibilities between departments contributed to something of a 'strategic policy collapse' (Stephens, 2005a), and regaining a strategic vision for housing policy is an important challenge.

In this chapter we examine the government's housing strategy, and provide a commentary on three key aspects of housing policy in England and Scotland. Many aspects of housing policy in Wales are similar to the situation in England, but the Welsh Assembly does have powers to make secondary legislation so it is often able to make its own regulations or standards within the framework of primary legislation passed by the Westminster Parliament. We do not discuss the distinctive features of Welsh policy here, but readers wishing to pursue this further are directed to the National Assembly for Wales (2001) and Richard (2004). However, we do consider developments in Scotland separately as the Scottish Parliament is able to pass primary legislation in the field of housing.

Housing strategy

The government's housing strategy since 1997 is somewhat difficult to discern. In part this reflects the lack of strategy when the Labour Party returned to power and the dispersal of responsibility for housing between government departments. While some progress has been made with more papers issued jointly by departments, the picture is further clouded by the escalation in the numbers of documents issued by government, often unnecessarily lengthy, repetitive and with an increased emphasis on presentation (for example, through photographs) over clarity. The status of papers is similarly diffused, with a growth in the number of 'consultation papers'. It is also notable that much policy development is occurring without new legislation – for example, stock transfers. The days of crisp and clear Green Papers followed by White Papers and a Bill are gone, seemingly lost in a sea of postmodern confusion posted somewhere on the Internet.

However, despite the difficulty in following housing policy developments, a housing strategy can be discerned. It has been shaped by two key documents. The first was the Green Paper (DETR, 2000), which remains the driving force behind the reforms to the social rented sector in England. The Paper is critical of the 'residualised' nature of the social rented sector. Under-investment in the sector is blamed for the poor quality of much of the housing, contributing to its lack of popularity, a problem that the government began to address early on. The policy of encouraging stock transfers from local authorities was partly connected to the improvement of property, but was also part of the strategy of changing the governance of housing in which local authorities step back from their role as the providers of housing and become strategic managers. Within this framework the government hoped to increase choice within the social rented sector through three principal reforms: (1) the introduction of choice-based lettings; (2) the restructuring of rents so that they better reflect the value of the property; and (3) the reform of Housing Benefit.

The second document to shape housing policy at a strategic level has been the Barker Report on housing supply (Barker, 2004). The report was commissioned by the Treasury in response to the persistence of house price inflation that was attributed in part to the diminishing responsiveness of the supply side to house prices. Although a formal response to Barker was not made until December 2005, the *Sustainable Communities* plan (ODPM, 2003) outlined the commitment to support the provision of some 200,000 additional houses in the Thames Gateway and other growth areas by 2016, a commitment repeated in the five-year plan, published in January 2005 (HM Treasury/ODPM, 2005; ODPM, 2005a). The formal response to the Barker Report addressed both planning and infrastructure requirements necessary to support additional housing supply (ODPM, 2005b). The response included the publication of a new draft planning policy statement for housing, which is intended to make the planning system more responsive to housing markets and to ensure a better supply of land to meet long-term housing need (ODPM, 2005c). A consultation paper on 'planning gain supplement' (PGS) was also issued (HM Treasury et al, 2005). It is hoped that PGS will provide local authorities with an incentive to approve applications, with landowners being taxed on the increase in land values arising from the granting of planning permission to build residential property.

Following a recommendation in the Barker Report, the government announced the merger of regional housing and planning functions by September 2006 to ensure that a strategic approach is taken to housing and infrastructure requirements. A cross-departmental review will consider how better to coordinate the strategic delivery of the infrastructure necessary to support housing growth in the run-up to the 2007 Spending Review. Meanwhile, a fund to support infrastructure projects in 'new growth points' was also announced, with local authorities able to bid for 'new growth point status'. The government's target is to raise housing production from 150,000 units to 200,000 units per year over the next decade, with the private sector providing most of the increase. The proposals, announced in the Chancellor's pre-Budget statement in December 2005, were met with some scepticism from the building industry, apparently frustrated by attempts to make it an arm of social policy and by others who believe that the measures are inadequate to address the underlying problem (*Financial Times*, 7 December 2005, news report). Meanwhile, measures to increase the level of home ownership to 75% – largely through demand-side measures – are connected unconvincingly to the strategy of expanding supply.

The third area of development in 2005 originated in the early 2000s and addresses homelessness and related support issues within the government's broader *Sustainable Communities* agenda (ODPM, 2003). *Homes for All* (ODPM, 2005a) included an emphasis on the provision of support to those households who would otherwise have difficulty in sustaining a tenancy. In 2005 the long-awaited review of the *Supporting People* programme (ODPM, 2005d), which funds housing-related support for vulnerable groups including those at risk of, or experiencing, homelessness, was published, as was another statement of strategy on homelessness, *Sustainable Communities: Settled Homes, Changing Lives* (ODPM, 2005e).

From strategy to policies

We now examine how policy developments fit in with the wider housing strategy in the three broad areas of: housing choice in the social rented sector; developments in the home ownership and private rented markets; and homelessness and housing-related support.

Housing choice in the social rented sector

Choice has become an important theme, particularly in the third term of the Blair Labour government. The public sector reform agenda has focused on proposed reforms to the health service and to school education. In each of these cases choice is interpreted as an individual consumer choice of a particular provider, that is, parental choice in schools and patients' choice of hospital. Importantly, the budget constraint is borne by the government, not the individual consumer. The key debates have centred on the utilitarian question of whether choice will act as a driver for greater inequality or as a means of pushing up standards across the board.

The vision of choice in social rented housing is fundamentally different. It can be characterised as an attempt to create a social market, whereby rents are kept below market levels, but reflect better the relative value of the property. The proposed reform of Housing Benefit (under the banner Local Housing Allowance, LHA), whereby the eligible rent is fixed for a particular household type in an area, is intended to provide the incentive for households to make a choice between housing costs and the quantity and quality of housing consumption. If the rent is below the level allowed for, then the tenant is able to retain the difference, but once the rent rises above the allowance, the individual pays the difference, that is, the marginal cost of housing rises to 100% (compared with 0 in the current system). Pilots on the LHA continued in 2005 (see Rhodes and Rugg, 2005; Stephens, 2005b). Meanwhile, choice-based lettings are intended to provide the means for households' preferences to be matched to properties with the desired characteristics (and rent). While the social market in social rented housing is also based on individual consumer choice, the key difference from the proposed introduction of choice into education and health is that it is the individual consumer, and not the government, that faces the budget constraint.

In social rented housing the individual consumer is expected to decide how much housing (in terms of quantity or quality) they wish to consume, whereas in health and education the choice is about the provider. Curiously, in the social rented sector the question of choice between providers is far from prominent. To the extent that there is choice, it is a collective one, arising from proposals for stock transfers. While there has been a move away from the large-scale public sector monopoly provider, in many cases this takes the form of a stock transfer housing association. The numbers of providers and developers among 'traditional' housing associations is diminishing, and apart from the opening up of subsidy to private developers (a provision contained in the 2004 Housing Act, with little immediate impact), there is little to propel choice between providers, which in turn may explain the government's heavy reliance on the micro-management of standards within the sector.

Much play is made of the fact that households have to apply for a house under a pure choice-based scheme, but this merely alters the method of application, and could coexist with a purely needs-based system. The fundamental difference between a needs-based system and a 'choice'-based system is that the 'currency' changes, with the emphasis shifting away from need and towards the ability to wait. One might expect this to favour the less desperate households over the more desperate ones.

But there are circumstances where choice-based lettings would increase choice for everyone. The conditions that must be met are as follows. First, the stock of housing, or more precisely the stock of housing available for letting, must be diverse. Second, the diverse housing stock must be matched by diverse consumption preferences among potential tenants. This provides us with the possibility that preferences might be better matched to individual properties than under traditional systems. Moreover, these consumption preferences must be unpredictable, in other words not capable of being detected by a purely needs-based system. It is also vital that there is an excess supply of *valued* characteristics in the housing stock available for letting. Finally, there must be an availability of alternative landlords so that tenants can exercise 'exit' power in order to maintain (especially maintenance) standards.

Conversely, a particular set of conditions would be likely to increase inequality. Once again we need a diverse stock of housing available for letting, but consumers have uniform and predicable consumption preferences. The situation is worsened by an insufficient supply of properties available for let with valued characteristics. Finally, there are no alternative landlords and hence no 'exit voice' can be exercised.

Rent restructuring and Housing Benefit reforms will also come into play to affect outcomes. To the extent that an applicant has a choice between properties (availability), they must make trade-offs between housing and other consumption. The difficulty here is that with social assistance benefits for working-age adults set at very low levels with no allowance for housing costs, 'excess' housing consumption must be bought out of income intended for non-housing purposes. The reduction of choice to one between limited housing preferences and the maintenance of post-rent income at social assistance levels is a very limited one indeed.

These reforms mark a shift in housing policy away from its traditional role as a merit good – one from whose consumption society derives some benefit. While in principle individual consumers should know best their consumption preferences, it is difficult to separate this from the resource implications arising from Housing Benefit reform. In principle, there could be greater choice in the sense that individuals might be better able to choose house A or house B, but it is difficult to construe choices that are highly constrained by cost as choices at all.

Developments in the home ownership and private rented markets

One of the consequences of the failure of supply and the resultant upward trend in real house prices has been the diminishing ability of new households to access home ownership. As house prices have increased, the proportions of first-time buyers have fallen and their average age has begun to increase. While there is some evidence that younger households suffered a relative deterioration in their incomes in the 1990s and that there might be some shift in tenure preferences away from home ownership and towards private renting, it is clear that many households (or would-be households) have been priced out of the market. While the UK has a liberalised mortgage market with wide access to 100% mortgages, as house prices rise more households become unable to afford mortgages that cover all of the value of a property.

While the strategy to increase housing supply is clearly the only one that can fundamentally improve access to home ownership (without the huge hardship and economic damage that a full-scale housing market recession would entail), there are questions about how the market can or indeed should be managed. Principal responsibility has fallen on the Bank of England's MPC through its control of interest rates. However, it is important to note that its remit is concerned with house prices only so far as they threaten to undermine the MPC's duty to meet inflation targets. Unlike the Treasury in the late 1980s when the link between housing wealth and consumption was not incorporated into the models of the economy, the MPC has been able to maintain low inflation alongside persistent house price inflation. Access to home ownership is not its responsibility per se. Interestingly, the Barker Report did not recommend the use of land or property taxation to control house price inflation, or indeed to increase the supply of housing. In 2005, of notable importance has been the government's post-election U-turn (in September), by which it decided to postpone the revaluation of property for Council Tax purposes. This was justified by the expansion of the remit of Michael Lyons' inquiry into local authority funding and the alteration of its timetable. The decision means that revaluation will not occur before the next General Election, provided Parliament runs for its usual four- to five-year course. However, it also means that the opportunity to use property taxation to limit speculative rises in house prices has been lost.

Meanwhile there have been signs of significant revival in investment in the private rented sector since the introduction of the Buy to Let initiative in the mid-1990s. While it seems likely that the additional finance that has been brought into the housing market by Buy to Let mortgages has contributed to house price inflation, and hence to the pricing out of households, it has also provided housing for many people either unable or unwilling to enter homeownership. However, the distinctive feature of the British privately rented sector remains its dependence on small-scale landlords and the lack of institutional ownership or funding. The dependence on small-scale landlords means that the sector is likely to be viable only if their assets – the housing – are relatively liquid, which explains the dependence on assured shorthold tenancies that can be terminated after six months. Although the evidence suggests that many Buy to Let landlords intend to remain in the market for the long term (Rhodes and Bevan, 2003), the dependence on short-term tenancies is likely to limit the attractiveness of the tenure to people who might otherwise wish to live in it long term.

The proposed expansion of the Self Invested Personal Pensions (SIPPS) to include second homes (and so receive privileged tax treatment) was abandoned in the pre-Budget Statement in December. The scheme had been criticised by many commentators as being likely to contribute significantly to house price inflation, although the announcement of its abandonment brought warnings of the collapse in the market for smaller flats, much favoured by Buy to Let investors and of which there were already suspicions of an over-supply.

However, the government intends to proceed with the inclusion of provisions for UK Real Estate Investment Trusts (REITs) in the 2006 Finance Bill. REITs might act as a vehicle for increasing long-term institutional investment in commercial and residential property for rent. The basic principle is that the investment trusts are exempt from paying corporation tax on their rental income, but they must pass on almost all of their profits to their individual investors. The individual investors would be taxed at their own marginal rate of tax. If these worked – and much will depend on the details that are so far not finalised – they could produce a less risky means of property investment for individuals as well as bringing long-term institutional funding into the sector. Since investors are unlikely to wish to manage property, an opportunity for housing associations might emerge.

The government has responded to immediate access problems for potential first-time buyers with two demand-side initiatives. In the 2005 Budget, the threshold for stamp duty was raised from £60,000 to £120,000. The 'slab' structure of stamp duty (whereby stamp duty is charged at the relevant rate on the entire value of the transaction once a threshold is passed) means that the deadweight costs of the initiative will be limited, although the obvious objections are that it is insensitive to regional variations in house prices and is likely to be capitalised into higher prices.

In April the ODPM issued a consultation paper to expand the HomeBuy scheme (ODPM, 2005f), and the intention to go ahead with it was confirmed in the Chancellor's pre-Budget statement in December. Under the new 'open market', HomeBuy scheme, eligible households are key public sector workers, social tenants, people on the housing register and other potential first-time buyers identified as being in need by regional housing boards (*The Guardian*, 6 December 2005, news report). Participants will take out a mortgage for 75% of the property's value from one of the three lenders that have agreed to participate in the scheme (HBOS, Nationwide and the Yorkshire Building Society; Abbey withdrew from the scheme). The government will meet the remainder. A pilot is scheduled to begin in October 2006. The scheme has been criticised on the one hand for being too small to make much of a difference, and on the other for being likely to push up house prices still further in the absence of additional supply (for example, *Financial Times*, 24 May 2005, leading article). Moreover, the scheme allocates negative equity risk in the first place with the government, then with the lenders and finally with the household. A similar scheme ('HomeStake') has been introduced in Scotland (see below).

Behind the post-Barker measures intended to tackle the underlying structural imbalances in the housing market, the government is in the process of introducing initiatives that are intended to assist households in the immediate or near future. However, the essential problem with demand-side measures, such as HomeBuy, is that they are likely to contribute to the upward pressure on house prices. This reflects the opposing interest of insiders and outsiders. If house prices fell, then access to home ownership would improve, but this is, of course, against the interests of existing home owners who are in the majority.

Homelessness and housing-related support: providing 'settled homes'

A third strand of housing policy in 2005 represented the continued development of a strategy to address homelessness and, alongside this, related housing and support needs of vulnerable households. The *Sustainable Communities* plan (ODPM, 2003) included a goal to achieve decent homes for everyone and to assist vulnerable people in securing and maintaining appropriate housing. *Homes for All* (ODPM, 2005a) also identified an aim to provide for those who need more support as well as containing a target to halve the numbers of households in temporary accommodation by 2010, following on from previous government targets to reduce the numbers of people sleeping rough and the use of bed and breakfast for families (except for up to six weeks in cases of emergency). More specifically, the 2002 Homelessness Act has already introduced a series of measures designed to deliver more coordinated and sustainable services for homeless households, including the extension of priority needs households (to young people, those leaving prison and those fleeing domestic violence) and the introduction of local homelessness strategies that required a new emphasis on the development of preventative support services.

Homelessness and support issues are now explicitly linked within government policy. In 2002, the government published *More Than a Roof* (ODPM, 2002), a report into tackling homelessness that recognised that the provision of housing alone, although important, was not sufficient to address the complex issue of homelessness and privileging the role of tenancy support services. Further, in 2003, the Homelessness Directorate within the ODPM merged with the Housing, Care and Support Division to create the Homelessness and Housing Support Directorate, overseeing both homelessness responses and the Supporting People programme. In 2005, the ODPM produced its latest document on homelessness: *Sustainable Communities: Settled Homes, Changing Lives* (ODPM, 2005e), which outlined government plans to tackle homelessness further and reduce the use of temporary accommodation. These plans included an increase in funding for homelessness, a consideration of further changes to the homelessness legislation, the rolling out of tested preventative initiatives, as well as area-based initiatives and the increase of the supply of new social housing. The agenda also placed coordination at the centre of the strategy, highlighting the need to build on links at the levels of local, regional and central government. The strategy represents a continuation of government policy that was broadly supported in the National Audit Office's (2005) report, which concluded that the government had made 'good progress' in improving the effectiveness of homelessness services. Other key documents have also welcomed changes, particularly the extension of priority need categories, the increased emphasis on prevention and more coordinated approaches following the 2002 Homelessness Act – although recognising that more still needs to be achieved, particularly with respect to increasing housing supply (ODPM Select Committee, 2005).

However, while the general direction of homelessness policy has been largely supported at the local and national level, the direction of Supporting People, the government policy and funding framework for delivering housing-related support to vulnerable people since 2003, was experiencing a more troublesome transition in 2005. The previous year had seen the publication of the critical Robson Rhodes independent review of Supporting People (Sullivan, 2004) that paved the way for severe Budget cuts in the 2005/06 programme. In October 2005, the Audit Commission, having reviewed nearly half of the 150 Supporting People authorities, produced its report on the programme. This concluded that while services had improved, delivery was not consistently good and that a refreshed strategy was required at both local and national level. The government followed with the publication of its awaited review and consultation document (ODPM, 2005d), which signalled possible changes to the programme, including removal of ring-fencing, redistribution and greater flexibility of use of funding, as well as individual budgets for vulnerable people to purchase services. Early concerns have been raised about the impact of any reorganisation on groups of users that may be perceived as less of a priority, including homeless households and those with drug and alcohol support needs. Clearly, the delivery of a coherent homelessness policy in the future will rely on the continued improvement of housing-related support services for a significant proportion of homeless households. While the direction of Supporting People does not in itself conflict with homelessness policy, it does have the potential to undermine its effectiveness.

Despite the problems surrounding the implementation of Supporting People, few commentators would argue with the underlying principles of attempting to assist households maintain independence, avoid homelessness and enjoy 'settled lives'. However, some housing developments in 2005 have not always directly supported this agenda. In particular, the strengthening of an enforcement agenda with respect to policies to address antisocial behaviour lies uneasily alongside a housing and support agenda. While it can be argued that the antisocial behaviour of a minority may need to be addressed to enable others to lead settled lives at a neighbourhood level, policy has tended to concentrate on making it easier to remove and evict potential perpetrators. The 2002 Homelessness Act had already given local authorities the power to deny households the right to a home if they believed the applicant or member of the household was guilty of unacceptable behaviour, and the 2003 Anti-social Behaviour Act allowed secure, assured and assured shorthold tenancies to be demoted on the grounds of antisocial behaviour.

The 2004 Housing Act gave permission for local authorities to extend introductory tenancies for six months; gave landlords of secure tenants the right to refuse mutual exchange applications; and suspended the landlord's obligation to complete a Right to Buy sale where some types of court action relating to anti social behaviour were pending. At the time of writing, the government has announced further measures, under its Respect agenda (www.homeoffice.gov.uk/documents/respect-action-plan?view=Binary), that include eviction powers to deal with occupants of 'properties from hell', regardless of tenure. Although the government acknowledges that a three-pronged response of prevention, enforcement and rehabilitation needs to be pursued in this area (SEU, 2000), most initiatives have concentrated on enforcement at the expense of more supportive initiatives. These policies have been criticised for actually resulting in the homelessness of vulnerable households that exhibit challenging behaviour. Early research has indicated that specially targeted supportive services can both prevent eviction and address antisocial behaviour concerns (Jones et al, 2004). Government policy documents have begun to acknowledge this potential (ODPM, 2005e) and some pilot services are presently being evaluated, but provision and policy in this area remains in its infancy and at odds with wider homelessness policy.

Developments in Scotland

Housing policy formation has also been affected by devolution, especially the establishment of the Scottish Parliament and Executive in 1999 with legislative powers. However, while formal responsibility for housing policy has been devolved to these institutions, social security and economic management are 'reserved' matters. The Scottish Executive has been very active in passing legislation concerning housing; indeed one of the arguments for devolution was to provide parliamentary time for legislation in areas including land policy under Scotland's separate legal system. However, asymmetries in devolution place another barrier in the way of devising a housing policy strategy in Scotland.

The early years of devolution were focused on the quality of housing in the social rented sector, and on strengthening the homelessness legislation. In particular, much energy was devoted to devising and seeing through the transfer of the City of Glasgow's housing stock to the new Glasgow Housing Association. This complex and politically contentious task, which involved a Treasury write-off of approaching £1 billion debt, is to be followed by 'second-stage' transfers to community-based landlords (Gibb, 2003). Meanwhile, in 2005 the proposal to transfer Edinburgh's stock was defeated.

In 2005 attention switched to promoting standards in the private sector, with the Housing (Scotland) Bill being passed and receiving Royal Assent in January 2006. This legislation followed the deliberations of the Home Improvement Task Force, which was established in 2000 and reported in 2003 (Berry, 2005). The Act gives local authorities powers to designate Housing Renewal Areas and obliges them to include details of how such areas will be identified in their local housing strategies. Local authorities are given a more flexible approach to providing assistance for improvements and adaptations, with provision for grants, loans and subsidised loans. The Tolerable Standard for housing is modernised with the inclusion of criteria for, inter alia, thermal insulation.

Meanwhile the Act strengthens the regulation of the private rented sector. Rent Assessment Panels are renamed Private Rented Housing Panels and are intended to provide tenants with an alternative route to the courts for enforcing repair standards. The licensing of Houses in Multiple Occupation (HMOs) that previously arose from secondary legislation under the 1982 Civic Government (Scotland) Act, is now given the status of primary legislation in this Act. The 2004 Anti-social Behaviour (Scotland) Act introduced the requirement for private landlords to be registered with local authorities and to pass a 'fit and proper person' test. The 2006 Housing (Scotland) Act gives ministers powers to issue a Letting Code that would be taken into account by local authorities as part of the 'fit and proper' person test. It also introduces a requirement for sellers of property to provide specific information for potential buyers (Scottish Parliament, 2006).

Meanwhile, the Scottish version of open market HomeBuy began a 12-month pilot in September 2005. In the pilot the scheme is operated by three housing associations in Edinburgh and the Lothians (where access to home ownership is most stretched by high prices), with the household's equity share normally in the range of 60%-80% of the property's value. The remainder of the equity will be paid for by a grant from Communities Scotland. The intention is that the scheme will be operated by Communities Scotland throughout the country, except in Glasgow and Edinburgh, where the local authorities will operate it. The scheme is aimed primarily at low-income households, although eligibility criteria will be set locally (Communities Scotland, 2005; Council of Mortgage Lenders, 2005).

These developments reflect in part the nature of housing problems and political culture in Scotland, but also the nature of devolution. It is natural that the Scottish Executive and Parliament should focus on the areas where they can exercise their regulatory powers. In many cases policy is moving in the same direction as in England – for example, with support for stock transfers, the registration of HMOs, the promotion of shared equity ownership and the introduction of sellers' packs – although there are differences in detail, as indeed was the case before devolution. In other areas, Scotland's approach will be influenced by measures, notably Housing Benefit reform, that lie with the Westminster Parliament. It is thus very difficult for the Scottish institutions to form a fully strategic vision of housing policy.

Conclusion

Given the complexities of housing problems and their frequent coincidence with other social and economic issues, it would be naive to expect every policy initiative to fit easily into a coherent overarching strategy. The Labour government elected in 1997 did not hit the ground running with housing policy, and much of its strategy has been developed when in office. Nevertheless, a strategy has emerged, with an acknowledgement that there are structural failings in the supply-side of the housing system. However, demand-side policies, including raising the stamp duty threshold and the announcement of a new equity sharing scheme, represent reactive policies that are likely to have undesirable spillover effects. The backing away from a revaluation of property values for Council Tax purposes may give cause to doubt that the government has the necessary courage to tackle the vocal 'insiders' in the interests of the less vocal 'outsiders' that will be necessary if supply-side policies are to succeed.

The advocacy of a social market in the social rented sector marks a very different conception of choice from other public service reforms, which is not in itself a bad thing. However, the reforms seem to neglect the starting point, which is a sector dominated by low-income households, whose ability to exercise market-like choices is limited. The government's strategy on promoting independence by providing support for homeless and other vulnerable groups appears to sit uneasily beside aspects of the 'enforcement' agenda, which relies quite heavily on housing sanctions.

The starting point for the formulation of a housing strategy in Scotland was effectively delayed until 1999 when devolution was implemented. Subsequently, the Scottish Executive and Parliament have devoted more time to housing and land issues than would have been likely within the pre-devolution framework. However, the ability of the Executive to take a fully strategic view of housing is limited by the partial nature of devolution, notably in relation to Housing Benefit.

References

Barker, K. (2004) *Review of Housing Supply: Final Report*, London: HM Treasury.

Berry, K. (2005) *The Housing (Scotland) Bill*, SPICe Briefing 05/16, Edinburgh: Scottish Parliament.

Communities Scotland (2005) *Helping You to Become a Homeowner: About the HomeStake Open Market Scheme*, Edinburgh: Communities Scotland.

Council of Mortgage Lenders (2005) 'HomeStake: a shared equity scheme operating in Scotland' (www.cml.org.uk/cml/policy/issues/758).

DETR (Department for Environment, Transport and the Regions) (2000) *Quality and Choice: A Decent Home for All*, Housing Green Paper, London: DETR/Department of Social Security (DSS).

DoE (Department of the Environment) (1977) *Housing Policy: A Consultative Document*, Cmnd 6851, London: HMSO.

Gibb, K. (2003) 'Transferring Glasgow's council housing: financial, urban and housing policy implications', *European Journal of Housing Policy*, vol 3, no 1, pp 89-114.

HM Treasury/Office of the Deputy Prime Minister (ODPM) (2005) *Housing Policy – An Overview*, London: HM Treasury/ODPM.

HM Treasury, HM Revenue and Customs and ODPM (2005) *Planning Gain Supplement: A Consultation*, London: The Stationery Office.

Jones, A., Pleace, N. and Quilgars, D. (2004) *Shelter Inclusion Project: Interim Evaluation Findings*, London: Shelter.

National Assembly of Wales (2001) *Better Homes for People in Wales: A National Housing Strategy for Wales*, Cardiff: National Assembly of Wales.

NAO (National Audit Office) (2005) *More Than a Roof: Progress in Tackling Homelessness*, London: The Stationery Office.

ODPM (Office of the Deputy Prime Minister) (2003) *More Than a Roof: A Report into Tackling Homelessness*, London: ODPM.

ODPM (2003) *Sustainable Communities: Building for the Future*, London: ODPM.

ODPM (2005a) *Sustainable Communities: Homes for All. A Five Year Plan from the Office of the Deputy Prime Minister*, London: ODPM.

ODPM (2005b) 'The Government's response to Kate Barker's review of housing supply', Press release, 5 December, London: ODPM.

ODPM (2005c) *Consultation Paper on Planning Policy Statement 3 (PPS3)*, London: ODPM.

ODPM (2005d) *Creating Sustainable Communities: Supporting Independence. Consultation on a Strategy for the Supporting People Programme*, London: ODPM.

ODPM (2005e) *Sustainable Communities: Settled Homes, Changing Lives: A Strategy for Tackling Homelessness*, London: ODPM.

ODPM (2005f) *HomeBuy – Expanding the Opportunity to Own*, Consultation paper, London: ODPM.

ODPM Select Committee (2005) *Homelessness*, London: The Stationery Office.

Rhodes, D. and Bevan, M. (2003) *Private Landlords and Buy to Let*, York: Centre for Housing Policy, University of York.

Rhodes, D. and Rugg, J. (2005) *Working with the LHA: Landlord and Agents' Early Experiences of the LHA in the Nine Pathfinder Areas*, London: Department for Work and Pensions.

Richard, Lord (2004) *Report of the Richard Commission: Commission on the Powers and Electoral Arrangements of the National Assembly of Wales*, Cardiff: National Assembly of Wales.

Scottish Parliament (2006) 'Explanatory notes to Housing (Scotland) Act 2006' (www.opsi.gov.uk/legislation/scotland/en2006/2006en01.htm).

SEU (Social Exclusion Unit) (2000) *Anti-social Behaviour*, Report of Policy Action Team 8, London: The Stationery Office.

Stephens, M. (2005a) 'The big picture', *Roof*, September/October, pp 42-4.

Stephens, M. (2005b) 'An assessment of the British Housing Benefit system', *European Journal of Housing Policy*, vol 5, no 2, pp 111-29.

Stephens, M., Burns, N. and MacKay, L. (2003) 'The limits of housing reform: British social rented housing in a European context', *Urban Studies*, vol 40, no 4, pp 767-89.

Stephens, M., Whitehead, C. and Munro, M. (2005) *Lessons from the Past, Challenges for the Future for Housing Policy: An Evaluation of English Housing Policy 1975-2000*, London: ODPM.

Sullivan, E. (2004) *Review of the Supporting People Programme*, London: Robson Rhodes.

FIVE

Social security policies in 2005

Paul Dornan

Introduction

2005 has seen three Secretaries of State for Work and Pensions – Alan Johnson, David Blunkett and latterly John Hutton. The year also saw a May General Election with the return to office of the Labour Party, albeit with a reduced majority. There has been particular concern over the delivery of the tax credit scheme, leading to both administrative and policy reform announcements within the year. The build-up to the Welfare Reform Green Paper, discussed and delayed through much of 2005 but not actually published until January 2006 (DWP, 2006), has led to much discussion around mechanisms of increasing labour market participation towards an aspiration of an 80% employment rate, focused particularly on lone parents and disabled adults. The staff reduction implications of the Gershon review of efficiency savings have begun to bite both in the Department for Work and Pensions (DWP) and Her Majesty's Revenue and Customs (HMRC), with concomitant fears around the quality of service delivery experienced by claimants. Ongoing concerns over service delivery go wider than the tax credit system, with the Child Support Agency described at the start of a Work and Pensions inquiry into its performance as 'a failing organisation which is currently in crisis' (Work and Pensions Select Committee, 2005a, p 3), and concerns over the delivery of some Jobcentre Plus services (covered by a separate Work and Pensions inquiry conducted during 2005) and especially those linked to the implementation of the Customer Management System within it (see Work and Pensions Select Committee, 2005b).

Social security is critical to government partly because it is so costly: in 2003/04 the DWP spent around £112 billion (DWP, 2005a, p 85) and the HMRC spent £15.8 billion on tax credits in 2004/05 (NAO, 2005, table 2). Indeed after eight years in office, Labour seems to have dropped none of its reforming zeal in social security policy. This chapter reflects on recent developments in social security, the background and current developments in 2005. Core to its argument is that there remain several touchstones for New Labour: increasing participation in paid work and poverty reduction, which have driven the agenda forward since 1997, but which have particularly influenced debate in this year with the development of the Welfare Reform Green Paper and, in particular, policy intended to increase labour market participation.

No department now bears the name 'social security', which Titmuss defined as 'transactions by Government (or agencies approved by Government) which increase individual money incomes in certain specific circumstance of income loss or need for income protection' (1968, p 173). From this definition it is worth emphasising the centrality of cash transfers or transfers to reduce outgoings (such as free school meals), and the specific needs associated with different groups. Beyond this it is worth noting the other interests the state may seek to serve through social security – around both increasing labour supply and incentivising saving, or control of different groups of the population. The provision of support under this headline of social security goes wide – including, among others, the DWP, HMRC, Home Office, local authorities and the Department for Education and Skills (DfES). The development of new forms of provision (such as the tax credits or Educational Maintenance Allowance) have increased this fragmentation and raise questions both for those experiencing policy (such as around delivery where systems are passported or around different ways in which departments assess income), as well as for those trying to study the aggregate or specific impact of diverse policies.

To further admit to the complications of studying such diverse policy, this chapter does not specifically examine the links between housing policy and social security, and particularly the provision and delivery of Housing Benefit. However, the move (reiterated in the Welfare Reform Green Paper) towards the Local Housing Allowance (in the private rented sector and potentially also in the social rented sector) has significant ramifications, including access to accommodation, housing quality, rental gaps between benefit and real cost (for an early evaluation, see Shelter, 2005). Nor does it deal with the debate associated with the reporting of the Pension Commission into long-term pension reform (see Turner, 2005) or the detail of the Pathways to Work pilots for those claiming Incapacity Benefit (evaluated by Corden et al, 2005). Since most of social security policy is governed by powers held by Westminster, this chapter does not profile differences by country. There have been some important exceptions to this in 2005, however, and since the path would appear to be for diversifying social policy across the different administrations, these differences are likely to grow in the future. Recent examples include the Greater London Assembly on reducing the costs of childcare for parents (GLA, 2005), the Welsh Assembly Government on school uniform grants policy (WAG, 2005) and the Scottish Executive's interest around school meal entitlements (see Schofield, 2005).

Poverty and inequality

Recent policy has focused on pensioners and children as key groups of concern; this section profiles recent performance on poverty reduction for these groups. Since there is a time lag between data collection and publication, the data predate 2005 at the time of writing. Although this lags the year of study, it is important both in terms of the broader trends and because the latest data (the 2003/04 financial year) covers the first of the new tax credits and also catches the start of the introduction of pension credit (although for the last half of the year). Whereas children and pensioners have been specifically targeted by policy, adults of working age have not received the same attention and poverty for this group has not fallen (see also Palmer et al, 2005, pp 28-9). Since the uprating of Income Support/Jobseeker's Allowance remains linked to a prices-based index, these have continued to fall in real worth as against average earnings.

Trends in income poverty demonstrate the challenge policy faces and some of the recent successes it has had. Income poverty is defined as being in a household that has an income below a particular threshold, adjusted for household size and composition (usually 60% of the contemporary median). This definition has been widely used in research and is explicitly used within the government's pledge to eradicate child poverty and in its social audit, *Opportunity for All* (DWP, 2005b). Data can be presented separately on a before or after housing costs basis; the former includes Housing Benefit as income without deducting housing costs, the latter deducts housing costs and in consequence gives a better feel for disposable income. Figure 5.1 uses after housing cost data from the Households Below Average Incomes series to track change since 1979 in the risk faced by children, pensioners and working-age adults.

The risk of income poverty grew over the 1980s and early 1990s, held broadly constant through much of the 1990s and fell for pensioners and children in the late 1990s and 2000s, while over this period the risk of poverty for those of working age did not fall. In 2003/04 children faced the highest risk of being poor, followed by pensioners and then by those of working age, with the risks faced by pensioners and working-age adults having converged.

Figure 5.1: After housing cost poverty rates (1979-2003/04)

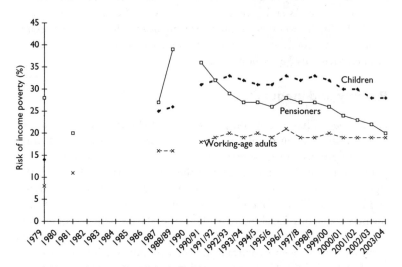

Notes: Data before 1994/95 are from the Family Expenditure Survey and cover the UK; data from 1994/95 onwards are from the Family Resources Survey covering Britain.
Source: DWP (2005c)

Figures 5.2 and 5.3 examine the income sources, as well as differences in gross income levels by decile for groups focused on.

Gross income is charted on the right axis to show the extent of inequality across the deciles, differences in income that are particularly pronounced at the top and bottom of the distribution. Sources are expressed as a percentage, not a cash sum, so the relative small size of the non-employment sources in the richest deciles is not necessarily an indication that these groups have less, rather that they have much more wage income. Employment income is key in all groups and provides a majority of income for all but the poorest. Non-contributory benefits (both means-tested and disability-related) make up a considerable proportion of income for the poorest deciles. Child Benefit – a flat-rate benefit – shows up on the figure as particularly important to the poorest families, as do the tax credits.

Again, gross income is plotted on the right-hand axis to indicate the degree of inequality, and other elements on the left-hand axis. Since this is a decile average, it is difficult to extrapolate to individual circumstances since not all have a given income source. This is particularly the case for pensioners where non-entitlement or non-take-up to income-related benefits may help explain why pension credit seems to play such a small role in the incomes of the poorest. The figure demonstrates the particular

Figure 5.2: Income sources averaged by decile for households with children (2003/04)

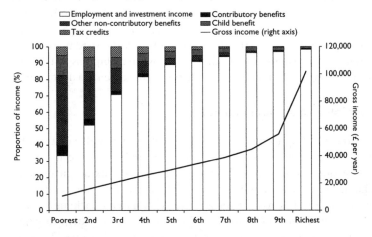

Note: Figures are for the UK.
Source: Jones (2005)

Figure 5.3: Income sources averaged by decile for pensioner households (2003/04)

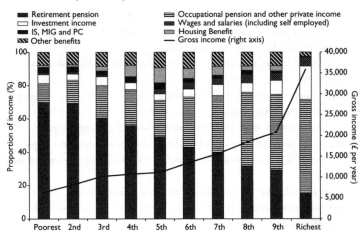

Notes: IS – Income Support; MIG – Minimum Income Guarantee; PC – pension credit. Figures are for the UK. Interpretation of this should be cautious since the PC was introduced in October 2003 (mid year of the data shown).
Source: Jones (2005)

importance of the state pension, providing more than half of all income right up to around the sixth decile. It also demonstrates the importance of occupational pensions; pensioners in higher deciles are often there precisely because they have an occupational pension. Although this is not broken down by gender, the importance of both the state pension and occupational pensions, since both rely on past contributions history, also indicates how this current income provision puts women at a disadvantage.

Principles of social security

With the build-up to the DWP Welfare Reform Green Paper, there has been significant discussion of the principles underlying social security. This section profiles some of this recent debate, linking current and ongoing concern with policy changes. The current Labour government has emphasised the role of social security by placing tackling poverty central to its reform programme and by increasing the extent to which income transfers are used to support labour market objectives. 2005 saw significant discussion of the principles of social security associated with the backroom work on the Welfare Reform Green Paper (eventually published as DWP, 2006). In October 2005 David Blunkett, then Secretary of State and working on the Green Paper, specified eight principles to inform welfare reform:

1. Help people to help themselves by offering a ladder to self-reliance and self-determination, not merely a safety net in time of need.
2. See work as the best route out of welfare.
3. Promote understanding and enable people to make informed choices for themselves.
4. Balance rights with responsibilities, while recognising the need for support and care where appropriate.
5. Recognise our mutual interdependence and obligation to each other, promoting solidarity between generations, and the importance of using the resources of Government to help people cope with rapid economic and social change.
6. Ensure the role of the state is active, liberating and enabling.
7. Address the root causes of poverty and overcome intergenerational disadvantage and exclusion.
8. Contribute to a stable and growing economy through investment in the potential of every individual, and flexibility of support in and out of work. (DWP, 2005d)

These principles were couched in language around 'enablement' and link to discussions of financial assets and social mobility. The subsections discuss overriding and underlying elements of these as: tackling poverty (raised in point 7 but inferred in others); meeting additional need (5); facilitating or encouraging paid work (2 and 8, but inferred in most points); and controlling behaviour (particularly in 4). The rest of this section links some of these underlying principles to policy developments in 2005.

Tackling poverty

Core to recent policy has been the direction of additional resources towards the poorest children and pensioners. In 2005 this commitment was maintained with earnings uprating for elements of child tax credit and pension credit. The pledge made by Tony Blair to eradicate child poverty 'within a generation' (Blair, 1999), along with a series of milestones that have been set and judged by Public Service Agreement (PSA) targets (the latest being to halve child poverty on a relative income poverty basis from the position in 1998/99 to 2010/11; see DWP, 2005a) demonstrates the political importance of this aim to the current government. Although there has been no equivalent pledge for pensioner poverty, it is monitored through the government's annual audit, *Opportunity for All* (DWP, 2005b), and a specific PSA to improve take-up of the pension credit (to have 3.2 million pensioner households in receipt of this credit by 2008; see DWP, 2005a).

There have been significant investments in both state pension (following a politically damaging 75 pence uprating of the single rate of the pension in April 2000; April 2001 saw a £5 rise) and to Child Benefit (which had a significant rise in April 1999 for the first child rate, but has since then risen only with prices). The thrust has been to direct resources through the means test with the pension credit introduced to tackle pensioner poverty and the child and working tax credits targeted at those of working age with children. Although the means-tested approach has come under attack (for many of the problems traditional to means tests: complexity, low take-up and administrative problems, together with new problems associated with the tax credits discussed below), the government continues to be committed to this approach.

Building assets

Whereas building savings has traditionally been encouraged by tax benefits (for instance around pensions saving and more recently through the savings credit element of pension credit), new asset-based welfare policies such as the Child Trust Fund take this aim more clearly into the realm of social security. The principle behind this mechanism, which ties in with broader debates around financial inclusion, has been that financial assets can be used to increase the choices available and aspirations to take these up. The two schemes developed under this heading – the savings gateway and Child Trust Fund – operate in very different ways. The former, which is currently being piloted (see Kempson et al, 2005, for an evaluation of the first wave of pilots), is targeted on poorer adults and provides a matched savings element for savings collected over an 18-month period, after which the asset could be saved or used by its owner (taking cash out of the account within the period was possible but forfeited the matched element).

By contrast, the Child Trust Fund has been rolled out nationally and backdated for babies born since 2002 when the scheme was first proposed. This scheme provides a fixed investment (of £250) for every child at birth with a top-up for children in lower-income households. The fund was left for parents to invest on behalf of children, with the possibility that they or other interested parties could invest up to £1,200 per year on behalf of the child into each fund, but with the income being invested until the child reached the age of 18. The principle behind the Child Trust Fund – although not borne out by research (see McKay and Kempson, 2003) – has been that an asset, provided at 18, may not only assist in taking up opportunities (for example, to study or train), but may have a separate effect on aspirations and so assist in increasing social mobility. The Child Trust Fund remains of significant interest to policy makers, with a commitment that the HMRC would top up each fund (with a progressive element) when the child reached seven years of age, the further progressive top-ups at age 11 being consulted on in 2005.

Since the Child Trust Fund is such a new policy, both in terms of its concept and its implementation, much is as yet unclear and merits research and analysis about its implications; however, early experience suggested low take-up of the scheme, with parents delaying or failing to invest the voucher sent to them by HMRC. In the first year, vouchers had been issued by November 2005; of 2,135,000 vouchers issued, only 1,164,000 had been invested (HMRC, 2005a). Vouchers not invested by parents would then be invested by HMRC on behalf of the child; however, this implies a level of disengagement by parents in the scheme. Further, given the scope for private saving into the scheme, there is also the potential for inequality to grow in fund value between children, and therefore in the assets available to young adults, which could undermine the intentions of the scheme in unblocking social immobility. Most fundamental is the extent of the impact that asset ownership may have on child outcomes –

and for the poorest children in particular (since the policy is one of 'progressive universalism'); here is clearly a case for more analytical investigation.

Facilitating the labour market

Since 1997 Labour has consistently followed a work-first policy, aimed at increasing labour market participation both to tackle poverty (perhaps most critically through the PSA to increase the employment rate of lone parents; see DWP, 2005a) and to meet macro-economic objectives. It has set a long-term aspiration of an employment rate of 80%, considerably higher than the current 74.9% rate (National Statistics, 2005), which is itself already high by international comparison (DWP, 2005a, figure 9). In reaching this, policy has focused on groups known to have a low employment rate, initially those facing high unemployment rates (such as the long-term unemployed or youth unemployed through the New Deal), but as the labour market has expanded attention has increasingly focused on the non-employed – those who may or may not be able and willing to work but who are not actively seeking it – including through the New Deals and through the Pathways to Work pilot scheme for non-working disabled adults.

Social security has been actively used to drive this labour market engagement by 'making work pay' (more than benefits). Working tax credit, the childcare element available within this and specific premiums arranged around specific work-focused activity are all used to increase the level of income or decrease the costs of those in work as well as other changes intended to protect the incomes of those who go into work following disability benefit receipt but then return to benefit, therefore assisting people to try work without the subsequent risk that future benefit levels might be reduced if work was not sustained. The extension of the working tax credit (now separated out from child payments and extended to allow low-wage childless adults to claim for the first time) has increased the level of subsidy the government provides to top up low wages (and thereby intended to increase labour supply), underwritten by a National Minimum Wage; but the increase in people claiming in-work means-tested benefits has also resulted in more people facing relatively high marginal deduction rates – the rate at which additional income (from wage increase or more hours) is reduced by lost entitlement to benefits/tax credits and additional tax.

Influencing behaviour

Alongside the controls over behaviour implied in work search requirements (with related sanctions) in Jobseeker's Allowance, social security continues to be used to control and to influence. At the extreme end of the use of control and sanctions is policy on support for asylum seekers. Provision, via the Home Office, under the National Asylum Support Service supports qualifying asylum seekers under highly controlled circumstances, at a lower rate (for adults) than the resident population receive through benefits and tax credits. Such provision may be withdrawn from those whose asylum claims are rejected or denied to those not registering as required. Here social security is used both to provide for need and to support other aims of the state. A second group of policies exist around incentivising behaviour the state views as beneficial (to individuals, society and tax yields). Recent examples include the Educational Maintenance Allowance, which provides some support to those from lower income households staying on in formal education to encourage increased participation, and the Sure Start maternity grant, for which entitlement is passported not only from receipt of other benefits but on the basis of recipients having come into contact with health care professionals.

Delivering social security in practice through the tax credits

Although the Labour government continues to consider policy changes, issues of delivery are also becoming increasingly important because of both the culmination of pre-existing problems (as has particularly affected the Child Support Agency) and the roll-out of new mechanisms of delivery. Tax credits are focused on here because of the considerable change brought by the development of this scheme, the problems that gained significant recognition in 2004 and 2005, and the policy action subsequently taken. Before looking at some of the challenges presented by the delivery of tax credits, however, this section examines the fragmentation of delivery mechanisms which has in part driven this delivery.

The increased role of the HMRC in delivering social security is a particularly important aspect of the changes initiated by the Labour government. This policy takes us closer to the integration of the tax and benefits system (through co-residing functions and running the tax credits on an annual basis akin to the tax year). Despite the names, these do remain largely separate systems with limited apparent linking of records (such as between National Insurance or tax and the tax credits) and separate payment mechanisms (with the child tax credit being paid to the principle carer and a shift away from the payment of working tax credit through the wage). The use of the HMRC to deliver social security policy has turned the collections agency into one that also has to distribute income. In doing so, it has changed the client base the Inland Revenue has to deal with from being typically more affluent to an often very poor group of claimants, and has faced a significant delivery and cultural challenge in doing so.

Following the introduction of the new tax credit scheme in April 2003, significant concerns over the delivery appeared in 2004 (see Howard, 2004) and 2005, notably with reports from both Citizens Advice (2005) and the Parliamentary and Health Service Ombudsman (2005). The tax credit scheme, in adopting an annual model of income, has allowed within it greater scope than has existed within the social security scheme for the accumulation of both overpayments and underpayments of tax credits, as changes in income or family circumstances not reported to, or recorded by, the HMRC, in case of administrative error, could leave individual entitlements different to amounts being received. In the case of overpayment of tax credit, when discovered, it would alter ongoing payments both to account for a different annual entitlement and also to recover the overpaid tax credit. The mechanism by which this occurred varied by whether an overpayment was discovered in the financial year in which it occurred (for instance following a call to the telephone helpline), or following the so-called year-end reconciliation. In the latter case fixed percentage deductions were applied to recover overpaid tax credit out of future award; however, in the former, since the computer system running tax credits was set to calculate an award on an annual basis, it would similarly try to recover within the year – irrespective of how much of an award was lost. The most concerning set of problems reported with tax credits thus far in their operation has been their ability to create significant swings in income, and to place families in hardship by removing ongoing award entitlements. The problems encountered were accompanied and worsened by significant administrative problems, which surrounded both the complexity of the scheme, the staff resources to run it and the system on which the scheme was operated: including the award notices, telephone helpline and reliability of the computer system. The first statistics relating to overpayment and to underpayment of tax credits were released in 2005 and showed one third of awards had been overpaid and one in 10 underpaid at the end of the financial year in 2004 (HMRC, 2005b). Although much higher than previously expected, these statistics underestimated true variation since they undercounted overpayments or underpayments discovered within the financial year in which they occurred.

The problems with the tax credit system, having initially been attributed to early implementation problems, were recognised by government to be more systemic in May 2005, when an action plan published to improve the administration of the scheme was laid out by the minister responsible (Primarolo, 2005).The May statement dealt with aspects such as improving award notices, communication and the helpline, and in doing so did not engage with structural concerns. It was followed in December with the pre-Budget report (HM Treasury, 2005), containing a series of proposed changes to the underlying policy intended both to reduce the extent of overpayments and to soften the impact that the sudden recovery of these might have. Although 2006 is too early to fully judge how the tax credit scheme will fare in the longer term, and whether the problems discovered in its early operation will be solved by that policy developed to do so, the tax credit example, and the preparedness, after significant problems became evident, to make changes to the policy to improve the operation demonstrates continued commitment to the use of means-tested policy in both its pro-labour market and anti-poverty policy.

Conclusion

In the years towards 2005 we have seen significant political and financial investment, much of which this chapter has by necessity touched on only briefly. Much policy continues to be driven by an active Treasury and Chancellor, and a change in either may alter the long-term trend of policy. In concluding, this chapter this lays out several further areas of increasing interest in social security policy that have not been examined in detail but are worth exploring because they merit research and analysis, and may bear on the direction of future direction of policy:

Delivery: the policy thrust of New Labour is relatively well understood but delivery is understood less well and this tension is sharpened following reductions in staff at both the DWP and HMRC suggested by the Gershon review and the need to understand how effectively new policy is being delivered on the ground will grow. Related to this the approach adopted by the HMRC to low-income claimants (for instance, around hardship or accessible advice) is also key to effective delivery of social security.

Devolution: this chapter has not discussed the implications for social security of devolution, yet these issues become increasingly important for social security; examining the future implications could be significant as the Scottish Parliament and National and Regional Assemblies examine and pursue different social policy objectives.

The sustainability of means testing: the approach discussed in this chapter is heavily dependent on the means test, couched in terms of progressive universalism – targeting within schemes that deliver an (often small) entitlement to large numbers of people but the most to the poorest group of these. It remains to be seen if it will be possible to sustain this approach over the medium term, by reducing the associated problems and by using it to tackle poverty. Further, although policy has increased the levels of the progressive elements of pension credit and child tax credit, in neither case do these represent long-term commitments, raising a question over whether these will retain value over time.

Financial assets: the role of assets may become more important in the future, both as a result of wider trends (such as inheritance) and of specific asset-based policy (especially the Child Trust Fund). The interaction of this with social security policy, together with the implications this has for life chances, remains an underexplored area and merits further attention.

Rights and responsibilities: arguably in recent years rights have been eroded in several important ways, both by the growth in discretion (around labour market interventions such as the Advisor Discretion Fund) and by tax credits (over which the HMRC has significant discretion). This discretion raises traditional questions as to how administrators are using this and how this is, itself, monitored. Possible extension in the application of conditions to benefits, following welfare reform activity to facilitate labour market objectives, raises questions around the conflict between applying sanctions and providing for need.

Adequacy: the relatively strong policy focus on income poverty has ignored income adequacy standards, illustrated both by resistance in government to such research and by the low relative value of out-of-work benefits and consequently high poverty levels associated with these. When the 2004/05 Family Resources Survey data are released (in March 2006) we will also have new material deprivation data which, following this release, will be developed into an indicator that will become politically important (in measuring child poverty), and will offer further data to gauge progress.

References

Blair, T. (1999) Speech at Toynbee Hall, East London, 18 March.

Citizens Advice (2005) *Money with Your Name on it?*, London: National Association of Citizens Advice Bureaux.

Corden, A., Nice, K. and Sainsbury, R. (2005) *Incapacity Benefit Reforms Pilot: Findings from a Longitudinal Panel of Clients*, DWP Research Report No 259, London: DWP.

DWP (Department for Work and Pensions) (2005a) *Department for Work and Pensions Five Year Strategy*, London: DWP.

DWP (2005b) *Opportunity for All Seventh Annual Report*, London: DWP.

DWP (2005c) *Households Below Average Incomes Series*, London: National Statistics.

DWP (2005d) 'Equality, opportunity, fairness and social justice to underpin the welfare state', Press release, 10 October.

DWP (DWP) (2006) *A New Deal for Welfare: Empowering People to Work*, Green Paper, London: DWP.

GLA (Greater London Authority) (2005) 'Mayor hails historical childcare deal for London', Press release, 2 December.

HMRC (Her Majesty's Revenue and Customs) (2005a) 'Child Trust Fund statistics' (www.hmrc.gov.uk/stats/child_trust_funds/child-trust-funds.htm, accessed December 2005).

HMRC (2005b) *Child and Working Tax Credits Statistics 2003-04: Supplement on Payments in 2003-04*, London: National Statistics.

HM Treasury (2005) *Pre-Budget Report, Britain Meeting the Global Challenge: Enterprise, Fairness and Responsibility*, London: HM Treasury.

Howard, M. (2004) *Tax Credits One Year On*, London: Child Poverty Action Group.

Jones, F. (2005) 'The effects of taxes and benefits on household income, 2003-04', *Economic Trends*, National Statistics No 620, London: National Statistics.

Kempson, E., McKay, S. and Collard, S. (2005) *Incentives to Save: Encouraging Saving among Low-income Households*, London: HM Treasury.

McKay, S. and Kempson, E. (2003) *Saving and Life Events*, DWP Research Report No 194, London: DWP.

NAO (National Audit Office) (2005) *Comptroller and Auditor General's Standard Report on the Accounts of the Inland Revenue 2004-05*, London: NAO.

National Statistics (2005) 'Employment rate rises to 74.9% in 3 months to Sept 05' (www.statistics.gov.uk/cci/nugget.asp?id=12, accessed 16 November 2005).

Palmer, G., Carr, J. and Kenway, P. (2005) *Monitoring Poverty and Social Exclusion 2005*, York: Joseph Rowntree Foundation and New Policy Institute.

Parliamentary and Health Service Ombudsman (2005) *Tax Credits: Putting Things Right*, HC 124, London: The Stationery Office.

Primarolo, D. (2005) Written statement, *Hansard*, 26 May, 23WS, House of Commons.

Schofield, K. (2005) 'Executive could extend free school meals into holidays', *The Scotsman* (http://news.scotsman.com/ topics.cfm?tid=773&id=2175782005, accessed 1 November 2005).

Shelter (2005) *On the Right Path? The Interim Findings of Shelter's Research into the Housing Benefit Pathfinders*, London: Shelter.

Titmuss, R. (1968) *Commitment to Welfare*, London: George Allen & Unwin Ltd.

Turner, A. (2005) *A New Pension Settlement for the Twenty-First Century, Second Report of the Pensions Commission*, London: The Stationery Office.

WAG (Welsh Assembly Government) (2005) 'Jane Davidson launches £750,000 School Uniform Grant', Press release, 22 June.

Work and Pensions Select Committee (2005a) *The Performance of the Child Support Agency*, HC 44-1, London: House of Commons.

Work and Pensions Select Committee (2005b) *The Efficiency Savings Programme in Jobcentre Plus*, Written evidence, London: House of Commons.

Part 2
Health and well-being

SIX

More than a matter of choice? Consumerism and the modernisation of health care

Janet Newman and Elizabeth Vidler

Introduction

The current cycles of health service modernisation open up important questions about the future of the welfare state and of the solidaristic citizen identifications with which it is traditionally associated. The figure of the demanding citizen-consumer who strides assertively through the pages of policy documents and the scripts of ministerial speeches stands as a central icon of the current reforms in general, and of the increasing significance of choice in particular. However, alongside choice, notions of 'challenge' and 'responsibility' inform the modernisation process. 'Challenge' is linked to ideas of a newly informed and potentially querulous citizenry – what the Patient Czar termed the 'standing up' patients of the future rather than the 'lying down' patients of the past (Cayton, 2003). 'Challenge' suggests some dismantling of the knowledge–power knot at the heart of professional claims to authority. But this sits somewhat uneasily with notions of 'responsibility' that derive from a new articulation of professional and governmental power. Here professional good practice is associated with high levels of patient involvement in treatment decisions, and the 'responsibilisation' of patients for their own good health through initiatives such as the expert patient scheme[1]. It denotes a shift of focus from expert-led interventions to greater collaboration with patients, not only in the interests of better health outcomes but also in order to manage resources in a more effective way.

In this chapter we begin by exploring some of the ways in which the 'consumer' is situated in New Labour's narrative of modernisation. We then examine how health care organisations are responding to the consumerist imperative, paying particular attention to how they attempt to resolve some of the political and policy tensions that arise. Finally, we examine the new relationships and patterns of identification that are configured in the interface between health services and their publics. The chapter is based on the results from an Economic and Social Research Council (ESRC)/Arts and Humanities Research Board (AHRB)-funded project entitled 'Creating Citizen-Consumers: Changing Relationships and Identifications'[2]. This project compared how three different public services (primary health care, policing and social care) in two geographically and demographically contrasting areas (here designated as 'Old Town' and 'New Town') responded to pressures to develop a more consumerist approach (see also Clarke et al, 2005). Our focus in this chapter is on the potential relationship between shifts in policy discourse and a reconfiguration of relationships and identifications. That is, how far, and in what ways, this image of the modern consumer and the consequent need for a modernised health service simply *reflect* a pre-existent and taken-for-granted reality, or can be viewed as *constituting* new relationships and patterns of identification. In order to do so, we draw on data from our analysis of policy documents; from interviews with senior health service managers; and from front-line staff and service users. More details on the research can be found at www.open.ac.uk/socialsciences/citizenconsumers.

New Labour and the construction of modernity

In political speeches and policy documents New Labour has repeatedly asserted the need for health services to be more strongly consumerist. Indeed, the idea of the consumer represents the 'new' or 'modern' image of health and other services in the narratives of change through which policy is explained:

> Thirty years ago the one size fits all approach of the 1940s was still in the ascendant. Public services were monolithic. The public were supposed to be truly grateful for what they were about to receive. People had little say and precious little choice. Today we live in a quite different world. We live in a consumer age. People demand services tailor made to their individual needs. Ours is the informed and inquiring society. People expect choice and demand quality. (Milburn, 2002)

> The NHS is too much the product of the era in which it was born. In its buildings, its ways of working, its very culture, the NHS bears too many of the hallmarks of the 1940s. The rest of society has moved on. On July 5th 1948, the day the NHS was founded, the high street banks were open between 10am and 3pm. Today, the public has 24 hour access to banking services.... In 1948, deference and hierarchy defined the relationships between citizens and services. In an era of mass production needs were regarded as identical and preferences were ignored. Today, successful services thrive on their ability to respond to the individual needs of their customers. (DH, 2000, paras 2.9-2.11)

These narratives construct a particular view of a modern service built around an image of a modern consumer. They suggest ways in which New Labour has been attempting to reconcile the social democratic conception of a free, universal health service with a range of modernising strategies that draw on private sector investment and resources. They offer a simplified version of history in which several post-1940s decades of change, including the response to the challenges of new voices and movements of the 1960s and 1970s, magically disappear. The narratives are constructed around two familiar New Labour themes. One is the need to move on from the days when needs were regarded as identical to a situation where services need to be tailor-made in order to respond to the individual needs of customers. This does something interesting to the traditional conception of equality at the core of the social democratic state, substituting a shallow and individualised conception of difference in its place. The second theme is the need to build services around the interests of users rather than the convenience of producers. This duality neatly places government on the side of users while at the same time calling on users to be the new driver of change:

> We live in a consumer age. Services have to be tailor-made not mass-produced, geared to the needs of users not the convenience of producers. The NHS has been too slow to change its ways of working to meet modern patient expectations for fast, convenient, 24 hour, personalised care. (DH, 2000, para 2.12)

The assumption underpinning the image of the patient as 'discriminating customer' is that people have become used to flexible, responsive, user-centred services delivered in the marketplace and want the same when they come to the NHS. It is possible to identify a few difficulties inherent in such an assumption. The first relates to whether or not consumers do actually get what they want from the commercial sector. As one of our respondents put it,

> These days the private sector isn't what it used to be. You are left dealing with call centres and people you didn't really want to speak to. You are left pushing buttons on the phone, left holding for hours on end. If the National Health [Service] acted in that manner I think you would probably have world war three on your hands. (Old Town, user respondent 1)

The second concerns whether people really do expect or want the NHS to behave like a company or whether it has a rather different place in the popular imagination, a theme to which we return later. But the third difficulty centres on the role and status of 'choice' in the reform programme and the tensions between this and other political discourses – notably those of 'equality' and 'need' – that remain significant in Labour's political lexicon. Equality is not a concept that the Labour government – however New Labour it might be – could reject out of hand. Rather it reworks it, detaching it from the social democratic discourse and its associations with rights and entitlements, and repositioning it in a more 'modern' set of discursive couplings between choice and equity:

> Extending choice – for the many, not the few – is a key aspect of opening up the system in the way we need. But choice for the many because it boosts equity. It does so for three reasons. First, universal choice gives poorer people the same choices available only to the middle classes. It addresses the current inequality where the better off can switch from poor providers.... Second, choice sustains social solidarity by keeping better off patients and parents within the NHS and public services. Third, choice puts pressure on low quality providers that poor people currently rely on. It is choice with equity that we are advancing. Choice and consumer power as a route to greater social justice not social division. (Blair, 2003)

However, choice is not the only concept around which the new policy agenda is based. We want to highlight the significance of the ways in which professional discourses of empowerment and responsibilisation are woven into the narrative of change:

> The era of the patient as the passive recipient of care is changing and being replaced by a new emphasis on the relationship between the NHS

and the people whom it services – one in which health professionals and patients are genuine partners seeking together the best solutions to each patient's problem, one in which patients are empowered with information and contribute ideas to help in their treatment and care. (DH, 2001, p 9)

These images of partnership imply a fundamental shift in the role and status of the health practitioner, one in which their knowledge and power loses some of its authoritative status. This aspect of consumerism – in which the empowered user is constituted as knowledgeable and able to participate in the treatment process as well as to be responsible for their own good health – implies something rather different from the shallow transactions between doctors and patients associated with 'shopping around' between alternative health providers.

Consumerism, then, is not a single phenomenon but elides a number of different developments. Some are concerned with legitimating the reform and restructuring of the welfare state (in the name of a 'modern' service for a 'modern' people). Here a narrative is constructed that collapses history and reconstructs the postwar welfare state as producing, rather than ameliorating, inequalities. Some appropriate professional concerns about how best to secure better health outcomes through a partnership-based and person-centred model of care. Some promulgate consumerism as a driver for change, with the government looking 'over the heads' of professionals and managers to the health user as a means of opening up the health service to new ways of working. Some are concerned with installing new commissioning processes and funding regimes organised around the idea of patient choice. The interaction between these different developments produces tensions that are then devolved to service delivery organisations to resolve. In the next section we explore ways in which consumerism is understood by senior health service managers, and how they experience – and negotiate – the tensions that are produced as they respond to the consumerist imperative.

Institutional adaptations

Rather than seeing the consumer as the all-powerful driver of a more accountable, responsive and user-oriented service, the interviews with senior managers in strategic roles offered a number of different conceptions of the service user. Indeed, they suggested ongoing struggles to reconceptualise the user in ways that drew on developments in professional conceptions of best practice, that responded to some of the challenges of user movements, and that acknowledged the need for legitimacy in the eyes of patients and the community. In Newman and Vidler (2006: forthcoming) we traced a number of different professional conceptions of the service user. One focused on a holistic conception of the patient, implying a need for a more 'joined-up' approach to service design:

> There is no point in having [a] super duper health centre if they are not on a bus route, … [or] if the people are too frightened to come in because of crime….We have to deliver services in a way that working people can access without having to have time off work and things. (Old Town, strategic interview 1)

However, the conception of the relationship between provider and service user still tended to be dominated by clinical models of care, albeit models in which patient experience was accorded a higher value because of its impact on health outcomes. The idea of the *expert patient* signified rather different changes in the relationships between provider and service user:

> The idea is that these patients who are going to be sent on the expert patient programme are the patients that present, sort of every week, that they do have … a chronic illness, but they just seem to need reassurance about all other aspects of their health and so will present week after week. So there is a place now where they can learn how to be more independent. Um, and that is a government initiative. (New Town, strategic interview 3)

The language of 'expert patient' was sometimes rejected in favour of a more professionalised concept of 'guided patient self-management' (Old Town, strategic interview 4: a senior clinician with a general practice background). The aim was to secure better health outcomes, but the change of language explicitly rejected the linking of 'patient' and 'expertise': the challenge to professional power was thus minimised.

One point of correspondence between policy texts and professional discourse was the idea of patient empowerment through access to information:

> Going to the doctor and just standing there like a stuffed dummy and expecting him to tell you what is wrong with you is, I think, almost a thing of the past.You've got to be proactive whenever you go and see a health professional and there's no better way of being proactive than learning about it before you go.Therefore you have got to have patient

involvement and public involvement.... It enables you to be more self -
aware about your own body, about your own condition, and to try to
get the best from the system you possibly can. (New Town,
strategic interview 1)

This could mean anything from equipping patients with information to
'empowering' people by giving them more choice. Empowerment also
encompasses more collective conceptions of participation in which service
users are consulted and involved in deliberations about service planning.
But the boundary between conceptions of the *empowered service user* (linked
to knowledge) and *discriminating customer* (linked to choice) was slippery:

> If you talk to people about choice how a lot of people will think is that
> it is about choosing whether you go to this hospital or that hospital. But
> from my point of view it is around choice right down to the patient
> level, and it is a bit greater than what hospital you go to, it's around how
> do you want the service delivered to you.... There are these options
> available for treatment, which one fits you best? (Old Town, strategic
> interview 1)

Here we can see the government discourse of 'choice' – denoting access
to alternative providers where patients have been on a waiting list for a
particular time – being reworked to signify a more professionally
recognised concept of 'choice', defined as involving patients in treatment
decisions.

The concept of choice, then, provided a bridge between professional
and consumerist discourse. It was welcomed where it was viewed as
extending or amplifying a pre-existing professional ethic, especially one
associated with the empowerment of particular groups such as people
with learning disabilities or mental health service users. However, this
was rather different from choice as elaborated in government policy. In
professional discourse choice meant involving patients in decisions about
appropriate treatments in the interests of more effective health outcomes
(rather than giving a choice of provider). Any more expansive conception,
linked to patients expressing wants or demanding particular treatments,
was viewed as a source of difficulty, since it raised the problem of how
clinical definitions of 'needs' might be aligned with the 'wants', 'preferences'
or 'choices' of the service user.

'Needs' and 'wants' are contested concepts, and form a point of conflict
between clinician and patient; the tension between them was a frequent
theme in discussions about the new choice agenda. The interviews

suggested that senior managers and clinicians had a sophisticated understanding of the concept of choice and were well able to deconstruct it:

> It depends, um, in health – what you mean actually by choice, whether there is choice to be had in that particular area and actually who that choice is ultimately going to benefit. (New Town, strategic interview 3)

Nevertheless, they were having to engage with the government's policy agenda – at the time based on the requirement that health authorities offered patients an alternative provider where they had been on a waiting list for six months or longer. In Old Town the authority was establishing a number of choice centres, essentially call centres through which patients could be offered an alternative provider where the hospital to which they were originally referred found that it could not meet the waiting list target. The region was also piloting new treatment centres, where simple operations could be performed in a more streamlined way. In contrast to the professional discourses of choice described above, these developments meant that choice was coupled to a more managerial agenda of processing patients, redesigning systems and meeting government targets in the most efficient way possible.

But the opportunity to seek an alternative provider was limited to certain categories of patient: those with high blood pressure or who were overweight, and therefore a higher risk in clinical terms, were less likely to be offered treatment in the new centres. And, although managers and senior clinicians were forging ahead on implementing the choice agenda, they remained deeply concerned about equity and were pursuing it in at least two different forms. One was what one respondent termed a 'global' strategy, focusing on improving health inequalities through programmes to persuade people to stop smoking or to eat more healthily. A second was to target resources to particular groups – travellers, asylum seekers, young people with drug or alcohol habits and so on. Consumerism was viewed as undermining both:

> The old adage is that we shouldn't be going down to a medium level, we should be trying to raise everything to a higher level. [But] as soon as you start taking resources away from somewhere else, they are going to start shouting, the self-empowered consumer in that area is going to start complaining. (Old Town, strategic interview 3)

The smoothing over of the tension between choice and equity in policy documents and political speeches, where choice is presented as driving up standards for all, was clearly not convincing those who had to deal with the reality of resource decisions on the ground. Indeed the idea of choice driving up standards for all, at the core of the Blair quote cited earlier (see p 104), is dismissed as an 'old adage'. The tensions between needs, wants and resources stubbornly refused to go away. But although the source of these tensions lay in the general programme of modernisation, they were experienced as problems for the *specific* authority, the *particular* practitioner, the *individual* budget holder or commissioning manager. The material questions about resources, rationing and priority setting were passed on to the 'empowered' clinicians and managers responsible for delivering services. This was well recognised by many of our respondents:

> Choice combined with payment by results could easily lead to bankrupt hospitals, it could also lead to hospitals saying we're not going to carry out that particular treatment because it costs too much. It could lead to patients travelling up and down the country ... then any sort of green policy goes out of the window, doesn't it? (Old Town, strategic interview 3)

Patients, too, identified similar problems associated with the choice agenda:

> The logistics of the thing are just ridiculous. Because, you know, if somebody's really ill and they want to go to see a particular consultant and he's some considerable distance away from where they live this sets up all sorts of problems. Not just for themselves, but for the family, close relatives, you know. It's a very, very difficult situation. So, whilst it sounds very nice and it's a good vote puller actually it isn't very practical at all. In fact it's quite impractical actually. (New Town, user respondent 2)

> Perhaps to choose to go further from home because you could be sorted quicker could be a choice, but then you don't want to go millions of miles from home. Because you want to be visited once in a while. And you want to get know you can get home. (New Town, user respondent 5)

However, such comments need to be set in the broader context of service user understandings of their relationships with health providers. They also raise questions about how far patterns of identification are shifting in the ways conceptualised in the policy documents and political speeches cited earlier. Do those using health services think of themselves as the modern citizen-consumers represented there? How do staff and users understand their relationship? Are service user allegiances and expectations in line with the transformative changes that underpin the drive towards health service modernisation?

New relationships and identifications?

In this section we draw on questionnaire and interview data from front-line staff and service users to address the issues outlined above. In each location we administered a questionnaire to a random selection of 100 front-line staff and 100 users. We then interviewed a selection of those who had completed the questionnaire, and finally explored some of the emerging issues through scenarios presented to focus groups in each location.

The first part of the questionnaire explored responses to issues of challenge, choice, responsibility and inequality, asking respondents to indicate their agreement or disagreement (on a five-point scale) with a series of statements. Questions were phrased differently on the questionnaires to users and to front-line staff, but were designed to elicit responses from each on the following issues:

Challenge: Are people becoming less deferential, less trusting and more willing to challenge the authority of service providers and to make demands on services? Do providers welcome the challenge posed by more informed, empowered, consumers?

Choice: Do staff and service users welcome the prospect of more choice, and perceive it as a driver for improving public services?

Responsibility: Do service users and staff expect individuals to take on greater responsibility – for example, for their own health and well-being?

Inequality: Do staff and service users believe that increased voice and choice would disproportionately benefit those with either the skills to negotiate the system or with the loudest voices?

The results of these sections of the questionnaire are presented in Figure 6.1.

The results can be interpreted in different ways. The vertical axis represents the degree of agreement or disagreement with the statements presented in the questionnaire, presented as a percentage. For example, if all users had ticked 'strongly agree' to all of the statements on 'challenge', the bar chart reading would be 100. If equal numbers had agreed as had disagreed, the result would be 0. None of the scores are dramatic in terms of actual ratings; what is perhaps more interesting is that 'choice' and 'inequality' received much more positive ratings than 'challenge' and 'responsibility' among service users. So, service users both wanted more choice, and were concerned about its potential effects in terms of exacerbating inequalities. They were apparently more willing to challenge health staff, but were, on balance, unwilling to take on new responsibilities for their own health and well-being. Figure 6.1 also suggests some differences between the responses of staff and of users. Users were more positive about the benefits of challenge and of choice, suggesting that the shift to a more assertive and demanding public was producing some discomfort among staff. However, staff were much more positive about the new ethos of patient responsibility than were service users. These results are not altogether surprising. Rather more interesting, however, are the responses on inequality. While both service users and staff were concerned about the potential for consumerism to exacerbate inequalities, fears about inequality arising from the introduction of choice were more strongly expressed by service users. This apparently challenges the idea, so strongly expressed in policy documents, that the citizen-consumer

Figure 6.1: Health care user and staff responses

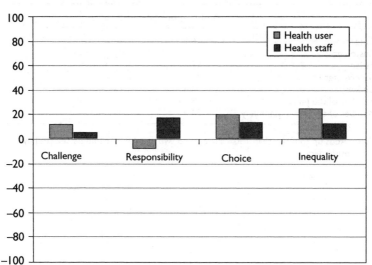

represents a more individualised and self-concerned orientation that potentially dismantles collective support for publicly funded and provided services (for example, Needham, 2003).

This question was also addressed in the second part of the questionnaire. Here we asked respondents to consider a number of possible identifications and relationships (citizen, consumer, member of the public and so on) and to select those that they felt best reflected who they thought they were when interacting with the service in question. They could select more than one category, and most did so. They were then invited, on the questionnaire itself, to add comments about why they had chosen particular categories. The text of this part of the questionnaire is presented in Table 6.1 and the results in Table 6.2.

Table 6.1: Health care user questionnaire

Which of these words best describes your relationship to the NHS? (please tick TWO at most)

Consumer	❏	Citizen	❏
Customer	❏	Member of the public	❏
Patient	❏	Member of the local community	❏
Service user	❏		

Table 6.2: Health care user identifications

	% of responses[a]
Consumer	6.2
Customer	4.5
Patient	51.5
Service user	46.1
Citizen	8.4
Member of the public	38.0
Member of the local community	24.0

Note: [a] Adds up to more than 100% since up to two categories could be selected by each respondent.

What is most striking from the data is the low scores for both consumer and customer. This was replicated in the comments people added to the questionnaires and in the interviews and focus groups. For example:

> I feel more than just a customer because you are paying for a national service for everybody's benefit. Whether you actually need to consume that service or not, is not the primary consideration. So it's wider than being a consumer; I feel more of a citizen than a consumer.

> I don't want to be a customer. I want to be a patient.... I think once you become a customer you are lumped with customers in a shop ... whereas as a patient you have that personal relationship which is very difficult to break.

The first of these extracts suggests the strength of citizen, rather than consumer, identification with the National Health Service (NHS). The second suggests that, in focusing on choice of provider, the government has subordinated other forms of choice that users may prefer – including the choice to have continuous care from a known doctor. Nevertheless, few people ticked the 'citizen' box. We might suggest that this is perhaps because of the close identifications between health service users and the NHS as an institution, not least because of the high scores for the categories 'service user' and 'patient'. Interviews suggested, however, that while many people wanted to continue to think of themselves as patients, this was a more informed and assertive conception of patient rather than a continuation of the image of the 'patient patient' associated with a more passive and dependent relationship with the medical profession.

There were also relatively high scores for the categories 'member of a local community' and 'member of the public'. While this suggests continuities with the solidaristic forms of citizenship associated with the social democratic welfare state, the 'community' or 'public' of the present is not necessarily the same as that of the past; but nor is it in line with the individuated consumer beloved of policy documents. In the focus group in Old Town, for example, it was evident that community activism was seen as the driving force behind improvements in the provision of health services. While emphasising a range of problems with the individual complaints procedure they nevertheless expressed great faith in the *collective* efficacy of the local community, as demonstrated by the following exchange (in which people cut across and followed on from each other in rapid succession):

Respondent 1: I think people of Old Town would complain and get things improved, whereas in other areas they are not doing the same amount of complaining and things are not moving. Old Town the whole place is full of complainers and they want better things. All you have to do is look at the Internet and see what services Old Town has got – they are leaders in so many things.

Respondent 2: A really strong sense of identity and community and wanting to make the place a better place for children, and....

Respondent 3: Unselfish, really. For some people it's about making it better for them personally. But for most people it's about making it better for the wider community.

Respondent 4: Old Town people are doing it for themselves, rather than government doing something to improve it. It's not coming down. These star ratings, choice and everything else, that's not what is driving improvement, it's the people in the....

Rather than the passive recipients of services and a high degree of trust in the NHS as a national institution, we can see here much more engaged and active relationships. Elsewhere the responses suggested a strong continuing attachment to the NHS as an institution, alongside some subtle distinctions about the different kinds of relationships at stake in an individual's interactions with it. The following are all taken from the section of the questionnaire that invited respondents to comment on the categories they had ticked (see Table 6.2):

I am a user of the NHS service when I am in need of it. I consider a patient to be someone who is more intensely dependent on the NHS. I like to be involved in making decisions about my healthcare, and question 'professionals' when I feel the need: yet I don't feel autonomous enough to be labelled a 'customer' or 'consumer'. (Old Town, user 20: ticked 'service user' and 'member of the public')

I have a chronic illness and have therefore been treated by the NHS over a long number of years. I feel involved in my case, but am nevertheless very dependent upon the care given by professionals – doctors and nurses. This relationship – doctor/patient – is right for me, and I feel more than a consumer or customer. I am also very involved in the more recent patient involvement/enablement programme and view myself as a member of the public, putting forward the view of the ordinary patient. (Old Town, user 11: ticked 'patient' and 'member of the public')

Service user: ... this is a two-way partnership between person who is ill and the medical adviser.

Member of the local community: ... because I am concerned about the quality of this public service for all its users in the community. (New Town, user 16: ticked 'service user' and 'member of the local community')

I am registered as a patient with a GP practice and as such I am entitled to receive consultation and treatment and/or referral for health issues. The practice (I believe) received NHS funding for having me registered as a patient.

As a member of the public my relationship to the NHS extends beyond that of only a patient. As a long-term (unpaid) carer for my elderly mother I had extensive experience of dealing with the NHS on her behalf when she became old and frail. I have been involved in voluntary work through the Carers Project on a GP initiative project. Also as a member of the public with a vote I consider a political party's policy on NHS issues when I cast that vote. (New Town, user 13: ticked 'patient' and 'member of the public')

The last three of these extracts are interesting for the ways in which they combine an individual conception of patient-hood, closely based on a personalised relationship with medical practitioners, with wider collective identifications and, in some cases, active commitments. These different identifications are held together by differentiating between support for the NHS as a public institution in general, and the kind of response people want to their individual needs when ill. That is, different identifications may be held at different moments in time, with 'public' and 'personal' shifting in importance. People appear to be able to hold more complex understandings of their relationship with health institutions and the medical profession than the simple policy narratives highlighted in the first section of this chapter suggest.

Conclusion

This chapter began by discussing extracts from policy texts and political speeches as examples of policy discourse, following Ball (1993), Fischer (2003) and others. Policies may be developed in a way that loosely stitches together a range of different goals, and that attempt to reconcile multiple interests. However, they are presented as part of a 'story' that situates new initiatives, drives or targets into a history, and that draws on images of societal change and/or institutional problems to legitimate their proposals. Such an approach views policies – and the political speeches that surround their presentation – as providing a linguistic repertoire on which managers, professionals, user groups and other stakeholders can draw. The language of political and policy texts is therefore interesting in its own right, not because it tells us about the policy content but because it provides clues about what tensions are having to be negotiated in the construction of a credible narrative, and how successful that narrative is. The Labour government has sought to call into being modernised conceptions of the service user. No longer the universal 'patient', we can trace, in successive policy documents, a shift to conceptions of the discriminating consumer, expert patient, responsible health user, demanding consumer and so on. These conceptions – and the narratives of change in which they are located – serve to shift the balance of power not only between health users and providers but also between government and health practitioner, with the government standing as the symbolic champion of consumer power in the face of what are presented as entrenched 'producer interests'.

However, we do not want to suggest that policy discourse is necessarily effective in constituting new relationships and identifications. In the second section (see p 105) we described a number of processes of 'discursive articulation' in which consumerist discourse was reworked through professional vocabularies of meaning. In the process some meanings were amplified – for example, the idea of patient involvement and empowerment – while others were marginalised. This was not, we suggest, a case of professional refusal or resistance to governmental imperatives, but can be understood as a more positive attempt to appropriate elements of consumerist discourse in order to secure the professional goals of improved health outcomes. Such outcomes were to be supported through enabling patients to make informed treatment choices, enhancing their expertise and finding ways to make them more 'responsible' for their own health. All of these ideas can be traced in the political and policy documents we discussed in the first section of this chapter. However, their meaning is subtly detached from the political narrative of change supporting the modernisation of the NHS and reworked into a more professional narrative of progress towards better models of clinical practice based on a partnership model of health care.

One might conclude that consumerism is a site of resistance and struggle. However, simple formulations of resistance would not be justified because of the many subtle ways in which the senior managers we interviewed were attempting to install more user-centred and customer-responsive services. They were doing so in a way that attempted to reconcile two very different imperatives. One was to meet government targets and to reconfigure services in line with policy imperatives (as in the establishment of 'Choice Centres' in Old Town). This was a matter of redesigning systems and procedures. The second was to pursue developments to secure professionally defined goals. The excitement expressed by some respondents to the idea of the 'expert' patient or the 'responsible' health user can be viewed as an attempt to secure more effective treatment alongside moves towards better demand management. The interviews suggest how many of the professional developments taking place in health – more emphasis on health promotion, more person-centred care, and more effort to inform and involve the patient in their treatment – were being elided with the idea of a more consumerist approach. In the process, the consumer was being decoupled from the market-oriented government discourse of choice and reworked into a more professional narrative of improved treatment outcomes. But this strategy could not overcome the more structural problems associated with the new discourses of choice – those that produced an individuation of the tensions between needs or demands on the one hand, and resources on the other. Despite oscillations and inconsistencies as consumerism is overlaid on different trajectories of change, and interpreted through different professional discourses, the move towards a more consumerist, choice-based conception of health serves to mask the continued need for rationing and priority setting at the local level.

However, the disjuncture between professional and governmental interests should not be over-emphasised. The interaction between consumerism and professional practice is messy, uneven and contested. Consumerism itself provides a new linguistic repertoire and a new set of institutional logics of appropriateness on which both professionals and service users may draw. It may be used to legitimate claims on the part of groups of professionals with a commitment to user-centred services (examples in our study included those with backgrounds in user advocacy or learning disability services). Senior managers may use it to challenge forms of professional power (as in the attempt to redesign services around locality-based multidisciplinary teams in Old Town). Service users – and user groups – may use it to make new claims or articulate new demands.

The new discursive repertoire, then, does have important consequences. New practices, based on the idea of a more informed, more empowered, more articulate, more demanding service user, open up the possibility of a shift in the relationships between health providers and users, one in which the 'knowledge–power knot' of professional authority is partly disentangled. Our data from service users appear to support such a shift. There was, as we have argued, a strong rejection of the language of consumerism and choice, but at the same time an awareness of the benefits of information sharing and an image of a more partnership-based relationship between clinicians and patients. There was also an explicit rejection of the transfer of models of service provision from private to public sectors. At stake here were concerns about the potential disruption to the personal relationship between doctor and patient implied by the idea of 'shopping around'.

Service users, then, had a rather different conception of modernity from that espoused by policy documents. They wanted more information and more involvement in treatment decisions (although they also wanted to be able to trust doctors to make decisions on their behalf in times of crisis). They also wanted more voice (including a voice that might challenge professional power). Those who were regular users of private medical facilities also wanted the raising of standards of cleanliness, food and so on in NHS hospitals. However, none of this mattered more than the quality of medical care (seen to be superior in the public sector) and the continuity of relationship with health professionals. And, perhaps most strikingly, alongside higher expectations of what the individual patient-practitioner relationship should offer, there was a continued willingness to identify with the NHS, or with local 'community' health services, as collective public resources whose benefits should be shared equitably.

Notes

[1] Expert Patient Programme (EPP), at www.expertpatients.nhs.uk/what.shtml.

[2] Part of the Cultures of Consumption programme. Further project details at www.open.ac.uk/socialsciences/citizenconsumers.

References

Ball, S.J. (1993) 'What is policy? Texts, trajectories and toolboxes', *Discourse*, vol 13, no 2, pp 10-17.

Blair, T. (2003) *Progress and Justice in the 21st Century*, The Inaugural Fabian Society Annual Lecture, 17 June, London.

Cayton, H. (2003) 'Trust me, I'm a patient: can healthcare afford the informed consumer?', Speech by the Director for Patients and the Public, Department of Health, to the Royal College of Physicians, BUPA Health Debate, 2 September, London.

Clarke, J., Smith, N. and Vidler, E. (2005) 'Constructing citizen-consumers: inequalities and instabilities', in M. Powell, K. Clarke and L. Bauld (eds) *Social Policy Review 17: Analysis and Debate in Social Policy, 2005*, Bristol: The Policy Press, pp 167-82.

DH (Department of Health) (2000) *The NHS Plan: A Plan for Investment, a Plan for Reform*, London: The Stationery Office.

DH (2001) *The Expert Patient: A New Approach to Chronic Disease Management for the 21st Century*, London: The Stationery Office.

Fischer, F. (2003) *Reframing Public Policy: Discursive Politics and Deliberative Practices*, Oxford: Oxford University Press.

Milburn, A. (2002) Speech to the Annual Social Services Conference, 16 October, Cardiff.

Needham, C. (2003) *Citizen-Consumers: New Labour's Marketplace Democracy*, Catalyst Working Paper, London: The Catalyst Forum (at www.catalystforum.org.uk/pdf/needham.pdf#search='Needham').

Newman, J. and Vidler, E. (2006: forthcoming) 'Discriminating customers, responsible patients, empowered users: consumerism and the modernisation of health care', *Journal of Social Policy*, vol 35, no 2.

SEVEN

Being well and well-being: the value of community and professional concepts in understanding positive health

Elaine Cameron, Jonathan Mathers and Jayne Parry

Introduction

Increasing attention to 'positive' health within public health can be seen in the way the term 'health' in policy documentation and discourse has more frequently become 'health and well-being' (Lazenbatt et al, 2000; DH, 2001, 2003; HDA, 2002, 2004). This emphasis on positive health (rather than a focus solely on negative, ill health) seems to chime with other changes and shifts, in particular the opening up of the traditional territory of public health to now be the proper concern and responsibility of all agencies and individuals (see, for example, DH, 2002), and widespread acceptance that health generally is now set free from an outdated dominant medical model (Acheson, 1998).

At first sight, this appears to be both a welcome development (there seems to be a ring of progress about it) and quite straightforward. After all, being healthy is something that is more readily agreed about and more widely understood than ill health. And the changes should lead to 'better' measurement of community health generally. Also this may be a timely shift given the search for measures that now focus on 'upstream' influences and indicators on health, rather than downstream 'medical' ones, and current priorities that include the reduction of health inequalities (see, for example, DH, 2001, 2003; HDA, 2001; Wanless, 2004).

We suggest, however, that while this new emphasis on positive health might indeed be welcome, much of the ground on which this and accompanying ideas are founded, is rather more crumbly and precarious than is typically assumed. Underlying definitions around positive health are typically unclear, unaddressed or value-laden. Associated assumptions that these changes lead to 'better' indicators of health may prove less robust under closer scrutiny.

This chapter offers some contributions to these issues. First, we reflect briefly on some current thinking and challenges around concepts of health (positive and negative) within sociology and social research. Second, we consider the notion of 'well-being' within public health discourse and its link with positive health. Through reviewing 'well-being' in wider social discourse, we offer a critical view of its current application in public health. Third, we draw on findings from our recent research (HealthCounts), a two-year project, funded by the Department of Health under its health inequalities programme, which set out to find common ground between community groups and professionals about better ways to measure health. We discuss communities' and professionals' perspectives on positive health and how they conceptualise it. We suggest that development of a clearer understanding of positive health is usefully served through exploration of these, and that incorporation of grassroots community concepts in public health policy and practice can counter the current more problematic use of 'well-being'. Moreover, inclusion of indicators reflecting community views of influences on positive health might contribute to better 'upstream' measurement of health.

Concepts of health

Social research and sociology has a long history of substantive contributions to knowledge and understanding of health and illness concepts and states, but has tended to focus more on exploration and analysis of negative rather than positive health (Blaxter, 2004). This is in no small part due to the dominance and widespread impact of biomedicine, and its focus on disease and ill health. However, as Lawton (2003) indicates, it is healthy bodies, rather than those that are sick or diseased, that are increasingly becoming the sites for medical attention and interventions.

Blaxter (2004) also points out the current lack of a conceptual base and associated measures for positive health, with existing health indicators distributed toward the 'unhealthy' end of the continuum. Her substantial and influential work around the core area of health concepts has provided frameworks and important insights into the many complexities involved. These include a useful framework for identification of lay concepts of positive health, 'healthy', which we draw on in the analysis of our HealthCounts findings below. She identifies health as not ill, as function, as social relationships, fitness/vitality, lifestyle and psychosocial well-being

(Blaxter, 1990). Psychosocial well-being is here defined as referring to health as a purely mental state, instead of, or as well as, a physical condition. However, understanding how people conceptualise positive and negative health is not straightforward. It is now well established that people's health concepts, as both social constructs and socially constructed, are complex, diverse, connect to other areas of people's lives and typically may be contradictory or inconsistent (Blaxter, 1990; Popay et al, 2003). Moreover, the setting, circumstances and type of researcher approach are all known to have an important bearing on what people will tell us about health (Blaxter, 1997, 2004). Disentangling perceptions of what people consider health to be, from perceptions of those things that influence it, is arguably an artificial exercise, as health is often perceived in ways that conflate the two (Blaxter, 1990). These complexities and the relative neglect of positive health within sociological work mean there is only a limited knowledge base from which public health can draw, in order to address the challenges it faces, as it engages with positive health in the context of wider changes.

Well-being and discourse

Sociological perspectives, however, can contribute in other ways to the issues at hand. As the term 'well-being' is widely used to signify positive health, an exploration of notions of 'well-being' in social and public health discourse can offer some critical insights into its use and meanings in the context of social structures and processes, and hence its value in 'capturing' positive health.

Well-being discourse in the wider social context

Whatever 'well-being' might be, it seems to have become more evident in social discourse generally and features increasingly across more areas in people's lives – from transport and the arts, to the media and community life (see, for example, Cairns, 1999; Glendinning et al, 2003; Sointu, 2003; British Council, 2004). We hear of 'carer well-being' (Lyonette and Yardley, 2003) or 'men's well-being' (Courtenay, 2000), 'economic well-being' (Bardasi et al, 2000) or 'spiritual well-being' (Waite et al, 1999). Well-being even greets the shopper in the supermarket. A range of products labelled 'well being' (including selected foodstuffs, complementary remedies and supplements, environmentally responsible household products, beauty and fair trade products) is said to embrace 'the customer's voracious interest in the well being of the planet as well as the body and mind' (J Sainsbury plc, 2001). And government responsibility for people's 'well-being' across a range of areas is recently underlined in a well-being manifesto (NEF, 2004). Well-being therefore appears to embrace many aspects of people's lives and is applicable in a range of settings and domains, private and public, but typically remains only loosely defined. It is generally something worthy, something desirable, something we ought to be aiming for, something positive.

Different applications and interpretations of the concept appear across an array of disciplines, including psychology, gerontology, economics and sociology (see, for example, Bartlett and Coles, 1998a, 1998b; Hilleras et al, 2000; Blanchflower and Oswald, 2004; Siegrist et al, 2004). Yet apart from psychology (for example, Brief et al, 1993), more often than not assumptions again take the place of definitions, and where interpretations are spelled out, they vary from the more open-ended (Cornwall et al, 2003) to the formulaic (Oswald, 2003). The complexities and challenges of conceptualising and measuring well-being across a range of disciplines are discussed by Gasper (2004), who adds that promoting well-being does not always require more work on measuring it. Within the sociology of health and illness, the slow broadening of enquiry from disease and illness to include an emphasis on positive health has also afforded the notion of well-being more prominence (for example, Beattie et al, 1993). However, as with its appearance elsewhere, well-being, even here, remains rather elusive in terms of precise definition or systematic use (for example, Grundy and Sloggett, 2003). And, to underline an earlier point, apart from Blaxter's framework where well-being features as a part of positive health, theoretical development around positive health generally remains limited (Williams, 2003).

Well-being's high profile in the different social arenas, often mirrored, reproduced or fostered within media discourse, can be explored using theoretical explanations that centre on power relations, ideology and cultural mediation. Sointu's interesting analysis of well-being as a general notion draws on media representations of the concept over the past 20 years or so (1985-2003) to explore and link changes in both conceptions of well-being and changes in wider society (Sointu, 2003, 2005). Although (positive) health is implicit in much of the analysis, there are explicit health issues that are discussed.

Sointu argues that contemporary dominant discourses of well-being relate to wider societal changes in subjectivity. In particular, changes in conceptualisations of well-being link to the move from subjects as citizens ('body politic') in the mid-1980s, to subjects as consumers ('body personal'), to growing individualisation and to the growth of dominant social discourses of interconnectedness. The choosing consumer now actively produces well-being. As a social norm, well-being is now seen as desirable, and viewed as something extra – an aid or resource in busy life, where there is obligation for care of the self. Well-being practices become meaningful because they enable people to reproduce themselves as subjects who are living out prevalent social norms and values. And well-being is seen to bring enjoyment, better coping and increased performance at work. Against a backdrop of a decline in biomedicine's authority, the state now acts as an enabling rather than a providing force in the self-responsible creation of personal well-being by active individual citizens. This extends to health, and Sointu cites Stacey's concept of 'self-health' (Stacey, 1997, 2000) in support of this idea. Well-being is increasingly commercialised and seen as outwith the terrain of mainstream healthcare institutions and experts in a world characterised by consumer culture and plurality of expertise. This analysis, then, sheds light not just on meanings and messages of 'well-being', but on the changes, structures and workings of society in which these ideas are reproduced.

Well-being and health discourse

If, as Sointu argues, well-being is now seen as something extending beyond the territory of mainstream healthcare institutions and experts, how can well-being within public health discourse itself be interpreted? What can an exploration of this tell us about public health and the nature of its work and thinking around positive health?

Well-being is not a new term within public health. The influential World Health Organization's definition placed positive health as a central part of health and gave the notion official recognition and status some time ago (WHO, 1948). As noted above, the term has come to feature increasingly in mainstream health, although, typically, it remains undefined and apparently detached from any lay perceptions of the concept (DH, 1997; DWP et al, 2005). Analysis of the term within public health discourse suggests that particular ideologies and political positions may be in play, the term itself imbued with particular, implicit meanings and messages.

Seedhouse's analysis of well-being within health promotion provides insights into well-being as part of official health discourse, identifying two different approaches taken by health promoters in the absence of clear definition or theorising around the term (Seedhouse, 1995). He shows how ideas of subjectivity, implicit in well-being, are typically hijacked by what he calls 'hardline' health promoters in line with particular value positions (claiming privileged knowledge of 'objective' well-being), leading to health interventions (and associated success measures) that reinforce these positions. Alternatively, 'optimistic' health promoters simply assume a causal relationship between their activities and the increase of well-being. His conclusion is that neither position is acceptable and that well-being should be discarded by health promoters altogether. In other words, the term 'well-being' within health promotion discourse has become part of the mechanism whereby particular powerful agencies reinforce and reproduce particular value positions.

A useful exploration by Carlisle (2001) of the politicised research field of health inequalities may shed further light on current public health use of well-being in public health discourse. Three identifiable but contested explanations of health inequalities (poverty/deprivation, psychosocial stress, individual deficit), with potential policy solutions, are linked to different types of discourse. She draws on a model by Levitas (1988, 1989) which distinguishes redistributionist, moral underclass and social integrationist discourses. Within this framework, each discourse suggests differing sources of health inequalities, explanatory levels, causal mechanisms, solution and action. The redistributionist discourse more readily links with poverty/ deprivation, the moral underclass with individual deficit, and the social integrationist with psychosocial stress explanatory models. Carlisle argues that current contested explanations of health inequalities allow for flexibility of interpretation and political manoeuvring at policy-making level. This means that the present government can claim leadership in tackling health inequalities while simultaneously assigning responsibility to individuals and communities. Carlisle describes the utilisation of redistributionist-type solutions as an uphill task for government, as they require political will to action that extends beyond the life of any one parliament. The more prominent social integrationist discourse, which places community as the locus for action, rather than the individual (moral underclass discourse) or socioeconomic policy (redistribution discourse), has become more evident, for example via regeneration initiatives. Well-being would seem to link well to this social integrationist discourse, just as the powerful concept of lifestyle can be seen as a central part of moral underclass discourse. The picture Carlisle paints of the prominent social integrationist discourse, with community as the locus for action, seems likely to extend beyond the UK setting and be part of wider Western trends, as research into sustainability of health and well-being via communities within a Canadian setting might imply (Vingilis and Sarkella, 1997).

East, in her analysis of neighbourhood residents' and voluntary and professional workers' perceptions of the health of their community, adds further weight to the view that prominent health gap solutions via community as partner in public health and urban regeneration initiatives are limited. She argues that community diversity, complexities of health influences, subjectivity and place as a contested space contribute to unworkable regeneration policies: 'Like many rallying cries in public health policy, "regenerating health in communities" unravels under scrutiny' (East, 2002, p 171).

We suggest that current use of well-being in public health discourse links with both the social integrationist and moral underclass discourses, in that it implies responsibility/locus for action that lies with the individual and community, yet control over what form the subjective aspects take remains more within the power of public health itself. The concept of 'lifestyle', which links more with the moral underclass discourse, has, of course, held considerable sway in framing health inequalities within policy and professional practice. It has also, as our findings below show, become a key feature of community discourse on health and health influences. But, as we point out below, 'well-being' seems to sit rather uncomfortably in the everyday language of health among the community groups in our study, more so than with professionals. If shifts in dominant discourses in public health are set to continue, it might well be that 'well-being' may follow the concept of 'lifestyle' in becoming more prominent in everyday health discourse in communities.

East's work on professional and community perceptions of community health suggests that the shift from a medical to social model of health may be superficial and only partial. She argues that despite engagement with a social model of health, professionals continue to identify health as 'ill health' and influences as ones that have a negative rather than positive impact (East, 2002). A further interpretation of the 'well-being' tag to health may concern underlying fragmentation or differential power relations within and between health organisations. So 'well-being' is more often tagged on to health by specific sectors within health as a means to challenge other health sectors, where the medical model is more firmly embedded. Well-being's high profile within the discourse of public health may support this view.

How useful then is the concept of 'well-being' as used in public health and in wider social discourse, in helping to understand or define the territory of positive health? The limitations begin to stack up. The term is used in a wide range of social arenas and contexts, more often within formal than informal settings and may come with extra, unwanted baggage or serve to reproduce and support particular agencies' power positions or values. Our recent research suggests that more clarity in health concepts generally is needed in public health (Cameron et al, 2006: forthcoming), and importantly, that communities' and professionals' perspectives may prove a useful and different starting point for a clearer understanding of positive health (Mathers et al, 2004).

The HealthCounts Project: concepts of positive health

Unravelling questions around positive health was not the main concern of this research; rather, they emerged as interesting issues during the course of the analysis. The project itself set out with a different agenda. We now provide details of the research before moving on to discuss findings on positive health.

HealthCounts was a two-year project carried out in the Black Country and Shropshire by a multidisciplinary team from the Health Impact Assessment Research Unit, University of Birmingham and the University of Wolverhampton. It sought to identify measures of influences on health that could be used to monitor health and inequalities in health and that had resonance with, and would help bridge any 'gap' between, professionals and community members. Such measures are potentially more useful than the traditional 'downstream' measures of mortality, morbidity and service utilisation, which are typically insensitive to short-term and small effects and probably discordant with lay perceptions of health. Furthermore, the long timescale between an intervention and change in morbidity and mortality makes it difficult to assess the cause–effect relationship.

HealthCounts aimed to achieve this by the explicit linkage of non-medical, routinely available data to the everyday experience of the target community. The work incorporated two interrelated aspects: a quantitative assessment of existing and available data items collected routinely by non-healthcare organisations and a qualitative investigation whereby professional and community groups were asked to prioritise the items that best reflect their perceptions of health. We identified over 1,000 measures, available from routine datasets, of non-medical factors that might influence health. These were discussed and prioritised by participants drawn from various identity groups within disadvantaged communities and from professionals working in the healthcare, statutory, voluntary and community sectors.

The foundation for the whole project was a detailed exploration of participants' perceptions and concepts of health – both negative and positive – and their perceptions of factors influencing health and how these can best be measured. The bottom-up methodology ensured that findings on health measures were systematically grounded in community and professional stakeholders' own experiences rather than based on more typically implicit, institutionally based assumptions of health concepts.

The qualitative data were collected via 16 two-stage focus group sessions with disadvantaged groups in the community (community 'experts'). Two-stage focus group sessions were also held with nine groups from the statutory, voluntary and community sectors (professional experts). In addition, in-depth interviews were carried out with 26 individuals selected from the focus group participants and from people who worked with disadvantaged groups not represented in the focus groups. These included the homeless and also so-called 'hard-to-reach' groups such as gypsies.

The two-stage focus groups were structured in the same way for both community and professional groups. In order to ground later considerations about health measurement in people's own perceptions of health, focus group members started by discussing and exploring their concepts of health along with their views and ideas on health influences. The researchers introduced the idea of well-being, along with other health concepts (being well and being ill), as structured prompts at the first session, and the groups discussed what they felt were influences on each of these. Participants then chose what they felt were the main influences on health overall. In the two-week gap between sessions, researchers reviewed findings from session one, and the groups' choices about health influences were matched against a list of indicators within 68 datasets. These datasets were identified in a review at the start of the project as routinely collected non-medical datasets that might be used to measure and monitor wider influences on community health and inequalities in health. From this list, researchers selected those that most closely matched the focus group members' choices of influences, to be evaluated by the group at the second session.

At the start of the second focus group session members were presented with a summary reminder of their discussion about health concepts, influences and their choice of most important health influences, from the first session, by the researchers. This served as a check mechanism and also allowed for further clarification and additional views. Group members then reviewed the indicators presented to them. They discussed which ones best measured their choice of main health influences, gave ideas for changes and suggested new indicators for some health influences. In the case of some influences, the groups found they had no suggestions for possible indicators.

Focus groups were used as they are considered more fruitful for tapping publicly acceptable accounts and demonstrating contrasts in the accounts of different social groups (Prior et al, 2000). Interviews with individual people from disadvantaged groups gave additional context, detail and depth and complemented the focus group data, affording opportunities to tap more 'private' rather than 'public' accounts of health (Cornwell, 1984). (For full details of the methodology, see Mathers et al, 2004.)

As noted above, disentangling perceptions of what people consider health to be from perceptions of those things that influence it is arguably an artificial exercise, as health is often perceived in ways that conflate the two (Blaxter, 1990). However, because the structure of the two sessions allowed for considerable revisiting of ideas within each group, and also involved activities where influences were specifically sought, identified and prioritised in discussions, we feel there was quite close consideration of these aspects within the groups, despite the limitations set by the approach overall, as indicated above.

Overall, the complexities of positive health and the impact and significance of agency and structure, as well as subjectivity in what counts as positive health for people, were evident in the research. Contradictions and inconsistencies, differences in meanings and contexts also emerged in the discussions, but six points are of particular note.

Value of positive health

Our analysis shows first, that positive health generally was seen as an important part of health by both professional and community groups. This is interesting, as it suggests that public health's embracing of positive health sits well with widespread attitudes, perceptions, beliefs and experiences. Both groups also generally subscribed to a social model of health. The important place of positive health in health generally was evident in their ideas following prompts about well-being and being well, and also by their subsequent choices of what they considered to be the main influences on health overall. Some of these choices related to factors previously discussed as seen to influence both positive and negative health. However, where they related to either positive or negative health only, almost all groups gave greater emphasis to influences that had been previously discussed as affecting positive health than to those seen as impacting on negative health.

'Well-being' and concepts of health

Compared with other health concepts (being well and being ill) introduced and discussed in the focus groups, 'well-being' as a term did not readily seem to form part of the everyday narrative or language people use to describe their ideas or experiences of health, nor possibly other parts of their lives. It seemed to be a much less accessible concept than other positive or negative health concepts, for both community and professional groups, when they were asked what they understood by it.

> ... no idea – haven't got a clue.... (woman from a disadvantaged urban estate within a rural area)

However, once prompted further, and once group members were in the more familiar territory of their own health language and accounts, discussions about areas of positive health did open up in both the community and professional groups, although there were signs that even for professionals, the term was not part of their everyday working health concepts. The professionals, however, were much more readily able to give interpretations than the community groups, seemingly drawing on greater familiarity with the term from more formal discourse around health. The following definition, given by a professional member of a regional body, suggests an 'official' line:

> ... a mental and physical state where no impediment exists related to health, preventing full functioning as related to my expectation of full functioning capability.

A member of a professional focus group, who was employed by a local authority, picked up on the impact of well-being in official discourse, in terms of boundary setting. He felt that recent policy shifts and use of terminology – such as talk of economic, social and environmental well-being – have had repercussions for what is seen as the main arena of work around health. He said that many professionals he encounters now see health as being to do with doctors, and public health to do with front-line delivery of services, leaving well-being out on a limb, and environmental issues (his area of work) as no longer relevant to the business of public health.

Positive health: being well and well-being

How did people's perceptions of positive health as 'well-being' and 'being well', both tapping aspects of positive health, compare? Our findings suggest interesting differences. Overall, the territory accessed via the term 'well-being' was linked to a considerably broader set of ideas of positive health than 'being well', both among communities and professionals, although patterns across the groups showed that being well is not simply 'subsumed' within well-being and many of the main analytical categories were shared. For communities, lifestyle, psychosocial aspects and fitness were the most emphasised interpretations for both, but lifestyle most prominent for being well, and psychosocial aspects, with wide-ranging ideas, for well-being. Social relationships had a higher profile for well-being than being well, although moral aspects and values were given similar emphasis for both.

For professionals, psychosocial interpretations of both well-being and being well were given greatest emphasis in all groups, although function and fitness were given much less emphasis for well-being than being well. Similarly, negative definitions of being well were more prominent than for well-being, and interpretations involving balance/harmony and holistic aspects were more often stressed for well-being. Negative interpretations of being well among the community groups included all the black and minority ethnic groups. When comparing the sets of groups, lifestyle was more prominent in interpretation of both aspects of positive health across community groups, and there was relatively much less emphasis on values and moral aspects of positive health among professionals.

Range of perceptions of 'well-being'

There was wide variation in perceptions about the nature of the well-being area in both sets of groups, with some definitions, as expected, given in terms of influencing factors, and many falling outside Blaxter's 'psychosocial well-being' category. All groups perceived well-being in a multiplicity of ways. What did these interpretations include? Community groups, taken overall, gave most emphasis to well-being as what might be described as psychosocial – contentment, happiness, feeling at ease, feeling good in one's self, self-respect, a positive outlook, or confidence.

> ... having confidence in yourself and what you do.... (man in urban area, lone parent)

> ... content in all aspects of life.... (older black woman, urban area)

One young man from a disadvantaged urban estate said it was thinking good things and not bad things, such as his local Premier League football team winning the next day. All of the professional groups saw well-being as psychosocial.

Other perceptions of well-being can be seen as falling within Blaxter's other domains for positive health. Among community groups, around half of the groups defined well-being negatively, as the absence of illness or symptoms, as physical fitness, behaviour/lifestyle, energy, social relationships, or function.

> ... healthy living.... (Asian woman, urban area)

> ... eating properly.... (unemployed person, urban area)

> ... it's loving and being loved, isn't it? (younger unemployed man, rural area)

Although the majority of people in the community groups did not view well-being as balance, in an interview an older disabled man told us how for him creating and maintaining a balance achieves well-being. With a history of mental health problems and now suffering from arthritis and thrombosis, he said how important it is for him to be involved in social activities, gaining confidence and taking his mind off himself. He finds it challenging to balance the benefits against his limitations and the dangers of being overstretched.

Some community members viewed well-being in terms of values or as having moral aspects, such as inward goodness, a theme also recognised within Blaxter's work (1990).

> ... treat others as self ... if you respect yourself, you respect others.... (younger man, urban area)

Among the professionals, about half the groups saw well-being as holistic, about function, balance and harmony; and some groups stressed the interrelationship of physical and non-physical aspects.

> ... body, mind, spirit at one with the rest of the world.... (woman staff member, primary care group in a rural area)

> It's feeling at ease with your – it's an internal equilibrium, isn't it.... (member of an urban regional group)

Some said well-being can be present despite physical health difficulty. In an urban secondary care group, it was felt that a person can lose a limb and still have a perfectly good sense of well-being. Two of the nine professional groups said well-being was the absence of disease, illness or symptoms.

Interestingly, some perceptions of well-being seem to extend beyond the main domains associated with positive health. For example, a third of community groups saw well-being in material or economic terms, most speaking of this in terms of income to meet essential needs, rather than referring to riches.

> ... well-being is feeling that you've got all the things you really need by the time you're 55 or so, so you're able to retire. (black older man in an urban area)

Both professionals and community members spoke of well-being as being in some way unattainable or a perfect state.

> But aren't we being unrealistic here, because there is no way anyone in the world can achieve this so it is even pointless talking about this. (member of an urban secondary care focus group)

> I don't think you can ever get a hundred percent, to be honest.... (disabled woman, urban area)

Commonalities and differences

Commonalities and differences between the groups suggest points of interest relating to the significance of identity, context and the professional and lay gaze. Discussions of the well-being area seemed particularly sensitive to these important concerns.

> ... knowing that you do something for somebody in your lifetime ... caring and sharing.... (unemployed woman in an urban area)

> ... having a bath without the children screaming at you.... (young father in a rural area)

> ... being settled, yourself, able to sleep, feel safe.... (woman in a new town refuge)

> ... buzzing ... out on the town – clubbing ... bumping your gums.... (women, disadvantaged urban estate)

... doing your knitting ... being able to read well.... (older women in residential accommodation, urban area)

... knowing your limits ... well, say there was a meltdown at a nuclear power station, I wouldn't run in and 'oh I'll sort it out', because I know that I wouldn't be able to help, you know ... achieve your goals ... they might just be simple – something simple, like cleaning up the living room, or doing the washing up, or it could be something simple like that, or it could be bigger things, it could be saving a baby from a burning building. Yeah – so basically, anything that you feel is worthwhile to get done. (younger unemployed men, rural area)

Subjectivity was a key strand running through both groups' interpretations of well-being in its many forms, but it is noteworthy that in some of the black and minority ethnic community groups, well-being was defined as referring to something shared and collective, rather than seen as individualistic.

... [well-being is] ... when the family is happy too.... (Asian woman in an urban area)

Interestingly, some professional groups tended to think of well-being in terms of others, to do with 'their' lives.

... they link it, don't they, with health – fitness.... (woman in rural voluntary sector organisation)

... satisfied with their life.... (member of urban primary care group)

This was also evident in the way professionals thought about wellness and illness, perhaps reflecting different ontological considerations around health between professionals and communities (Popay et al, 1998).

Other points of difference concerned lifestyle. Professional groups gave much less emphasis to definitions involving lifestyle than community groups, not just for well-being but also for all aspects of health (negative and positive). Community groups gave lifestyle high priority in their interpretations of health across the board.

Also, unlike community groups, well-being was not seen by professionals in terms of a moral dimension or values; they gave relatively more emphasis to well-being as an interrelationship between physical and non-physical aspects.

When the groups specifically considered influences on well-being, following discussions of their well-being concepts, other points of similarity and difference were apparent. Almost all community and all professional groups said that social relationships are an important influence on well-being.

> ... if you're really old and you can't get out and you're lonely, I mean that must be the worst thing, you know because you feel trapped in your situation. (woman worker in voluntary and community sector, rural area)

> ... it's made a big difference to me to see both my grandson and my son this week.... (older woman in residential accommodation, urban area)

Community groups also emphasised lifestyle/behaviour, money/economic factors, personal qualities/characteristics and housing as influential. Professional groups stressed personal qualities/characteristics, money/economic factors and the physical environment, and were much more likely than community groups to cite health and social care services as influential; community groups, again, were much more likely to stress lifestyle than professionals.

Community groups generally spoke of influences as having a positive impact on well-being, although with money and housing, negative impact was mentioned. The professionals were more likely to see influences as having either a positive or negative impact.

Measuring positive health

The business of measuring positive health is often thought to be trickier in principle than measuring negative health within official health circles. The people in the focus groups, however, did not seem to lack views or ideas in respect of positive or negative health. Voluntary and community sector workers, included in the 'professional' groups, had useful views and ideas here that seemed to link with their experiences, role and position in relation to the communities with whom they worked. All groups recognised difficulties in the measurement of some key influences on positive and negative health. When discussing indicators of influences on all aspects of health, both community and professional groups showed, for example, the importance of the need to take account of context, local settings and the significance of 'place'. The concept of 'place', of course, in particular the interaction between its normative, material and social aspects, has already been highlighted as important in shaping people's lives and identities, and its potential in mediating structural factors in health (Popay et al, 2003). Challenges of measurement of place effects on health have also been raised (Macintyre et al, 2002). The focus group discussions, which linked a range of identified health concepts, specific influences, and meaningful indicators of these influences within a particular context and setting, generated a particularly rich arena in which to explore these issues across a range of identity groups. As part of this, for example, many people in the community groups emphasised the need for indicators, particularly those concerning influences on positive health, that move beyond quantitative approaches and take account of meanings and understanding. Positive health seemed especially open to all of these issues – the idea of place, different aspects of health, specific contexts, particular groups of people and the need for qualitative measures. As such, positive health ideas may provide a good starting point for further work developing ways to combine qualitative and quantitative health measures, an issue that already seems to be moving up the official health agenda (Dixon-Woods et al, 2004).

Conclusion

There is arguably a pressing need to clarify and better understand positive health, both within public health and sociology. HealthCounts findings showed that positive health matters to people, and that it occupies a substantial part of their view of what health is. The concept of 'well-being', which is often used as a pointer to positive health within public health, might seem a useful starting point, but is problematic in that it at best lacks sufficient definition and at worst comes with unwanted baggage. As such it is likely to be unhelpful as a heuristic device, unless used in specified and well-defined ways. Apart from Blaxter's work (1990, 2004), there is little sign of progress here to date.

Sociological analysis of 'well-being' within social and health discourse, however, is useful in exploring and explaining the laden nature of the concept, the different ways in which health and health influences (including positive health) are framed by institutions, including public health, and how these are reproduced. This analysis provides further understanding of how these are situated and operate within wider social and political contexts and ideology.

How can positive health then be explored? We argue that the focus for further research, much needed to develop theoretical frameworks around positive health, should lie at grassroots levels with community groups and voluntary, community and statutory sector workers. Our research shows that community and professional experts are just as able to identify, access and discuss positive health as they are negative health. We suggest also that social research has a key role to play in helping to clarify and articulate the contributions of different and sometimes competing 'knowers' in any situation, by generating and providing theoretical frameworks. Reference also needs to be made to the way health may occupy different ontological positions for professionals and communities, the status of different kinds of knowledge – such as experiential knowledge – and the ways in which these may be interpreted and combined in the search for causality and meaning within health. Although people's accounts may be limited or seen as plain wrong in some quarters (Prior, 2003), the nature of the narratives provide more than simply more or less valid knowledge; they can generate all-important theorising around the shaping of health and health as experienced. As noted by Popay et al (1998), lay accounts provide potential for exploring and identifying the finegrain pathways between health and its influences. We suggest that positive health, with its particular emphasis on subjectivity, has potential for affirming the status of lay knowledge within these processes.

Exploration of people's perceptions of positive health, however, is not readily accessed by the term 'well-being'. It was not found to be part of everyday lay discourse around positive health, but appeared to be linked more to formal or official discourse. Uncritical inclusion of the term in exploration and development of grounded frameworks for positive health is therefore likely to act as a barrier. When used as a probe, 'well-being' led to aspects and ideas of positive health that extended beyond Blaxter's psychosocial well-being domain. Development of theoretical frameworks to shed more light on the black box of positive health is more likely to be fruitful if constructed around people's own concepts of positive health that link with identity, context and subjectivity.

We argue that drawing on concepts of health (positive and negative) and health influences held by all stakeholders is important in establishing more valid pictures of health and its influences within a given locality or setting. This is likely to lead to better health measures, and a clearer fix on which specific interventions are likely to connect with particular aspects of health. The persistence of a powerful tendency to measure the measurable means there is a rather uneven playing field that typically favours ill health over health and quantitative over qualitative data.

> In practice, the definition of health has always been the territory of those who define its opposite.... (Blaxter, 2004, p 10)

So, incorporation of stakeholders' concepts and suggestions for differing and qualitative health indicators may be fertile ground for generating a much-needed knowledge base to challenge health measurement skew. One of the offshoots of HealthCounts' findings was the indication that looking to 'better' measure health is likely to give better theoretical understanding of positive health. Efforts to understand positive health arguably also keep open productive constructionist–objectivist debates. This is of particular relevance for public health research and adds weight to any move toward decentring methodologies and combining or synthesising different kinds of knowledge and types of data called for by Popay and Williams (1996). If, as others suggest, the difficult business of measuring positive health is something that can really only ever be aspired to by involving those in the frame (Seedhouse, 1995), then some of the ideas generated in the HealthCounts groups may be useful.

> ... no sensible test exists by which to tell whether or not someone has 'well-being' independent of his or her beliefs. (Seedhouse, 1995, p 64)

Acknowledgements

This work was undertaken by the authors, who received funding from the Department of Health. The views expressed in the publication are those of the authors and not necessarily those of the Department of Health. We are grateful to the many people – residents and workers in the Black Country and Shropshire – who gave their views, ideas and time so enthusiastically to the project.

The chapter presents work on a related but different theme to a paper to be published in *Critical Public Health* (Cameron et al, 2006: forthcoming).

References

Acheson, D. (1998) *Independent Inquiry into Health (The Acheson Report)*, London: Department of Health.

Bardasi, E., Jenkins, S.P. and Rigg, J.A. (2000) *Retirement and the Economic Well-being of the Elderly*, Colchester: Institute for Social and Economic Research, University of Essex.

Bartlett, C.J. and Coles, E.C. (1998a) 'Psychological health and well-being: why and how should public health specialists measure it?, Part 1: Rationale and methods of the investigation, and review of psychiatric epidemiology', *Journal of Public Health Medicine*, vol 20, no 3, pp 281-7.

Bartlett, C.J. and Coles, E.C. (1998b) 'Psychological health and well-being: why and how should public health specialists measure it?, Part 2: Stress, subjective well-being and overall conclusions', *Journal of Public Health Medicine*, vol 20, no 3, pp 288-94.

Beattie, A., Gott, M., Jones, L. and Sidell, M. (eds) (1993) *Health and Wellbeing: A Reader*, Basingstoke: Macmillan, in association with The Open University.

Blanchflower, D.G. and Oswald, A.J. (2004) 'Well-being over time in Britain and the USA', *Journal of Public Economics*, vol 88, pp 1359-86.

Blaxter, M. (1990) *Health and Lifestyles*, London: Routledge.

Blaxter, M. (1997) 'Whose fault is it? People's own conceptions of the reasons for health inequalities', *Social Science & Medicine*, vol 44, no 6, pp 747-56.

Blaxter, M. (2004) *Health*, Cambridge: Polity Press.

Brief, A.P., Houston Butcher, A., George, J.M. and Link, K.E. (1993) 'Integrating bottom-up and top-down theories of subjective well-being: the case of health', *Journal of Personality & Social Psychology*, vol 64, no 4, pp 646-53.

British Council (2004) 'Arts and well being' Seminar, advertised to be held 14-18 February 2005 (www.britishcouncil.org/seminars/seminars-themes-artsnew/seminars-arts-0406.htm, accessed 24 June 2005).

Cairns, S. (1999) 'Moving towards well-being', *Town and Country Planning*, vol 68, pp 252-3.

Carlisle, S. (2001) 'Inequalities in health: contested explanations, shifting discourses and ambiguous policies', *Critical Public Health*, vol 11, no 3, pp 267-81.

Cameron, E., Mathers, J. and Parry, J. (2006: forthcoming) 'Health and well-being: questioning the use of health concepts in public health policy and practice', *Critical Public Health*.

Cornwall, A., Lall, P. and Owen, F. (2003) 'Putting partnership into practice: participatory wellbeing assessment on a South London housing estate', *Health Expectations*, vol 6, pp 30-43.

Cornwell, J. (1984) *Hard Earned Lives: Accounts of Health and Illness from East London*, London: Tavistock.

Courtenay, W.H. (2000) 'Constructions of masculinity and their influence on men's well-being: a theory of gender and health', *Social Science & Medicine*, vol 50, pp 1385-401.

DH (Department of Health) (1997) *Health and Well-being: A Guide for Older People*, London: DH.

DH (2001) *The National Health Inequalities Targets*, London: DH.

DH (2002) *Building Healthy Cities – What Works in Regeneration*, London: DH.

DH (2003) *Tackling Health Inequalities: A Programme for Action*, London: DH.

Dixon-Woods, M., Agarwal, S., Young, B., Jones, D. and Sutton, A. (2004) *Integrative Approaches to Qualitative and Quantitative Evidence*, London: Health Development Agency.

DWP (Department for Work and Pensions), DH and HSE (Health and Safety Executive) (2005) *Health, Work and Well-being – Caring for Our Future: A Strategy for the Health and Well-being of Working Age People*, London: DWP, DH and HSE.

East, L. (2002) 'Regenerating health in communities: voices from the inner city', *Critical Social Policy*, vol 22, no 2, pp 147-73.

Gasper, D. (2004) *Human Well-being: Concepts and Conceptualizations*, Discussion Paper No 2004/06, Finland: World Institute for Development of Economics Research, United Nations University.

Glendinning, A., Nuttall, M., Hendry, L., Kloep, M. and Wood, S. (2003) 'Rural communities and well-being: a good place to grow up?', *The Sociological Review*, vol 51, no 1, pp 129-56.

Grundy, E. and Sloggett, A. (2003) 'Health inequalities in the older population: the role of personal capital, social resources and socio-economic circumstances', *Social Science & Medicine*, vol 56, pp 935-47.

HDA (Health Development Agency) (2001) *Closing the Gap: Setting Local Targets to Reduce Health Inequalities*, London: HDA.

HDA (2002) 'Workplace health and wellbeing', Web-based resource (www.hda.nhs.uk/html/about/press/14102002.html).

HDA (2004) *Improving the Health and Wellbeing of People in Mid-life and Beyond: Making the Case for the National Health Service*, London: HDA.

Hilleras, P.K., Pollitt, P., Medway, J. and Ericsson, K. (2000) 'Nonagenarians: a qualitative exploration of individual differences in wellbeing', *Ageing & Society*, vol 20, pp 673-97.

J Sainsbury plc (2001) News release, 8 August (www.j-sainsbury.co.uk, accessed 21 July 2004).

Lawton, J. (2003) 'Lay experiences of health and illness: past research and future agendas', *Sociology of Health & Illness*, Silver Anniversary Issue, vol 25, pp 23-40.

Lazenbatt, A., Orr, J., Bradley, M., McWhirter, L. and Chambers, M. (2000) 'Tackling inequalities in health and social well-being: evidence of "good practice" by nurses, midwives and health visitors', *International Journal of Nursing Practice*, vol 6, pp 76-88.

Levitas, R. (1998) *The inclusive society? Social exclusion and New Labour,* Basingstoke: Macmillan.

Levitas, R. (1999) 'Defining and measuring social exclusion: a critical overview of current proposals', *Radical Statistics,* vol 71, pp 10–27.

Lyonette, C. and Yardley, L. (2003) 'The influence on carer wellbeing of motivations to care for older people and the relationship with the care recipient', *Ageing & Society,* vol 23, no 4, pp 487–506.

Macintyre, S., Ellaway, A. and Cummins, S. (2002) 'Place effects on health: how can we conceptualise, operationalise and measure them?', *Social Science & Medicine,* vol 55, pp 125–39.

Mathers, J., Cameron, E. and Parry, J. (2004) *HealthCounts. Bridging the Gap between Experts: Finding Shared Ways between Communities and Professionals to Measure Community Health,* Birmingham: Health Impact Assessment Research Unit, Department of Public Health and Epidemiology, University of Birmingham.

NEF (New Economics Foundation) (2004) *A Well-being Manifesto for a Flourishing Society,* London: NEF.

Oswald, A.J. (2003) 'How much do external factors affect wellbeing? A way to use "happiness economics" to decide', *The Psychologist,* vol 16, pp 140–1.

Popay, J. and Williams, G. (1996) 'Public health research and lay knowledge', *Social Science & Medicine,* vol 42, no 5, pp 759–68.

Popay, J., Bennett, S., Thomas, C., Williams, G., Gatrell, A. and Bostock, L. (2003) 'Beyond "beer, fags, egg and chips"? Exploring lay understandings of social inequalities in health', *Sociology of Health & Illness,* vol 25, no 1, pp 1-23.

Popay, J., Williams, G., Thomas, C. and Gatrell, T. (1998) 'Theorising inequalities in health: the place of lay knowledge', *Sociology of Health & Illness,* vol 20, no 5, pp 619-44.

Prior, L. (2003) 'Belief, knowledge and expertise: the emergence of the lay expert in medical sociology', *Sociology of Health & Illness,* Silver Anniversary Issue, vol 25, pp 41-57.

Prior, L., Chun, P.L. and Huat, S.B. (2000) 'Beliefs and accounts of illness. Views from two Cantonese-speaking communities in England', *Sociology of Health & Illness,* vol 22, no 6, pp 815-39.

Seedhouse, D. (1995) '"Well-being": health promotion's red herring', *Health Promotion International,* vol 10, no 1, pp 61-7.

Siegrist, J., von dem Knesebeck, O. and Pollock, C.E. (2004) 'Social productivity and well-being of older people: a sociological exploration', *Social Theory & Health,* vol 2, no 1, pp 1-17.

Sointu, E. (2003) 'The imperative of wellbeing: tracing a changing discourse', Paper given at British Sociological Association Medical Sociology Group 35th Annual Conference, part of PhD thesis in progress, 'The spirit of wellbeing', Department of Sociology, Lancaster University.

Sointu, E. (2005) 'The rise of an ideal: tracing changing discourses of wellbeing', *The Sociological Review*, vol 53, no 2, pp 255-74.

Stacey, J. (1997) *Teratologies: A Cultural Study of Cancer*, London, Routledge.

Stacey, J. (2000) 'The global within', in S. Franklin, C. Lury and J. Stacey (eds) *Global Nature and Global Culture*, London: Sage Publications, pp 97-145.

Vingilis, E. and Sarkella, J. (1997) 'Determinants and indicators of health and well-being: tools for educating society', *Social Indicators Research*, vol 40, pp 159-78.

Waite, P.J., Hawks, S.R. and Gast, J.A. (1999) 'The correlation between spiritual well-being and health behaviors', *American Journal of Health Promotion*, vol 13, no 3, pp 159-62.

Wanless, D. (2004) *Securing Good Health for the Whole London Population*, London: DH.

WHO (World Health Organization) (1948) *Constitution*, Geneva: WHO.

Williams, G. (2003) 'The determinants of health: structure, context and agency', *Sociology of Health & Illness*, Silver Anniversary Issue, vol 25, pp 131-54.

EIGHT

Happiness and social policy: barking up the right tree in the wrong neck of the woods

Tania Burchardt

Introduction

Research on happiness is currently enjoying a higher profile than at any time since Jeremy Bentham and the utilitarians in the 18th century. In particular, some economists have in recent years turned their attention to possible connections between happiness and various aspects of economic behaviour (see, for example, Frey and Stutzer, 2002). This builds on work by psychologists over many decades on the relationships between happiness, personality traits and experiences (for a review, see Diener, 1994). This chapter considers whether there are insights to be gleaned for social policy from this resurgence of interest in the idea of happiness. Is happiness a useful way to conceptualise well-being and is promoting it an appropriate goal for social policy? What light, if any, does the accumulating evidence on the determinants of happiness shed on the optimal design of social policies?

The next section briefly outlines the motivations behind the development of the 'economics of happiness' and describes the indicators commonly used to measure happiness or subjective well-being (SWB), as it is sometimes called. A review of empirical findings on the determinants of SWB is then offered, and the possible policy implications are drawn out. In some cases, this offers a new rationale for an existing area of policy; in other cases, the happiness perspective indicates that aspects of individuals' circumstances that have received little policy attention should be afforded a higher priority. However, I argue that an exclusive concern with happiness as a policy objective would be mistaken for two reasons, the first relating to the plurality of human ends and the second relating to distributional issues. The chapter concludes that while research on the economics of happiness is a useful corrective to the overly materialistic focus of traditional welfare economics (it is barking up the right tree), the philosophy on which it is based does not provide a secure foundation for the development of social policy (it is in the wrong neck of the woods).

Development of the economics of happiness

Current interest in the economics of happiness can be traced back to its roots in classic utilitarianism, as advocated by Bentham (1789). Classic utilitarianism held that states of affairs were to be judged solely on the basis of the total sum of utility that they produced, with utility interpreted as the balance of pleasure over pain ('the greatest happiness of the greatest number'). Preference utilitarianism developed from the classical version, in response to concerns about the incommensurability of different kinds of pleasures, and indeed of pleasure and pain. By interpreting utility as preference satisfaction (or desire fulfilment), preference utilitarianism avoided the need to specify how individuals weighted the components of their personal utility function to arrive at their preference for state x over state y. In a further twist, preferences can be inferred from the choices people make: preferences are revealed by the option an individual chooses from a given set of options.

This interpretation of utilitarianism provided the foundation for welfare economics (for a brief account, see Sugden, 1993). Social welfare was assumed to be a function of individual utility, with utility interpreted as revealed preferences. The task of welfare economics, then, was to analyse the economic arrangements that would maximise social welfare, given other constraints.

For a given set of prices, the principal constraint is a budget constraint; at an individual level, the limit on preference satisfaction is defined by the income available to the individual[1]. Increasing income relaxes the budget constraint and hence allows greater preference satisfaction.

This condensed account of intellectual history illustrates that there are many links in the chain between the theory of utilitarianism, with its foundational concept of utility as well-being, and the proxy for individual well-being that has become most widely used in economics (and indeed social policy), namely income. Unease about the validity of income as a proxy for utility was voiced periodically, but it was not until Easterlin (1974) that a convincing empirical representation of the gap between income and intuitively more direct measures of utility, based on subjective well-being, was provided. Easterlin showed that although there had been large increases in real incomes in the US since the 1950s, average happiness had remained static. He posited an aspirational shift: as average standards of living rise, so do aspirations and the standards of living of the groups to which individuals compare themselves, such that there is little net gain in SWB.

Since Easterlin, a number of studies have confirmed that income is not associated in the expected way with life satisfaction, happiness, or other measures of subjective well-being (see below). This has provoked a number of economists to examine alternative measures more seriously. Could they provide a better match to the original concept of utility?

Two main groups of measures have emerged. The first aims to capture moment-by-moment mood or 'affect'. This is perhaps closest to the classical utilitarian position, with no attempt to distinguish between higher and lower pleasures, or to give greater weight to more considered preferences. The Experience Sampling Method works by issuing participants with a buzzer, set to go off at random times during the day. Participants are asked to record what they are doing and their mood on a range of dimensions each time the buzzer sounds. The results can then be aggregated to give an index of overall positive or negative affect, and the relationship with particular activities can be analysed. The Day Reconstruction Method has the same objective but involves less interruption of the activities themselves and lower respondent burden: participants are asked to recall the sequence of activities in which they were engaged in the previous 24 hours and to rate their mood during each activity on 12 dimensions (happy, warm/friendly, enjoying myself, frustrated/annoyed, depressed/blue, hassled/pushed around, angry/hostile, worried/anxious, criticised/put down, competent, impatient, tired). The two methods have been shown to produce similar results (Kahneman et al, 2004).

Proponents argue that the mood interpretation of utility is conceptually clearer and more scientifically robust than the alternatives. Experiments have shown that changes in mood correspond to alterations in brain activity and other physiological changes (Davidson, summarised in Layard, 2005). Whether this evidence helps to establish the validity of this measure as a proxy for utility depends, of course, on many other assumptions, such as the relationship between mind and body, and the preferred interpretation of utility.

The second group of measures that have been investigated in some detail aim to capture a more reflexive assessment of subjective well-being. Respondents are asked questions like, 'How satisfied are you with your life overall?', sometimes supplemented with questions about specific domains (job, family, leisure time, etc). Responses are recorded on scales from 'completely satisfied' to 'not at all satisfied'. Scales may have short ranges (for example 1 to 5) or be much longer (1 to 100). An alternative formulation explicitly refers to happiness: 'Taking all things together, would you say you were very happy, fairly happy, or not too happy these days?'.

Precisely which interpretation of utility this second group of measures reflects depends on what one imagines respondents consider in answering the questions. Qualitative research unpicking the process respondents undergo in reaching their rating might be revealing. Whatever their precise meaning, life satisfaction and happiness measures of this kind have been found to have some reassuring characteristics: responses show a reasonable degree of test–retest reliability over the short term, and variations over the longer term or between people correspond to life events and circumstances which psychological and sociological theories predict to be significant (Myers, 1993). Responses also correlate well with other people's observations of the individual, both close friends and strangers (Sandvik et al, 1993). More objective measures like frequency of smiling or laughing, health, and likelihood of committing suicide also turn out to be correlated in the expected direction with self-reported life satisfaction (Pavot, 1991; Shedler et al, 1993). One eminent researcher in the field concluded that these kinds of measure of well-being 'appear to possess adequate psychometric properties' (Diener, 1994, p 114).

None of this establishes that either mood or life satisfaction is the correct interpretation of utility; it simply serves to show that each approach succeeds in measuring *something,* rather than just random noise. Moreover, the 'something' that each construct measures has some degree of face validity as a proxy for utility.

Determinants of happiness

A very wide range of personality traits, individual relationships, demographic characteristics, socioeconomic circumstances, cultural values and institutional settings has been hypothesised to influence subjective well-being[2]. A number of those that have been empirically tested are reported below, selected on the basis that they have interesting potential implications for social policy. These implications are discussed in the following section.

Income

Numerous studies have examined the relationship between individual income and SWB (see Frey and Stutzer, 2002). Most of these are based on life satisfaction type measures, rather than mood. To summarise the empirical findings:

- income is positively correlated with SWB;
- income explains a relatively low proportion of the differences in SWB between people;
- there are diminishing marginal returns to income;
- relative income matters;
- inequality matters over and above the individual's own income;
- individuals adapt (partially) to changes in income.

The positive correlation between income and SWB is reassuring to those who would defend income as a proxy for utility. However, the fact that many other factors, including, for example, age, health, education and personality, affect the relationship between income and happiness gives pause for thought. The same level of income does not translate into the same SWB for these different groups. Moreover, each additional unit of income is associated with a decreasing addition to SWB, suggesting that if income is to be used as a proxy for utility, it should be used in a non-linear form[3].

The evidence suggests that the subjective value of income to an individual depends on comparisons with other incomes, whether consciously or otherwise. This manifests itself in a number of different ways. Firstly, individuals compare themselves with their peers – for example, their work colleagues, members of their extended family, or even as broadly as others of their gender, age and social class (Clark and Oswald, 1996; Frey and Stutzer, 2002). This lends support to the possibility of 'aspirational shift', discussed above in relation to Easterlin's pioneering work (Stutzer, 2004). Similar concerns have led to the idea that the frame of reference – that is, the standards of living that people aspire to – should be regarded as a public good, and that in so far as conspicuous consumption shifts the frame of reference upwards, the negative externality it creates should be taxed accordingly (Frank, 1999; Layard, 2005).

Secondly, the level of income inequality itself affects levels of SWB, over and above the individual's position in the income distribution. Alesina and colleagues (2004) found that SWB is lower when income inequality is high, comparing across years and across regions (states in the US and countries in Europe), and controlling for individual-level income, employment status, education and other personal and macro-economic characteristics. The effects are large: for Europeans, a 10 percentage point increase in the Gini-coefficient for income would correspond to a 27% rise in the proportion of people reporting themselves as 'Not very' or 'Not at all' satisfied. Interestingly, although these results hold for both sides of the Atlantic, the relationships between inequality and happiness are different. In Europe, high levels of inequality more adversely affect the SWB of the poor than the rich, while in the US, the reverse is the case. Alesina and colleagues suggest that this may reflect differences in beliefs about mobility: 71% of Americans believe that the poor have a chance of escaping from poverty, compared with 40% of Europeans. Thus for the poor in Europe, high inequality may be perceived to mean being trapped in poverty, while for the rich in America, high inequality may be perceived to make their wealth insecure.

Finally, there is some evidence that individuals compare their income levels with their own previous incomes, but that the positive effect of an increase in income on SWB wears off over time (Burchardt, 2005). This effect is referred to as adaptation, or sometimes as the 'hedonic treadmill'. Interestingly – and unfortunately – adaptation to falls in income is less pronounced.

Employment, unemployment and family life

For people in work, job satisfaction is one of the most important domains of life satisfaction. It is likely that there is interaction between job and life satisfaction: high job satisfaction contributes to life satisfaction; high life satisfaction contributes to job satisfaction (Judge and Watanabe, 1993). The correlates of job satisfaction have been widely studied (for an overview, see Warr, 1999). Opportunity for making decisions over work tasks, interacting with others, variety, and a supportive environment have all been found to be important. So too are the more obvious features such as pay, physical working conditions and job security.

The relationship between satisfaction and financial reward is complex, however. Job satisfaction and propensity to remain in the job seem to be related to changes in wages more strongly than levels of wages, implying that workers subjectively adapt to wage rises (Clark et al, 1998; Clark, 1999; Grund and Sliwka, 2003). Studies of voluntary work indicate that financial rewards do not always enhance satisfaction (Le Grand, 2003). Volunteering increases life satisfaction (over and above the fact that happier individuals are more likely to volunteer), but this can be 'crowded out' if the exchange becomes too much like a market transaction (Meier and Stutzer, 2004).

Conversely, unemployment has a strong and lasting adverse effect on subjective well-being. Indeed, it has consistently been found to be one of the most powerful predictors of unhappiness (Clark and Oswald, 1994; Korpi, 1997). Becoming unemployed is associated with a sharp drop in life satisfaction, even after controlling for loss of income, and individuals do not return to their former level of satisfaction, on average, even after they get a new job (Lucas et al, 2004). Subsequent spells of unemployment are again associated with sharp drops in SWB, indicating that there is no protective effect of having experienced the event before. Winkelmann and Winkelmann (1998) confirm the absence of evidence for a process of adaptation to unemployment. Unemployment is worse than other forms of non-employment such as being retired or looking after children, although in some estimations, the status 'sick and disabled' approaches a similar level of dissatisfaction as unemployment (Burchardt, 2005). These results suggest that status – the acknowledgement that you are engaged in a socially valued activity – is a critical component of subjective well-being.

Another domain of satisfaction that features significantly in individuals' overall evaluation of well-being is family life. The events of marriage, birth of a child and divorce, and the statuses of being married and being divorced all have strong and significant associations with subjective well-being. There is some evidence of selection into marriage, that is, happier people are more likely to get married, but panel evidence indicates that as well as this, marriage itself is associated with an increase in happiness (Clark et al, 2003). There is a honeymoon period, almost literally: after two years or so, the lift to life satisfaction associated with getting married begins to decline, but average satisfaction does not quite return to pre-marriage levels. Unsurprisingly, divorce is anticipated by a period of unhappiness for both men and women, but while men's SWB returns to its baseline level fairly swiftly following divorce, women's remains low.

Satisfaction with family life is potentially in tension with other satisfaction domains. For example, Nickerson and colleagues (2003) find that the more strongly individuals are motivated by a desire for financial success (including promotion at work) the less satisfied they are with family life. Similarly, being under time pressure at work is associated with strongly negative affect (Kahneman et al, 2004), which may spill over into lower overall assessments of well-being.

Hope, autonomy and freedom

Subjective feelings and beliefs about the future – such as whether there is any possibility of an improvement, and in particular whether you yourself are likely to be able to change things for the better – have been theorised as an important aspect of social inclusion or exclusion (Atkinson, 1998). Empirical research on subjective well-being shows that hope and fatalism are indeed closely bound up with happiness and unhappiness. The perception of the future as bright, both in terms of one's individual chances and more generally that of the society in which one lives, are strongly associated with positive subjective well-being (Kimweli and Stilwell, 2002; MacLeod and Conway, 2005). Indeed, Diener and colleagues (2002) argue that hope and 'constructive cognitions about the future' are so central that it is appropriate to conceptualise them as a constitutive part of well-being.

In addition to feeling positive about the future, the extent to which an individual perceives himself or herself as being in control, or having a say over future events, is also correlated with life satisfaction. As mentioned above, research on job satisfaction has shown that autonomy at work matters. More generally, having an external 'locus of control' (that is, a fatalistic attitude) is associated with lower overall life satisfaction (Klonowicz, 2001), while 'owning one's actions', including feeling that one's objectives are consistent with one's values and underlying beliefs, is associated with high subjective well-being (Sheldon et al, 2004).

More broadly, a large cross-country study (Veenhoven, 2000) found that three indices of freedom, political (democratic process and civil rights), economic (conditions of exchange of goods, services and labour) and personal (religious freedom, etc), were each strongly positively correlated with SWB. Economic freedom was especially important in poor countries, while political freedom was more important in rich countries (perhaps due to there being less variation in economic freedom among more developed countries).

Focusing on political freedom, Frey and Stutzer (2000) used differences between the 26 Swiss cantons as a natural experiment to assess the effect of direct democracy on SWB. They find that individuals in cantons with more referenda have significantly higher SWB, even after controlling for sociodemographic and other characteristics. This can be interpreted as showing that referenda are an effective way of aligning local policy with what makes the population happy, or that the opportunity to participate in decision making is itself highly valued. The latter interpretation is supported by the fact that it is the right to participate rather than actual individual participation that appears to make the difference.

Potential policy implications

Psychologists may be interested in the relationship between happiness and various characteristics for its own sake, and economists may be interested in the relationships with economic behaviour and decision making, but what insights are there for social policy from this area of investigation? As this section explores, evidence that social arrangements promote subjective well-being provides, in some cases, a new rationale for existing policies; in other cases, the happiness perspective indicates that aspects of individuals' circumstances that have received little policy attention should be afforded a higher priority.

Perhaps the first important finding is that income is a necessary but not sufficient condition of well-being. This is, of course, a familiar refrain from studies of poverty and deprivation: although low income is a convenient indicator, it has been clear since Rowntree's research at the beginning of the 19th century that the phenomenon of poverty is multidimensional, an insight restated and re-enforced by Townsend (1979), and much of the subsequent literature on deprivation. There is some overlap between the domains identified as important in happiness research and those most commonly used in studies of deprivation – unemployment, low income and leisure activities, for example – but happiness research also draws attention to *conditions* of employment, the quality of family relationships, and the extent of individual autonomy. Perhaps the key difference here is that while poverty and deprivation remain focused on material deprivation, happiness research indicates that other, non-material, dimensions may be equally important. This brings it closer to the more recent generation of research on social exclusion, which incorporates participation in social and political spheres as dimensions in their own right (Hills et al, 2002).

If one were to follow the lead provided by happiness research, this would imply, firstly, that more imaginative policy tools need to be developed to address the non-material domains. The record of policy initiatives that explicitly aim to promote positive social interactions is not encouraging: they have a tendency to be moralistic, patronising and hypocritical. One example from recent history in the UK is John Major's *Back to Basics* campaign, which preached family values despite the fact that more than one cabinet minister was subsequently revealed to be having an extra-marital affair. Tony Blair's recently announced *Respect* agenda seems destined to go the same way, with critics highlighting the inconsistency of statements like, 'It is about the duty I have to respect the rights that *you* hold dear. And vice-versa' (Blair, 2005), with simultaneous government attacks on civil liberties and derogations from the EU Convention on Human Rights.

Policies that have as their objective creating the conditions in which positive social interactions are more likely to take place may have more potential. Passing and enforcement of anti-discrimination legislation, for example, should enable a wider range of people to socialise freely and without fear of harassment, whether they are black, white, gay, straight, disabled or non-disabled. Curbing excessively long working hours would ease the time constraint on spending time with friends and family. Full-time employees in the UK work longer hours than in any other country in the EU (TUC, 2002).

Consideration of the interactions between material and non-material domains are also important in policy design. On the positive side, traditional forms of financial redistribution are likely to have beneficial effects in other areas (health and quality of environment, for example). On the other hand, a welfare to work policy that reduces financial hardship (improving satisfaction with income) through access to jobs that involve long hours and poor conditions is likely to have offsetting effects in the domains of satisfaction with work, health, friends and family relationships. The overall effect on SWB could be negative.

Moreover, the strongly diminishing marginal returns to income indicate that the deficit in SWB of, for example, fraught family relationships, cannot be easily made up with financial transfers. So policies that promote supportive relationships within and between generations would need to be given higher priority. This might take the form of more adequate statutory leave entitlements, for fathers as well as mothers, and for other carers too. Moreover, such entitlements would need to be paid; unpaid leave is of relatively little benefit to those on low household incomes, since they are often unable to afford the loss of earnings. Carers have consistently campaigned for better support to combine unpaid caring and paid employment roles, including, for example, the availability of longer breaks or greater flexibility in their paid employment, more 'respite' care services, and more responsive social services.

Evidence on the importance of hope, and conversely, fatalism, indicates an area of concern that has been relatively neglected in social policy, which could be called 'subjective dynamics'. The effects of government policy not only on the actual opportunities available to individuals but also on their perception of the future and on their confidence in their own self-efficacy need to be considered, if the overall impact on subjective well-being is to be assessed. At present, most policy evaluations do not include a balance sheet of changes in fulfilment, hope and confidence on one side, against frustration, disappointment and despair on the other.

Such considerations provide a different rationale for tackling child poverty than the arguments most often put forward by the current government, which focus on the consequences for these children as adults, particularly in terms of their economic activity. As well as these long-term material consequences, growing up in significant material disadvantage limits the aspirations of young people and their belief in their ability to control their own fate (Bynner et al, 2002; Schoon and Parsons, 2002).

Continuing obstacles, failures and pure bad luck in adulthood merit attention too. Repeated opportunities to recover from setbacks are needed to maintain hope and self-confidence. Some life events are obvious points for intervention, where the evidence suggests that the risk of a negative subjective trajectory is high: imprisonment, onset of impairment; and bereavement or divorce. In these cases, appropriate responses might include more intensive versions of programmes that already exist – resettlement for ex-offenders, rehabilitation for newly disabled people (focusing on sustaining or rebuilding aspirations, especially for people with mental health problems), and counselling or befriending. In other instances, thinking about the subjective dynamics would give rise to different kinds of policy response: with respect to unemployment, for example, interventions would need to be designed to counteract stigma, rather than re-enforcing it, as at present. This in turn might mean reconsidering a human capital approach to welfare to work, investing in adult education, supporting voluntary work and exploring ways in which existing skills can be used or developed.

What these interventions have in common is the attempt to expand people's capabilities, to set them on a different track from that which they were previously following (an approach John Hills has termed 'propulsion' – see Hills, 2002, p 232). These are often seen as expensive policy options, but long-term gains reduce the net costs and the potential benefits in terms of subjective well-being are considerable.

The significance of individual agency and autonomy for subjective well-being has implications for policy making and implementation as well as for policy content. It favours the subjects of a policy being actively involved in its development, rather than being passive recipients of a pre-formulated strategy. Area regeneration programmes under New Labour have been progressive in this respect, making greater efforts to involve local residents in decision making from an early stage than some previous programmes (Lupton and Power, 2005). But the tension between participative policy development, on the one hand, and targets and overall policy goals set by central government, on the other, has not been resolved. Are residents to have discretion over the ends as well as the means? How can this be reconciled with the need for accountability of funding raised and distributed centrally? Participation of this kind is also patchy. At the same time as some residents are being encouraged to get involved in designing regeneration schemes, the emaciation of other local forums, including local government itself, continues.

Other policy areas have paid lip-service to individuals taking an active role in formulating a programme; for example, many of the UK welfare to work 'New Deals' incorporate an element of choice for participants, but this is more often nominal than actual. For the subjective well-being of participants, it is possible that offering pseudo-choices is more alienating than giving a realistic assessment of limited employment opportunities (Mitchell-Smith, 2003).

Arguments against happiness

Before we wholeheartedly recommend reshaping social policy in these ways, it is worth pausing to consider whether happiness is, after all, the right objective to promote. There are two main concerns here. The first is that some policies that make or keep people happy are deeply unattractive for other reasons.

This is a line of criticism that reaches right back to the failure of classic utilitarianism to distinguish between different kinds of pleasure, or to allow for human ends other than hedonism. The argument has been made in various ways; the 'experience machine' in Nozick (1974) illustrated one version. People on the machine believe that they are popular, successful, engaged in the activities they value most in life, and so forth. In reality, none of those conditions holds, but for as long as people are on the machine, they get exactly as much pleasure as they would if they were genuinely popular, successful and so on. Clearly, an enlightened policy maker would hook as many people as possible up to these machines on a permanent basis. A similar point is made in fiction by Aldous Huxley's *Brave New World* (1932). Citizens are issued with a drug called soma, which soothes anxiety, gets you high, and does not have any unpleasant side-effects (although it may eventually kill you).

The 'mood' interpretation of utility, which was described above as being measured at the sound of a buzzer, is particularly vulnerable to this objection. If the objective is to maximise the amount of time people spend in a positive mood, widespread distribution of antidepressants should become a policy priority, even to people who are not clinically depressed. Layard (2005) in places seems to look forward to such an outcome with approval, and some psychiatrists have expressed concern that a similar trend is already occurring with respect to the prescription of drugs like Ritalin for children (Cooper, 2004). More generally, it may be tempting for governments to concentrate their efforts on creating or maintaining an illusion of well-being rather than engaging in the messy, long-term and difficult business of providing the objective conditions that would enable people to live the lives they want to lead. One need not look beyond Western democracies to find instances of governments stimulating vigorous public debate about trivial matters to avoid dwelling on more significant injustices, or endeavouring to create the impression that the 'consumer' of health services is in control when in fact he or she has little influence on the quality of care, the duration of waiting time or even the cleanliness of the facilities. The underlying objection is that the goal of social policy should be actual well-being, not just the cosy sensation of well-being. This formulation, of course, begs the question as to what 'actual' well-being really is, a problem to which the concluding section returns.

Even if we accept that subjective well-being or happiness is an appropriate goal for social policy, a further problem is whose happiness we should aim to promote. Utilitarianism itself, the philosophical wellspring of interest in happiness, provides little guidance on distributional matters, since maximising either the total sum or average happiness is consistent in principle with *any* degree of inequality of happiness. One might hope to motivate some redistribution from rich to poor with the observation that the evidence suggests that those on low incomes are generally more efficient at converting resources into utility than the wealthy (that is, there are diminishing marginal returns to income). Hence total utility will be maximised if more resources are directed to the poor. Exactly what share of resources depends on the shape of the income-utility curve.

To set against that, those with additional needs would be likely to lose out under a strictly utilitarian metric. A disabled person, for example, who incurs extra costs related to his or her impairment requires greater resources to obtain the same standard of living and may therefore require greater resources to obtain the same level of subjective well-being as a non-disabled person. They have a lower rate of conversion of resources into well-being and a purely utilitarian calculation could result in diverting resources to a more 'efficient' consumer.

In either case, viewing the situation in static terms is inadequate. If we add in the observation that levels of subjective well-being are particularly sensitive to *changes* in state, and moreover that losses are more keenly felt than gains (Kahneman and Tversky, 1979), then we are forced back to a position of non-redistribution. The ideal policy for achieving maximum social welfare in the presence of adaptive preferences of this kind would be to ensure continual and ever-lasting upwards social mobility for everyone. However, since upwards mobility for some is inevitably associated with downwards mobility for others where relative status is concerned (and the evidence outlined above indicates that in many areas, subjective assessments are made relative to others), one would have to balance the subjective benefits of upwards mobility with the dis-benefits of downwards mobility. Since gains are more quickly and thoroughly assimilated than losses, this would tend to tip the balance in favour of avoiding downwards mobility rather than promoting upwards mobility, which implies that the distributions of earnings, health, social status, and so on should be kept as static as possible. All forms of mobility should be reduced to a minimum so that no one has the frustration of no longer being able to achieve a level of earnings, or whatever, that they previously enjoyed. Solidifying inequality in society in this way, of course, runs directly contrary to most liberal political theory.

The deeper problem here is not whether some technical reason can or cannot be found within the research on happiness for redistributing resources from rich to poor, but that efficiency in maximising the total sum or average happiness is the wrong motivation for redistribution altogether. Inequality is objectionable because it is unjust, not because it is inefficient (although it may be that as well). The economics of happiness, and the utilitarianism that underlies it, can give us no guidance on this deeper issue.

Conclusion

So, what, if anything, can social policy learn from the economics of happiness? As the title of this chapter suggests, my own view is that there are useful insights to be gleaned from this area of research (it is barking up the right tree), but the philosophical foundation on which it is based is ill suited to social policy (it is in the wrong neck of the woods). To be more specific: welfare economics, and social policy, have relied for too long on income as the chief indicator of well-being. Turning, or returning, to more direct measures of utility, and exploring their relationship with individual and societal characteristics and circumstances, is a helpful reminder of the importance of non-material dimensions of well-being. Many of the findings that are emerging from that research agenda coincide with the concerns that have been investigated in the social policy world through concepts like multiple deprivation and, in particular, social exclusion. These general findings, include, for example, the way in which individuals evaluate their position in relation to others (relativity), the significance of changes in status not just levels (dynamics), the fact that no one domain can describe all the others (multidimensionality), and the importance of individual choice and control (agency). It is useful to have the significance of these features underlined by an alternative perspective and there is an opportunity for fruitful cross-disciplinary engagement here.

On the other hand, social policy is inescapably concerned with questions of distribution, questions that the economics of happiness cannot answer. We should not seek a technical fix; questions of distribution are normative and require a substantive theory of social justice to ground them. Such a theory is unlikely to be based on utilitarianism, not only because it does not match our intuitions about the injustice of wide inequalities, but also because it acknowledges only one object of value (namely happiness); an assumption that is at odds with the recognition of the plurality of human ends that has become so central to the modern liberal ideal. Fortunately, there are many other contenders. For example, Rawlsian egalitarianism adopts the 'difference principle': no inequality in the distribution of 'primary goods' (those things everyone is presumed to need in order to pursue their own goals in life) can be justified unless allowing such inequality improves the circumstances of the worst-off members of society (Rawls, 1971). Alternatively, there is a range of interpretations of equality of opportunity, such as Dworkin (2000), which require redistribution of resources in order to ensure that factors beyond individual control do not create unfair advantage or disadvantage. The capability approach, developed by Sen (1985, 1999), focuses attention on the distribution of capabilities: the range of valuable activities and states of being that individuals are able to engage in or achieve. Each theory provides a different answer to the question, 'equality of what?' and a different set of principles for determining whether a given distribution is just or unjust.

The benefits of the fresh perspective brought by the economics of happiness to questions of social policy can be retained, without risk of being led astray into absurd or unpalatable policy implications, provided the need for an alternative theory of social justice is recognised and put into practice by explicitly identifying the normative assumptions underpinning any analysis of inequality or disadvantage.

Notes

[1] Strictly speaking, the budget constraint should be defined in terms of resources (including, for example, financial, physical, human and social capital, access to public goods, and time), but income is very often used as an approximation.

[2] Much of the evidence refers to life satisfaction or happiness-type questions, rather than mood or affect. Although there are shades of difference in meaning between the different concepts, in those cases where the relationships between them and individual characteristics have been tested, the results have been broadly consistent. For this reason, the terms 'happiness', 'life satisfaction' and 'subjective well-being' are used interchangeably in the summary that follows. For more nuanced interpretations, readers are referred to the sources listed in the references.

[3] Oswald (2005) notes that the observed relationship is between *reported* SWB and income. The unobservable utility underlying reported SWB might nevertheless be linear with respect to income.

References

Alesina, A., Di Tella, R. and MacCulloch, R. (2004) 'Inequality and happiness: are Europeans and Americans different?', *Journal of Public Economics*, vol 88, pp 2009-42.

Atkinson, A. (1998) 'Social exclusion, poverty and unemployment', in A. Atkinson and J. Hills (eds) *Exclusion, Employment and Opportunity*, CASEPaper 4, London: London School of Economics and Political Science, pp 1-20.

Bentham, J. (1789) *An Introduction to the Principles of Morals and Legislation* (republished 1907), Oxford: Oxford University Press.

Blair, T. (2005) 'Respect action plan', Speech given at launch of plan at No 10 Downing Street, 10 January (reported at www.number-10.gov.uk/output/page8897.asp, accessed 17 January 2005).

Burchardt, T. (2005) 'One man's rags are another man's riches: identifying adaptive preferences using panel data', *Social Indicators Research*, vol 74, pp 57-102.

Bynner, J., Elias, P., McKnight, A., Pan, H. and Pierre, G. (2002) *Young People's Changing Routes to Independence*, York: York Publishing Services.

Clark, A. (1999) 'Are wages habit-forming? Evidence from micro-data', *Journal of Economic Behavior and Organization*, vol 39, pp 179-200.

Clark, A. and Oswald, A. (1994) 'Unhappiness and unemployment', *Economic Journal*, vol 104, no 424, pp 648-59.

Clark, A. and Oswald, A. (1996) 'Satisfaction and comparison income', *Journal of Public Economics*, vol 61, no 3, pp 359-81.

Clark, A., Georgellis, Y. and Sanfey, P. (1998) 'Job satisfaction, wage changes and quits: evidence from Germany', in S. Polachek (ed) *Research in Labor Economics*, vol 17, London: JAI Press.

Clark, A., Diener, E., Georgellis, Y. and Lucas, R. (2003) *Lags and Leads in Life Satisfaction: A Test of the Baseline Hypothesis*, DIW Berlin Discussion Paper 371, Berlin: German Institute for Economic Research.

Cooper, P. (2004) 'Education in the age of Ritalin', in D. Rees and S. Rose (eds) *The New Brain Sciences: Perils and Prospects*, Cambridge: Cambridge University Press, pp 249-62.

Diener, E. (1994) 'Assessing subjective well-being: progress and opportunities', *Social Indicators Research*, vol 31, pp 103-57.

Diener, E., Lucas, R. and Oishi, S. (2002) 'Subjective well-being: the science of happiness and life satisfaction', in C. Snyder and S. Lopez (eds) *Handbook of Positive Psychology*, New York, NY: Oxford University Press.

Dworkin, R. (2000) *Sovereign Virtue: The Theory and Practice of Equality*, Cambridge, MA: Harvard University Press.

Easterlin, R. (1974) 'Does economic growth improve the human lot? Some empirical evidence', in P. David and M. Reder (eds) *Nations and Households in Economic Growth: Essays in Honor of Moses Abtamowitz*, New York, NY: Academic Press, pp 89-125.

Frank, R. (1999) *Luxury Fever: Why Money Fails to Satisfy in an Era of Excess*, New York, NY: The Free Press.

Frey, B. and Stutzer, A. (2000) 'Happiness, economy and institutions', *Economic Journal*, vol 110, no 446, pp 918-38.

Frey, B. and Stutzer, A. (2002) *Happiness and Economics: How the Economy and Institutions Affect Human Well-being*, Princeton, NJ: Princeton University Press.

Grund, C. and Sliwka, D. (2003) *The Further We Stretch, the Higher the Sky: On the Impact of Wage Increases on Job Satisfaction*, Bonn Economic Discussion Paper 1/2003, Bonn: University of Bonn.

Hills, J. (2002) 'Does a focus on social exclusion change the policy response?', in J. Hills, J. Le Grand and D. Piachaud (eds) *Understanding Social Exclusion*, Oxford: Oxford University Press, pp 226-43.

Hills, J., Le Grand, J. and Piachaud, D. (eds) (2002) *Understanding Social Exclusion*, Oxford: Oxford University Press.

Huxley, A. (1932) *Brave New World*, London: Chatto and Windus.

Judge, T. and Watanabe, S. (1993) 'Another look at the job satisfaction–life satisfaction relationship', *Journal of Applied Psychology*, vol 78, no 6, pp 939-48.

Kahneman, D. and Tversky, A. (1979) 'Prospect theory: an analysis of decision under risk', *Econometrica*, vol 47, no 2, pp 263-91.

Kahneman, D., Krueger, A., Schkade, D., Schwarz, N. and Stone, A. (2004) 'A survey method for characterizing daily life experience: the day reconstruction method', *Science*, vol 306, pp 1776-80.

Kimweli, D.M.S. and Stilwell, W.E. (2002) 'Community subjective well-being, personality traits and quality of life therapy', *Social Indicators Research*, vol 60, no 1, pp 193-225.

Klonowicz, T. (2001) 'Discontented people: reactivity and locus of control as determinants of subjective well-being', *European Journal of Personality*, vol 15, no 1, pp 29-47.

Korpi, T. (1997) 'Is well-being related to employment status? Unemployment, labour market policies and subjective well-being among Swedish youth', *Labor Economics*, vol 4, no 2, pp 125-47.

Layard, R. (2005) *Happiness: Lessons from a New Science*, London: Allen Lane.

Le Grand, J. (2003) *Motivation, Agency and Public Policy: Of Knights and Knaves, Pawns and Queens*, Oxford: Oxford University Press.

Lucas, R., Clark, A., Georgellis, Y. and Diener, E. (2004) 'Unemployment alters the set point for life satisfaction', *Psychological Science*, vol 15, no 1, pp 8-13.

Lupton, R. and Power, A. (2005) 'Disadvantaged by where you live? New Labour and neighbourhood renewal', in J. Hills and K. Stewart (eds) *A More Equal Society? New Labour, Poverty, Inequality and Social Exclusion*, Bristol: The Policy Press, pp 119-42.

MacLeod, A. and Conway, C. (2005) 'Well-being and the anticipation of future positive experiences: the role of income, social networks and planning ability', *Cognition and Emotion*, vol 19, no 3, pp 357-73.

Meier, S. and Stutzer, A. (2004) *Is Volunteering Rewarding In Itself?*, Institute for Empirical Research in Economics Working Paper 180, Zurich: University of Zurich.

Mitchell-Smith, G. (2003) 'Choice, volunteering and employability: evaluating delivery of the New Deal for Young People's voluntary sector option', *Benefits*, vol 11, no 2, pp 105-11.

Myers, D. (1993) *The Pursuit of Happiness: Who Is Happy and Why?*, New York, NY: Avon.

Nickerson, C., Schwarz, N., Diener, E. and Kahneman, D. (2003) 'Zeroing in on the dark side of the American dream: a closer look at the negative consequences of the goal for financial success', *Psychological Science*, vol 14, no 6, pp 531-6.

Nozick, R. (1974) *Anarchy, State and Utopia*, Oxford: Blackwell.

Oswald, A. (2005) 'On the common claim that happiness equations demonstrate diminishing marginal utility of income', mimeo, Department of Economics, University of Warwick.

Pavot, W. (1991) 'Further validation of the satisfaction with life scale: evidence for the convergence of well-being measures', *Journal of Personality Assessment*, vol 57, pp 149-61.

Rawls, J. (1971) *A Theory of Justice*, Cambridge, MA: Harvard University Press.

Sandvik, E., Diener, E. and Sidlitz, L. (1993) 'Subjective well-being: the convergence and stability of self and non-self report measures', *Journal of Personality*, vol 61, no 3, pp 317-42.

Schoon, I. and Parsons, S. (2002) 'Teenage aspirations for future careers and occupational outcomes', *Journal of Vocational Behaviour*, vol 60, no 2, pp 262-88.

Sen, A. (1985) *Commodities and Capabilities*, Oxford: North Holland.

Sen, A. (1999) *Development as Freedom*, Oxford: Oxford University Press.

Shedler, J., Mayman, M, and Manis, M. (1993) 'The illusion of mental health', *American Psychologist*, vol 48, no 11, p 1117.

Sheldon, K., Elliot, A., Ryna, R., Chirkov, V., Kim, Y., Wu, C., Demir, M. and Sun, Z. (2004) 'Self-concordance and subjective well-being in four cultures', *Journal of Cross-Cultural Psychology*, vol 35, no 2, pp 209-23.

Stutzer, A. (2004) 'The role of income aspirations in individual happiness', *Journal of Economic Behavior and Organization*, vol 54, no 1, pp 89-109.

Sugden, R. (1993) 'Welfare, resources and capabilities: a review of *Inequality Re-examined* by Amartya Sen', *Journal of Economic Literature*, vol XXXI (December), pp 1947-62.

Townsend, P. (1979) *Poverty*, London: Penguin.

TUC (Trades Union Congress) (2002) *About Time: A New Agenda for Shaping Working Hours*, London: TUC.

Veenhoven, R. (2000) 'Freedom and happiness: a comparative study in 44 nations in the early 1990s', in E. Diener and E. Suh (eds) *Culture and Subjective Well-being,* Cambridge, MA: MIT Press.

Warr, P. (1999) 'Well-being and the workplace', in D. Kahneman, E. Diener and N. Schwartz (eds) *Well-Being: The Foundations of Hedonic Psychology*, New York, NY: Russell Sage.

Winkelmann, L. and Winkelmann, R. (1998) 'Why are the unemployed so unhappy? Evidence from panel data', *Economica*, vol 65, pp 1-15.

NINE

Using health and subjective well-being for quality of life measurement: a review

Robert A. Cummins and Anna L.D. Lau

Introduction

Until very recent times, the single statistic that best predicted the health and well-being of populations was wealth. Even as late as 1972 the economist Wilson remarked that the science of economics is 'nearest the core of any problem concerning the quality of life' and that 'the quality of life of any individual or community can in a direct and simple way be related to income' (Wilson, 1972, p 131).

Contemporary data from industrialised nations, however, indicate a far more complex picture. Indeed, even as Wilson made his pronouncement there was plenty of evidence that his broad attribution to 'any' individual or community was wrong. What is now abundantly clear is that wealth has its strongest, causative power over life quality in the context of poverty. When people are very poor, all of the other objective indicators such as education, housing and physical health are highly sensitive to degrees of wealth. Among more affluent populations, however, the relationship between wealth and other measures of well-being, such as health, are fragile and unreliable (for example, Subramanian et al, 2002). Thus, while such standard statistics as infant mortality rates and disease prevalence are useful to track the progress of developing countries, they have very limited usefulness beyond a certain level of economic development. Consequently, within middle-class samples, all of the individual objective variables, including health, are not strongly predictive of overall 'well-being'. While wealth can ensure good medical care, it is no safeguard against loneliness or lack of purpose.

As a consequence of this understanding, it has become clear that the simple statistics that reflect physical health no longer suffice to describe the well-being of the middle classes. New measures are required, including more refined measures of health. Various disciplines have become involved in the process of creating such measures. As a result, it has become clear that 'health' can be measured in many different ways, each of which provides a different view of population well-being to social policy planners.

This review examines these different measurement technologies with the aim of understanding, and critiquing, the hypothetical constructs each measurement style is intended to represent. The first section describes how the constructs of mental health and life quality have evolved in different ways within medicine and the social sciences. This is followed by a description and critique of the two dominant constructs within medicine as Quality Adjusted Life Years (QALYs) and Health-related Quality of Life (HRQOL). Subjective Well-being (SWB) is then introduced and described in terms of its active management by a homeostatic system. Finally, the relevance of SWB measurement for social policy will be discussed from both a rights and an economic perspective.

Defining health and well-being

The term 'mental health' signals the most basic dichotomy of health into its physical and mental components. Unfortunately this term has developed a wide variety of meanings. Most commonly, it is used as a composite term to refer to conditions of psychopathology comprising such states as anxiety, depression and stress. It is, thus; confusing that this positive term 'mental health' actually refers to various conditions of ill-health. Nor is this assisted by the addition of a negative term as 'mental health morbidity' (for example, McNair et al, 2005). The clear implication is that good 'mental health' is signified by the absence of pathology, and this is importantly misleading. The absence of psychopathology means simply that the person is not mentally ill. It does not mean that they enjoy 'good' mental health in possessing such attributes as enthusiasm for life, social competence, a sunny disposition, etc. It is also notable that some authors use the term 'mental health' to refer to QALYs (see, for example, Voogt et al, 2005), which involves a quite different technology devised by medical economists (see later).

The conceptual confusion created by this term was recognised over 40 years ago by Kornhauser (1962), who suggested mental health should be defined in a manner true to its name as 'a loose descriptive designation for an overall level of success, effectiveness, or excellence of the individual's functioning as a person. The emphasis is on mental health in a "normal" and positive sense [not] mental disease or illness' (p 44). Thus, even in 1962, three types of health were evident as: physical health, mental health (pathology) and mental health (perceived well-being).

During the 1980s further complexity was introduced, with the development of the 'Quality of Life (QOL)' concept within both medicine and the social sciences. Within medicine, Hollandsworth (1988) reports that 'quality of life' was first used as an index term by Index Medicus in 1977 and that 23 studies used the term over the period 1975-79.

Within the social sciences the concept of QOL arose from the Social Indicators movement (for a historical review, see Land, 2000), which had its origins as a reaction to the dominance of economic indicators as the primary measures of national well-being. As is well known, Gross Domestic Product (GDP), introduced during the Second World War as a measure of production capacity, is merely the sum of monetary exchange. As such it fails to distinguish between those transactions that add to national well-being and those, such as the cost of prisons, which represent damage control. It was never intended to be an indicator of economic progress and national well-being (for a good description, see Redefining Progress, 1995). Hence, social policy theorists began to look to other indicators of progress, selected either normatively or idealistically, with the aim of better informing policy development (for example, Knox, 1975; Young and MacCannell, 1977).

At first these new social indicators were confined to objective variables, such as population health, and this resulted in some widely used instruments such as the Physical Quality of Life Index (Morris, 1979) and the Human Development Index (Neumayer, 2001). However, the idea of asking 'subjective' questions had been gradually introduced into national surveys. In 1957, a team of researchers (Gurin et al, 1960) used an item format that became widely adopted. Their single question asks 'Taking all things together, how would you say things are these days – would you say you are very happy, pretty happy, or not so happy?'.

Over the next couple of decades, these subjective social indicators were found to produce interesting and anomalous data. In particular, researchers noticed that despite rising wealth, levels of population happiness were remaining static. Such data led the US Department of Health, Education and Welfare in 1969 to advise President Johnson 'Money income, of course, cannot buy happiness, and it is by no means obvious that satisfaction rises with income' (US DHEW, 1969, p 41).

Thus it was that, during the 1970s, researchers from the three disciplinary areas of economics, medicine and the social sciences were all developing alternative conceptualisations of population 'life quality'. This has resulted in three distinct forms of measurement, as follows:

- QALY: a product that shares the disciplines of economics and medicine;
- HRQOL: a product of the discipline of medicine;
- SWB: a product of the social sciences.

While each of these three approaches includes measures of health, their technologies are so different from one another as to yield indexes that have remarkably little in common. Each of these will now be reviewed.

Quality Adjusted Life Years (QALYs)

The technology of the QALY derives from both medicine and economics. It is recommended by the Panel on Cost-effectiveness in Health and Medicine, an expert group appointed by the US Department of Health and Human Services (Gold et al, 1996) to evaluate health benefits to society from reductions in both mortality and morbidity. The reason for the conception of the QALY, and for its continued use, lies in the harsh fact that medicine has become far too expensive for modern cures, palliatives and assistive devices to be made available to everyone in need. In OECD (Organisation for Economic Co-operation and Development) countries, for example, health care costs are rising faster than GDP. The figures for Australia are close to the average for these 28 countries. Health spending in Australia, as a percentage of GDP, rose from 7.8% in 1990 to 8.3% in 2000 (OECD, 2002). This trend is not sustainable, and already many medical procedures are now regarded as too expensive for general application. Medical treatment, in consequence, must be rationed on some determined basis; the QALY provides the rationale. It allows the apportioning of medical care based on the relative valuation of human life weighed against the cost of medical care (Kaplan, 1994): it allows the computation of comparative cost-effectiveness of different technologies (Engle and Bergsma, 1988).

QALYs have various derivative forms. These include the Healthy Years Equivalent (HYE) (Mehrez and Gafni, 1989), Disability Adjusted Life Years (DALYs) (Murray, 1994), Quality Adjusted Life Expectancy at birth (QALE) (Williams, 1988), and Healthy Life Years (HeaLYS) (Hyder et al, 1998).

QALY measurement is based on utility theory, derived from economic and decision theory. Galanter (1962) describes utility theory as based on choice behaviour, with the measurable outcome being the subjective probability of selection among a set of alternatives. This choice reveals an evaluative process concerning the relative desirability of the alternatives, or its 'utility.'

In determining QALYs, people are asked to make decisions based on a trade-off between the quantity and the quality of a life. The application of utility measurement to such decisions (choices) then allows outcomes to be calculated in economically relevant terms. As Torrance and Feeny note, 'QALYs are designed to aggregate, in a single summary measure, the total health [state] for a group of individuals, capturing improvements from impacts on both quantity of life and quality of life' (1989, p 572). A set of weights is applied to the health states to enable cost–utility analysis. The belief that QALYs represent an advanced form of quality of life measurement is widespread. Johannesson (1994), for example, describes QALYs as representing 'years of life multiplied with a weight reflecting quality of life' (p 1623).

In order to make such measurements, people are asked to choose between described health states in one of two ways. The first approach, known as the 'standard gamble', asks a respondent to choose between two alternatives: living in a particular health state (for example, with diabetes) with certainty, or taking a gamble on a treatment with an uncertain outcome. This treatment has a certain probability (p) of leading to perfect health, and another probability ($1-p$) of leading to immediate death. These two probabilities are then varied until the respondent is indifferent between them. The lower the indifference probability, the greater risk of death the respondent is willing to consider, and the lower the desirability of the health state in question.

Many people have difficulty in understanding such procedures when presented as probabilities, and hence an alternative procedure called 'time trade-off' may be used. In this case, a respondent is asked about the number of years lived in a certain health state (for example, with diabetes) he or she would be willing to trade for a shorter life span in full health. The periods can then be varied until the respondent has no distinct preference between them. The ratio of these durations (x/y) then places the condition in question onto a utility scale that ranges from 1.0 (perfect health) to 0.0 (death).

The major advantage of utility measurement is its amenability to cost–utility analysis (see, for example, Kaplan, 1985), allowing medical economists to assess the merits of alternative allocations of resources (Grabowski and Hansen, 1990). Lives are valued in dollar terms. McNeil and Segal (1999) present an example of this in relation to body weight. After adopting a commonly used acceptability threshold for cost per QALY of around US$40,000 (Kupersmith et al, 1995), they determine that people who are obese suffer a 'fall in quality of life [utility index score] of 0.16 of a life year' and so 'experience an average loss in quality of life of $5,500 per year' (p 28). Because the QALYs technology allows the cost of a medical procedure to be compared to the dollar value of human life quality gained as a consequence of the procedure, QALYs may form the basis for health care rationing (for example, Williams, 1988).

A critique

We have published a detailed critique of the QALYs methodology (see Cummins, 2005), a summary of which is as follows.

Rating task

The validity and reliability of questionnaire items is directly related to their simplicity. For general population samples, the more complex an item, the less the responses will reflect a true evaluation of the intended question. People will simply be unable to validly respond or be unwilling to make the effort. Consider then the observation by Carr-Hill (1989) that all QALY-type judgments involve the integration of three variables: remaining life expectancy, the discount rate adopted so as to transform future life years into current values, and quality adjustment. As Carr-Hill states, it is most unlikely that any of these variables could be individually calculated to an acceptable level of reliability and validity to warrant their inclusion in an index. The fact that the QALYs estimations require the simultaneous interaction of these items, again, makes the task too complex. Others have also reached this conclusion (for example, Boulding, 1972; Kaplan et al, 1993; Revicki and Kaplan, 1993). Consequently, these data have uncertain response validity.

Proxy responding

Respondents may be requested to imagine that they have the medical condition in question, and so respond as proxy for people who are actually ill or disabled. A review of proxy responding for subjective states (Cummins, 2002) concludes that such data are unlikely to be valid because the ratings that people provide are strongly determined by personal prejudice. The well-documented general tendency is to rate other people as having a lower level of well-being than oneself. Thus, people's utility ratings will reflect a whole series of systematic influences such as first-hand experience with the medical condition in question, their age, the social acceptability of the condition (for example, AIDS), and so on (see, for example, Gerard et al, 1991; Bjork and Norinder, 1999). These prejudices will be enhanced when the judgements are confined to negative evaluations. Proxy judgements, then, reveal more about the raters than the rated.

Sensitivity

If QALYs are to be used as a measure of outcome effectiveness, they should change as the patient's medical condition improves. In fact QALYs are poor performers in this regard. Even when an obvious improvement in the patient's condition is evident through direct measurement, QALYs may change hardly at all (for example, Feeny and Torrance, 1989; Sherbourne et al, 2001). Moreover, the QALY values derived from different instruments under such changing conditions differ very widely (Nord, 2001; Sherbourne et al, 2001).

Criterion validity

Criterion validity has not been established (for example, Richardson, 1991; Deverill et al, 1998). The three major contenders for criterion validity will now be considered.

* *HRQOL:* the closest related construct against which to validate QALYs are measures of HRQOL (for example, Patrick and Erickson, 1993; Feeny et al, 1996; McNeil and Segal, 1999). Revicki and Kaplan (1993) reviewed studies between 1985 and 1993 that combined health utility preference and the direct measurement of HRQOL. HRQOL measures accounted for 27-34% in preference values. HRQOL scores and time trade-off preferences shared 1-43% of their variance, and gamble utility scores shared 1-25% of their variance. The authors concluded that the two forms of measurement are not interchangeable (see also Dolan and Sutton, 1997).

* *Time lived:* the issue of time is confusing in relation to QALYs. In the DALY it forms the basis for judgements using the time trade-off technique, where people match a variable duration of life lived in perfect health to a longer time lived in a medically compromised state, to the point of indifference. This assumption, that time spent in perfect health equals life quality, is an over-simplification. Other life dimensions such as pain, boredom or social exclusion may make good health an issue of minor importance to the individual.

Time is also used in another, purely economic, sense. In the DALY (Murray, 1994) time is the years of productive life lost as a consequence of the medical condition. Thus, age represents a linear discounting of life worth based on productivity. Following Hyder, Rotlant and Morrow (1998), this would suggest a 60% reduction in productivity between the ages of 25 and 45 years. There is no evidence this is generally true.

- *SWB:* for reasons that will be explained in the following section, the presence of medical illness or disability usually plays a minor role in people's self-evaluation of their life quality. Consider, for example, the high levels of subjective well-being among people with quadriplegia (for example, Bach and Tilton, 1994) and the low correlation between subjective well-being and the standard gamble and time trade-off, of 0.09 to 0.25 respectively, for people on dialysis (Hornberger et al, 1992). Findings such as these have been replicated many times, such that there appears to be agreement that QALYs have no reliable relationship with subjective well-being (for a review, see Nord, 2001).

In summary, while QALYs are expedient devices to rationalise the allocation of medical resources, they fail when subjected to scientific scrutiny. They are not valid in terms of representing a broader view of life quality. They are not reliable in their use of proxy data and complex questions. They are not as sensitive as more direct instruments that target the life aspects that are changing. Importantly, their application has also been questioned on ethical grounds (for example, Faden and Leplege, 1992; Williams, 1996; Koch, 2000). It is our view that this whole family of measures fail to adequately represent the construct of life quality.

Health-related Quality of Life (HRQOL)

A crucial dichotomy when considering the human condition is the distinction between objective and subjective measurement. The former comprises such classic medical variables as blood pressure and longevity. The subjective side concerns how people feel about their health and how such feelings influence their overall sense of well-being. These are starkly different territories. For example, people with pathologically high blood pressure are often not consciously aware of their condition, hence, the objective pathology is not reflected in their own estimates of perceived health. However, there is little value in increasing longevity at the expense of poor perceived life quality. So measures of both objective and subjective health are important independent considerations for social policy.

Unfortunately, a schism has evolved between medicine and social sciences in terms of how to measure perceived health and overall life quality.

While both disciplines rely on self-reporting, they fundamentally differ in the type of information accessed. Within medicine, QOL is operationalised via the HRQOL construct. This utilises patient-reported symptoms. Consequently, an excellent level of HRQOL represents the absence of pathology as reported by the patient. Within the social sciences, on the other hand, QOL is operationalised by a construct called Subjective QOL or SWB. This utilises patient-reported satisfaction with their life. Here, an excellent level of SWB represents a highly positive state of mind and satisfaction with life in general.

These two different views would be congruent if a lack of pathology was proxy for SWB, but it is not, as has already been discussed in relation to 'mental health'. No matter whether the pathology is subjective (for example, perceived stress) or objective (for example, degree of physical disability), pathology does not have a simple linear relationship with SWB (see, for example, Cummins, 2000a; Cummins et al, 2004a). The reason for this non-linear relationship is that SWB is under homeostatic control, as will be explained in the following section.

The lack of a simple relationship between perceived health pathology and SWB is demonstrated in Figure 9.1. These data are derived from the AustralianUnity Well-being Index, which is a regular national survey involving 2,000 people, new to each survey, selected on a geographically proportional basis. Each survey measures SWB using the Personal Well-being Index (PWI) (International Wellbeing Group, 2005), which averages satisfaction across seven domains. Figure 9.1 shows the accumulated data over five surveys for people who are full-time volunteers (Cummins et al, 2005a).

The SWB of volunteers, as measured by the PWI, lies above the normal range. This range has been calculated for both the PWI and for each of the seven domains by combining the mean scores from the 14 surveys conducted to date (Cummins et al, 2005b). In terms of the individual domains, it is notable that health satisfaction lies below the normal range. This is consistent with the fact that these volunteers are generally older than the population average. However, this deficit has been more than compensated by their higher than normal satisfaction with four of the other domains. The end result is that their overall sense of life quality is excellent. Clearly the domain of health is not necessarily a dominating force, as assumed by the HRQOL technology.

HRQOL may be measured by either generic or specific scales. The most widely used generic scale is the SF-36 (McHorney et al, 1993),

Figure 9.1: Full-time volunteers (PWI)

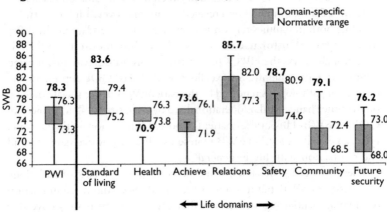

which is designed to measure HRQOL for diverse medical groups. One disadvantage of such generic scales is that their broad cover makes them insensitive to specific change. For example, an intervention for arthritis may increase joint flexibility yet has little impact, as judged through change in a generic HRQOL scale. Thus, condition-specific scales have been developed, which concentrate on symptoms relating to the body part or system in question.

We have published a detailed critique of HRQOL (Cummins et al, 2004b). The essential issues for concern are as follows.

Construct validity

It is not at all clear what HRQOL scales actually measure. Most require the patient to report their own perception of their medical status, that is, their symptoms of ill-being. In these terms HRQOL represents an inverse index of badness from the patient's point of view. And, importantly, the interpretation of this 'badness' scale is that 0 badness (no reported symptoms) equates to QOL excellence. This is demonstrably incorrect. The lack of symptoms signifies only that the person is normally healthy. It does not account for the fact that the individual concerned has just been fired from their job, run over the family's dog, and returned home to find their children have chicken pox.

Even more strangely, a 0 score on a HRQOL scale does not even equate to 'very good health'. A definition of excellent physical and mental health would invoke at least good physical fitness, an absence of disease whether consciously manifested or not, robust immunological functioning, a positive attitude to life, and so on. Clearly, therefore, excellent HRQOL is quite different from excellent physical and mental health. Excellent HRQOL is, simply, the absence of medical symptoms. How, then, should HRQOL data be interpreted?

Clearly, from what has been revealed, such data have no right to represent 'quality' in life. The term 'quality' implies that something is 'better than average' or 'better than normal'. Thus, a 'quality life' is a better than average life. HRQOL scales, however, do not generally allow such a determination. Since they are measures of pathology, the absence of pathology is as good as it gets.

The limitations imposed by using symptoms as proxy for life quality is depicted in Figure 9.2. This shows the full spectrum of perceived life quality, from very bad to very good. It demonstrates the truncated nature of the information available from symptoms alone. They do not permit the person being assessed to indicate a sense of positivity about their life. Symptoms tap only the well-being side of the feeling spectrum, thereby disallowing the expression of positivity.

What, then, do HRQOL scales really measure? In our view the output of such scales represents a mish-mash of medical ill-health, functional limitations and psychopathology. They 'correlate' with other measures of ill-being and well-being due mainly to the fact that the samples used for such 'validation' purposes include people who are severely compromised to the point that any measure of their status reflects their gross pathology. Generic HRQOL scales thus represent very blunt instruments that have lost even the diagnostic utility of their individually measured symptoms. For all of these reasons we cannot recommend HRQOL measurement as an indicator of life quality

Figure 9.2: The feeling dimensions represented by HRQOL and SWB

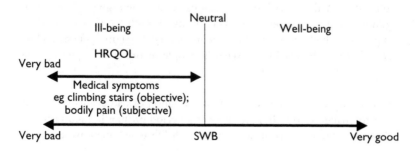

Subjective Well-being (SWB)

The systematic study of SWB is now over 30 years old. While there had been prior research, two extraordinary publications (see Andrews and Withey, 1976; Campbell et al, 1976) launched the idea that 'happiness', 'subjective quality of life', 'life satisfaction' and 'subjective well-being' could be reliably measured and that such measures exhibit trait-like properties. While each of these terms may legitimately be used to indicate somewhat different aspects of the well-being construct, they are operationalised by measures that produce far more shared than unique variance, and SWB is now widely accepted as the generic descriptor. The research base interrogating and describing this construct is now vast.

Perhaps the most important discovery is that these new measures are different from the traditional 'well-being' measures. Physically able and rich people are not necessarily more satisfied with their lives than people who are disabled and have less income. So, these purely subjective measures are accessing an alternative form of well-being.

Subjective Well-being homeostasis

In order to understand the relationship between the objective world of tangible quantities and the private world of perceived life quality, a theory of SWB homeostasis has been proposed. This posits that, in a manner analogous to the homeostatic maintenance of blood pressure or temperature, SWB is actively controlled and maintained by a set of psychological devices (for an extended description, see Cummins and Nistico, 2002) that function under the control of core affect (Davern and Cummins, in press). The operation of these devices is most evident at the level of general, personal well-being. That is, homeostasis operates at a non-specific, abstract level, as exemplified by the classic question 'How satisfied are you with your life as a whole?'. Given the extraordinary generality of this question, the response that people give reflects their general state of subjective well-being, which, it is proposed, is approximately the level at which the homeostatic system operates. As one consequence, the level of satisfaction people record to this question has the following characteristics:

- It is remarkably stable. While unusually good or bad events will cause it to change in the short term, over a period of time homeostasis will normally return global satisfaction with life to its previous level (see

Headey and Wearing, 1989; Hanestad and Albrektsen, 1992; Suh and Diener, 1996).

• The 'set point', around which an individual's SWB varies, lies in the 'satisfied' sector of the dissatisfied–satisfied continuum. That is, on a scale where 0 represents complete dissatisfaction with life and 100 represents complete satisfaction, people's set point normally lies within the positive scale range of 50-100 (see Cummins et al, 2002).

• At a population level within Western nations, the average SWB is 75. In other words, on average, people feel that their general satisfaction with life is about three quarters of its maximum extent (Cummins, 1995, 1998).

While this generalised sense of well-being is held positive with remarkable tenacity, it is not immutable. A sufficiently adverse environment can defeat the homeostatic system and, when this occurs, the level of SWB falls below its homeostatic range. For example, people who experience the chronic pain of arthritis or the stress of caring for a severely disabled family member at home have low levels of SWB (for example, Cummins, 2001). However, for people who are maintaining a normally functioning homeostatic system, their levels of SWB will show little relationship to normal variations in their chronic circumstances of living.

Set points

Central to the idea of homeostasis is the 'set point' for SWB, and a set of recent studies (Davern and Cummins, in press) point to its origin in a construct called 'core affect' (Russell, 2003). Core affect is not linked with any object but, like body temperature, can be brought to consciousness. It is 'free floating' in that, in the absence of challenge by experience, it will attain its genetically endowed level of positivity. Also, like body temperature, it is most evident to consciousness when the level of experienced affect lies outside the normal set point range.

As measured by Davern and Cummins, it can be represented as the combined affects of happiness, contentment and positive energy. These represent the activated and deactivated positive quadrants of the affective circumplex (for a review of affect, see Cropanzano et al, 2003). Core affect is envisaged as the tonic state of affect that provides the activation energy, or motivation, for behaviour. It also produces cognitive awareness in interaction with both genetic and experiential memory.

Core affect perfuses all cognitive processes to some degree, but the ones that are most strongly influenced are those rather abstract notions of the self (for example, I am a good person). These self-perceptions are held at a strength of positivity that approximates the individual's set point as determined by their level of core affect.

Homeostatic buffers

The set point range of well-being is under constant threat. Environmental experience is seldom neutral. Thus, interaction with the environment constantly threatens to move well-being up or down in sympathy with such experience. And to some extent this does occur. Strong and unexpected positive or negative experience will shift the sense of personal well-being to abnormally higher or lower values, at least for a brief period of time. Moreover, if the negative experience is sufficiently strong and sustained, it will cause SWB to remain below its set point range. This is exemplified for body weight in Figure 9.3.

As before, these data are derived from the AustralianUnity Well-being Index and show the relationship between Body Mass Index (BMI) and SWB. Parenthetically it can be seen that the number of people with a higher than normal BMI now dominate within the Australian population. That is the bad news. The good news is that, on average, people can continue to homeostatically manage their SWB even up to mild levels of obesity. Beyond that level, however, the negative consequences of high body mass start to dominate and average SWB falls below the normal range.

Figure 9.3: The relationship between Body Mass Index and SWB

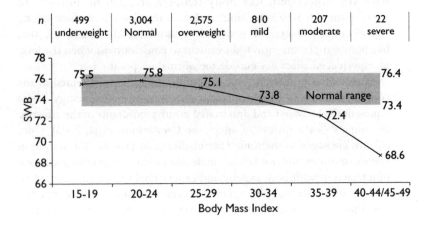

There are two kinds of defences against homeostatic defeat. The first is to avoid, or at least attenuate, negative environmental interactions. This is the role of the external buffers. The second is to ensure that the negative experience, when it does occur, does not diminish the positive sense of self, and this is the role of the internal buffers. The external buffers will be discussed first.

External buffers

Anything that protects people from the potentially negative experiences in their environment can be considered an external buffer. For example, the distinctive nuns' habit affords some protection within the population at large. Other people have personal characteristics that make people react to them more positively than usual. These attributes may be either physical (for example, being physically attractive) or behavioural (for example, friendliness). But the two most important buffers for people in general are money and relationships.

Money is a highly desirable commodity. But there are misconceptions as to what it can and cannot do in relation to personal well-being. What it cannot do is shift the set point. So, in this sense, money cannot buy happiness because, no matter how rich someone is, their average level of SWB cannot be sustained higher than their set point range. Moreover, people adapt readily to luxurious living standards, so genetics trumps wealth at the high-end of well-being. What wealth can do, however, is to maximise the probability that they will be able to maintain their set point range in conditions of potential adversity.

In these terms, money is a highly flexible resource in its capacity as an external buffer (Cummins, 2000b). Wealth allows people to minimise the negative potential inherent within their environment. Wealthy people pay others to perform the maintenance tasks they do not wish to do themselves. If they are bored they buy entertainment; if they are medically ill they buy the best medical care. Companionship, also, can be readily purchased. Poor people, on the other hand, lack such resources and are consequentially at the mercy of their environment to a far greater extent.

The other major type of external buffer is a relationship that involves mutual sharing of intimacies and support. Almost universally, the research literature attests to the power of such relationships as moderators of the relationship between potential stressors and SWB (for reviews see Henderson, 1977; Sarason et al, 1990).

Internal buffers

The nature of the internal buffering system in humans is complex. In lower order animals, such as slugs, we presume that core affect is the essential motivator for volitional activity. The relative lack of cognitive activity within such animals means that, aside from habituation and learned avoidance/approach behaviours, there is little in the way of internal buffering. Their set point for core affect is so dominating that there is little variation.

This lack of variation changes, however, as cognitive systems become more complex. Such systems confer the benefit of advanced information processing, but the downside is elevated levels of conscious awareness and imagination. Such systems have the potential to control the set point through the imposition of pathological thoughts concerning either the dark or the bright side of life. Since the set point is, presumably, the average optimum setting for the SWB system, the potential for such pathology must be controlled. Hence we speculate, in evolutionary terms, the homeostatic system needed to develop in parallel with increasing cognitive capacity. Its function is to protect the set point setting for SWB against the conscious reality of life. A detailed discussion of these systems is provided in Cummins and Nistico (2002) and Cummins, Gullone and Lau (2002).

Robustness and fragility

Homeostatic systems can be inherently robust or they can be fragile. To some extent this dimension is a product of the person's constitution and to some extent it is dependent on resources.

In terms of constitution, this attribute has been studied for many years, commonly under the rubric of 'resilience'. A resilient person is someone who functions normally even in the face of considerable environmental hardship and challenge. The term applied to children denotes that they have developed normally despite adverse living conditions. What allows people to function in such a robust manner has been much debated, but it may be simply a function of their SWB set point.

Someone with a high set point has the advantage that their normal level of SWB is far away from the 'danger zone' of 50 points that signals an increased probability of depression (see later). Moreover, their high core affect will enhance extraversion more than neuroticism, ensuring a socially oriented personality that is likely to garner the involvement of other people in the person's life. Thus, their social capital is likely to be high. In addition, their high core affect will deliver a robust sense of self-esteem, control and optimism, all of which will ensure a strong buffering system (Cummins and Nistico, 2002).

What, then, is the nature of the relationship between the circumstances of people's lives and their SWB? Almost universally, researchers assume the relationship to be linear. Necessarily, however, if homeostasis theory is correct, the linearity assumption is wrong. All homeostatic systems operate around a threshold. The purpose of homeostatic systems is to create relative stability in whatever variable is being defended. In the current context, the positive sense of self is being defended against challenge by sources beyond core affect. Thus, it is predicted, the strength of any source of environmental challenge will relate to SWB, as shown in Figure 9.4.

In the absence of any challenge, SWB will lie at the top of its set point range that averages about 80-82 points in population samples. In an extensive search for groups with high SWB conducted through our analyses of the AustralianUnity Well-being Index data, no demographically defined group has a mean score that reliably lies above this range.

As the presence of a challenging agent becomes increasingly evident, the SWB for each person will move down through its set point range until it approximates the bottom of the range. This downward progression will plateau as homeostatic processes are progressively activated to prevent further decrease. At about 70 points, on average, these homeostatic processes are fully activated. That is, even though the strength of the challenging

Figure 9.4: The relationship between negative experience and SWB

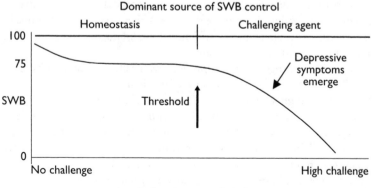

Level of environmental challenge

agent is increasing, homeostasis is 'holding the line' and preventing further change in the level of SWB.

At some higher strength of challenge, the capacity of the homeostatic system is exceeded. At this point the threshold for homeostatic maintenance is breached, and control of SWB shifts from the homeostatic system to the challenging agent. This causes a change in the correlation between SWB and the challenging agent, from a very weak relationship to strong interdependence as the threshold gives way. A description of this change is provided in Cummins (2000a).

As the challenging agent causes well-being to fall, this creates a progressive increase in the condition called depression. The pathological state of depression is hypothesised to be the loss of SWB, as shown in Figure 9.4.

Positive discrimination and homeostatic fragility

Any kind of disability is a potential source of challenge to the homeostatic system, over and above those faced by the general population. Whether the disability constitutes a serious challenge to homeostasis depends on the strength of the challenge and the individual's external and internal resources. If these resources are sufficient to neutralise the additional demands caused by the disability, the homeostatic system will manage SWB and the person will experience normal levels of well-being. If the demands exceed the resources, homeostasis will fail, and SWB will lie below the normative range.

It can be assumed that the genetically determined level of core affect is unaffected by disability. However, the external resources available to such people may well be lower than is average for the general population. Many people with a disability have a lower income than is age normative and many have reduced control of the income they do receive. Additionally, many will experience more difficulty than is normal in developing friendships or intimate relationships.

These factors, together with the negative challenge imposed by their disability in negotiating the routines of life, represent a double jeopardy. They have a higher probability of low external resources and a higher probability of encountering difficulties with daily living. As a result, their management of SWB will be more tenuous because their homeostatic systems will be under constant pressure. While this does not imply widespread homeostatic failure it does imply that people with a disability will have a reduced capacity to deal with unexpected negative experiences.

They are, thus, predicted to be more susceptible to depression than the general population.

SWB and social policy

There are several ways in which SWB measurement should impact on the development of social policy. These may be described from a rights perspective and from an economic perspective. Each of these arguments will now be presented.

Rights perspective

As a response to the treatment of disabled people during the Second World War, the 1948 General Assembly of the United Nations adopted the Universal Declaration of Human Rights as a common ethical basis for civilised nations. Article 25.1 states:

> Everyone has the right to a standard of living adequate for the health and well-being of himself and his family, including food, clothing, housing and medical care, and necessary social services, and the right to security in the event of unemployment, sickness, disability, widowhood, old age or other lack of livelihood in circumstances beyond his control.

The key aspect of this statement is the determination of the 'adequacy' of health and well-being. The criterion in regard to physical health is relatively simple, as the absence of disease and the treatment and amelioration of disability. Adequate well-being, however, is more difficult to determine.

Some conceptual assistance has been provided by the World Health Organization's definition of health as 'a state of complete physical, mental and social well-being and not merely the absence of disease or infirmity' (WHO, 1948). This clearly indicates a meaning for well-being that lies beyond the physical. Moreover, as has been argued, neither QALYs nor HRQOL are adequate for such measurement because they deal predominantly with ill-being, not well-being. So, SWB fits the bill, but how can a level of SWB be regarded as 'adequate'?

The answer lies within normative data and an understanding of the SWB homeostatic threshold. Normative tables for the Australian population (Cummins et al, 2005b) indicate that group mean scores within Australia should lie within the range of 73.4 to 76.7 points when SWB is measured using the PWI (International Wellbeing Group, 2005). That is, any group with a mean score of <73.4 points can be regarded as having insufficient resources to meet the needs of its members. Such determination for groups living in other countries would be dependent on the generation of relevant normative data.

To demonstrate the utility of such measures for public policy, the two major external resources of household income and partner support are mapped below against the SWB of people living with various forms of household composition (Figure 9.5).

It is evident that the best household composition for SWB is living only with a partner. Even the lowest household income allows couples, on average, to maintain normal-range SWB. Moreover, due to the genetically imposed ceiling, their SWB rises only marginally with increasing financial resources, changing only 3.7 percentage points over the entire income range.

The situation is more volatile when children are added to the household. Children drain parental resources and this compromises the SWB of adults living in households with annual incomes of less than $31,000. For sole parents the situation is even more extreme and it is well known that single mothers are more prone to depression than mothers with a partner (Cairney et al, 2003). At the lowest income, the score of 64.1 points for single parents indicates in no uncertain terms that additional resources are required. Moreover, while partners plus children enter the normal range at $31,000-$60,000, sole parents require $61,000-$90,000.

Figure 9.5: Effect of income and household composition on SWB

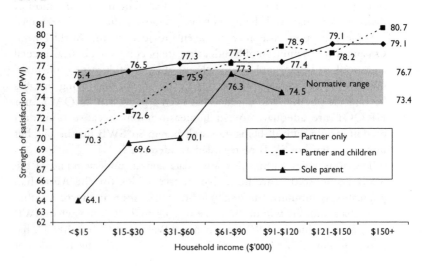

This is because the sole parents are missing the partner support resource and require more income support to compensate.

Through such analyses population subgroups can be identified that require additional resources in order to maintain normative levels of SWB. This argument for selective resource enrichment is from a rights perspective. The case can also be argued from the perspective that low SWB groups constitute an economic burden to society due to depression.

Economic perspective

Depression constitutes a terrible burden to individuals and a substantial economic burden to the state. When people are depressed they lack the normal motivation for living. They are less likely to sustain gainful employment and meaningful personal relationships (for example, Roberts et al, 2000; Burg et al, 2003). They also display increased morbidity (for example, Murphy et al, 1987; Davidson et al, 2004). As one consequence they are voracious consumers of medical and social resources. Moreover, there is evidence that the highest consumers of such resources are people with mild, subclinical depression (see Rose, 1992). In this context it is notable that the World Health Organization report (2001) ranked depression as the fourth leading cause of burden among all diseases.

The relationship between SWB and depression is shown in Figure 9.6. These data have been drawn from the AustralianUnity Well-being Project and appear in the doctoral thesis of Davern (2004). Depression has been measured using the Depression, Anxiety and Stress Scale (DASS) (Lovibond and Lovibond, 1995).

Figure 9.6: SWB versus depression

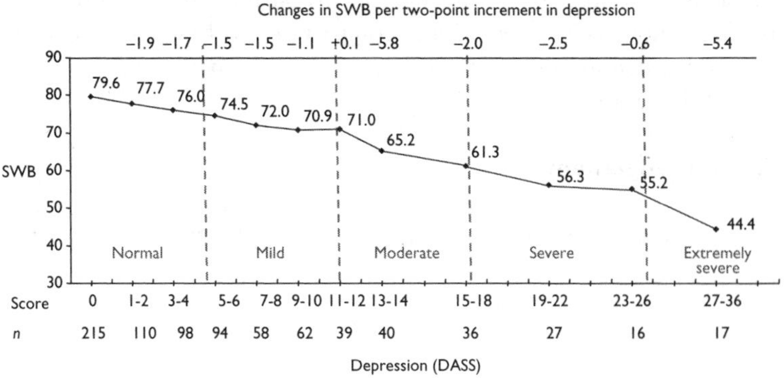

Changes in SWB per two-point increment in depression

Depression (DASS)

As can be seen, the data follow the homeostatic theoretical model previously outlined. Importantly, the threshold for homeostatic failure at 70.0 percentage points can be seen to be breached with moderate, but not mild, levels of depression according to the DASS scoring criteria. The advantages of using SWB to measure depression are two-fold. First, this form of measurement is consistent with the theoretical model of SWB homeostasis. This means that the nature and rationale for the measurement can be understood and be open to empirical investigation. In this it differs from the depression scales that are largely atheoretical groupings of depression symptoms.

The second advantage is that the questions people are asked are positive: 'How satisfied are you with …?'. This is very different from the items of depression scales that are usually targeting some negative life aspect such as sadness, loss of appetite or even suicidal thoughts. The positive nature of the SWB items means that the questions are less likely to exacerbate the respondent's low spirits. As such, such items are very suitable for general population surveys.

Conclusion

We have argued that there are very serious problems with the use of both QALYs and HRQOL as indicators of population well-being. The data generated by these measurement techniques reflect neither high-quality physical health nor SWB. For the purpose of social policy we recommend a different set of measures:

Policy makers and planners need data concerning the physical morbidity and mortality status of populations. The traditional indices are suitable for this purpose. However, the perceived life quality of populations should also be monitored through the construct of SWB. The PWI (International Wellbeing Group, 2005) is suitable for this purpose. Not only does this measure allow valid international comparisons to be made but it also allows the identification of population subgroups that have an increased risk of depression.

Acknowledgement

We thank Ann-Marie James for her assistance in the preparation of the typescript.

References

Andrews, F.M. and Withey, S.B. (1976) *Social Indicators of Well-being: American's Perceptions of Life Quality*, New York, NY: Plenum Press.

Bach, J.R. and Tilton, M.C. (1994) 'Life satisfaction and well-being measures in ventilator assisted individuals with traumatic tetraplegia', *Archives of Physical Medicine and Rehabilitation*, vol 75, pp 626-32.

Bjork, S. and Norinder, A. (1999) 'The weighting exercise for the Swedish version of the EuroQOL', *Health Economics*, vol 8, pp 117-26.

Boulding, K. (1972) 'Human betterment and quality of life', in B. Strumpel, J.N. Morgan and E. Zahn (eds) *Human Behaviour in Economic Affairs*, Amsterdam: Elsevier Scientific Publishing Company, pp 455-71.

Burg, M.M., Benedetto, M.C. and Soufer, R. (2003) 'Depressive symptoms and mortality two years after coronary artery bypass graft surgery (CABG) in men', *Psychosomatic Medicine*, vol 65, no 4, pp 508-10.

Cairney, J., Boyle, M., Offord, D.R. and Racine, Y. (2003) 'Stress, social support and depression in single and married mothers', *Social Psychiatry and Psychiatric Epidemiology*, vol 38, no 8, pp 442-9.

Campbell, A., Converse, P.E. and Rodgers, W.L. (1976) *The Quality of American Life: Perceptions, Evaluations, and Satisfactions*, New York, NY: Russell Sage Foundation.

Carr-Hill, R.A. (1989) 'Background material for the workshop on QALYs: assumptions of the QALY procedure', *Social Science and Medicine*, vol 29, pp 469-77.

Cropanzano, R., Weiss, H.M., Hale, J.M.S. and Reb, J. (2003) 'The structure of affect: reconsidering the relationship between negative and positive affectivity', *Journal of Management*, vol 29, no 6, pp 831-58.

Cummins, R.A. (1995) 'On the trail of the gold standard for life satisfaction', *Social Indicators Research*, vol 35, pp 179-200.

Cummins, R.A. (1998) 'The second approximation to an international standard of life satisfaction', *Social Indicators Research*, vol 43, pp 307-34.

Cummins, R.A. (2000a) 'Objective and subjective quality of life: an interactive model', *Social Indicators Research*, vol 52, pp 55-72.

Cummins, R.A. (2000b) 'Personal income and subjective wellbeing: a review', *Journal of Happiness Studies*, vol 1, pp 133-58.

Cummins, R.A. (2001) 'The subjective well-being of people caring for a severely disabled family member at home: a review', *Journal of Intellectual and Developmental Disability*, vol 26, pp 83-100.

Cummins, R.A. (2002) 'Proxy responding for subjective well-being: a review', *International Review of Research in Mental Retardation*, vol 25, pp 183-207.

Cummins, R.A. (2005) 'Measuring health and subjective wellbeing: vale, quality adjusted life years', in L. Manderson (ed) *Rethinking Wellbeing*, Perth: Australia Research Institute, Curtin University of Technology, pp 69-90.

Cummins, R.A. and Nistico, H. (2002) 'Maintaining life satisfaction: the role of positive cognitive bias', *Journal of Happiness Studies*, vol 3, pp 37-69.

Cummins, R.A., Gullone, E. and Lau, A.L.D. (2002) 'A model of subjective wellbeing homeostasis: the role of personality', in E. Gullone and R.A. Cummins (eds) *The Universality of Subjective Wellbeing Indicators: Social Indicators Research Series*, Dordrecht: Kluwer, pp 7-46.

Cummins, R.A., Lau, A.L.D. and Stokes, M. (2004b) 'HRQOL and subjective wellbeing: noncomplementary forms of outcome measurement', *Expert Reviews in Pharmacoeconomics Outcomes Research*, vol 4, pp 413-20.

Cummins, R.A., Eckersley, R., Okerstrom, E., Woerner, J. and Tomyn, A. (2005a) *AustralianUnity Wellbeing Index: Report 13.0 – 'The Wellbeing of Australians – Caregiving at Home'*, Melbourne: Australian Centre on Quality of Life, School of Psychology, Deakin University (www.deakin.edu.au/research/acqol/index_wellbeing/index.htm).

Cummins, R.A., Woerner, J., Tomyn, A., Knapp, T. and Gibson, A. (2005b) *AustralianUnity Wellbeing Index: Report 14.0 – 'The Wellbeing of Australians – Personal Relationships'*, Melbourne: Australian Centre on Quality of Life, School of Psychology, Deakin University (www.deakin.edu.au/research/acqol/index_wellbeing/index.htm).

Cummins, R.A., Eckersley, R., Lo, S.K., Okerstrom, E., Hunter, B. and Davern, M. (2004a) *AustralianUnity Wellbeing Index: Report 9.0 – 'The Wellbeing of Australians – Owning a Pet'*, Melbourne: Australian Centre on Quality of Life, School of Psychology, Deakin University (www.deakin.edu.au/research/acqol/index_wellbeing/index.htm).

Davern, M.T. (2004) 'Subjective wellbeing as an affective construct', School of Psychology, Deakin University, Melbourne (www.deakin.edu.au/research/acqol/theses/index.htm).

Davern, M.T. and Cummins, R.A. (in press) 'Subjective wellbeing as an affective construct', *Journal of Happiness Studies*.

Davidson, K.W., Rieckmann, N. and Lesperance, F. (2004) 'Psychological theories of depression: potential application for the prevention of acute coronary syndrome recurrence', *Psychosomatic Medicine*, vol 66, no 2, pp 165-73.

Deverill, M., Brazier, J., Green, C. and Booth, A. (1998) 'The use of QALY and non-QALY measures of health related quality of life. Assessing the state of the art', *Pharmacoeconomics*, vol 13, pp 411-20.

Dolan, P. and Sutton, M. (1997) 'Mapping visual analogue scale health state valuations onto standard gamble and time trade-off values', *Social Science and Medicine*, vol 44, pp 1519-30.

Engle, G.L. and Bergsma, J. (1988) 'Quality of life', *Health Policy*, vol 10, pp 215-16.

Faden, R. and Leplege, A. (1992) 'Assessing quality of life: moral implications for clinical practice', *Medical Care*, vol 30, Suppl 5, pp 166-75.

Feeny, D.H. and Torrance, G.W. (1989) 'Incorporating utility-based quality-of-life assessment measures in clinical trials. Two examples', *Medical Care*, vol 27, pp S190-S204.

Feeny, D.H., Torrance, G.W. and Furlong, W.J. (1996) 'Health Utilities Index', in B. Spiker (ed) *Quality of Life and Pharmacoeconomics in Clinical Trials* (2nd edn), Philadelphia, PA: Lippincott-Raven Publishers.

Galanter, E. (1962) 'The direct measurement of utility and subjective probability', *American Journal of Psychology*, vol 75, pp 208-20.

Gerard, K., Hall, J. and Cameron, S. (1991) 'Quality of life in the economic evaluation of the screening for breast cancer in Australia', in C.S. Smith (ed) *Economics and Health*, Melbourne: Monash University, pp 308-27.

Gold, M.R., Siegal, J.E., Russell, L.B. and Weinstein, M.C. (1996) *Cost-effectiveness in Health and Medicine*, New York, NY: Oxford University Press.

Grabowski, H.G. and Hansen, R.W. (1990) 'Economic scales and tests', in B. Spilker (ed) *Quality of Life Assessments in Clinical Trials*, New York, NY: Raven Press.

Gurin, G., Veroff, J. and Feld, S. (1960) *Americans View Their Mental Health: A Nationwide Interview Survey*, vol 4, Joint Commission on Mental Illness and Health, Monograph Series, New York, NY: Basic Books.

Hanestad, B.R. and Albrektsen, G. (1992) 'The stability of quality of life experience in people with Type 1 diabetes over a period of a year', *Journal of Advanced Nursing*, vol 17, pp 777-84.

Headey, B. and Wearing, A. (1989) 'Personality, life events, and subjective well-being: toward a dynamic equilibrium model', *Journal of Personality and Social Psychology*, vol 57, pp 731-9.

Henderson, S. (1977) 'The social network, support and neurosis. The function of attachment in adult life', *British Journal of Psychiatry*, vol 131, pp 185-91.

Hollandsworth, J.G., Jr (1988) 'Evaluating the impact of medical treatment on the quality of life: a 5-year update', *Social Science and Medicine*, vol 26, pp 425-34.

Hornberger, J.C., Redelmeier, D.A. and Petersen, J. (1992) 'Variability among methods to assess patients' well-being and consequent effect on a cost-effectiveness analysis', *Journal of Clinical Epidemiology*, vol 45, pp 505-12.

Hyder, A.A., Rotlant, G. and Morrow, R.H. (1998) 'Measuring the burden of disease: healthy life-years', *American Journal of Public Health*, vol 88, pp 196-202.

International Wellbeing Group (2005) *Personal Well-Being Index* (www.deakin.edu.au/research/acqol/inter_wellbeing/index.htm).

Johannesson, M. (1994) 'QALYs, HYEs and individual preferences: a graphical illustration', *Social Science and Medicine*, vol 39, pp 1623-32.

Kaplan, R.M. (1985) 'Quality of life measurement', in P. Karoly (ed) *Measurement Strategies in Health Psychology*, New York, NY: John Wiley & Sons, pp 115-46.

Kaplan, R.M. (1994) 'Using quality of life information to set priorities in health policy', *Social Indicators Research*, vol 33, pp 121-63.

Kaplan, R.M., Feeny, D. and Revicki, D.A. (1993) 'Methods for assessing relative importance in preference based outcomes measures', *Quality of Life Research*, vol 2, pp 467-75.

Knox, P.L. (1975) *Social Well-being: A Spatial Perspective*, London: Oxford University Press.

Koch, T. (2000) 'Life quality vs the "quality of life": assumptions underlying prospective quality of life instruments in health care planning', *Social Science and Medicine*, vol 51, pp 419-29.

Kornhauser, A. (1962) 'Toward an assessment of the mental health of factory workers: a Detroit study', *Human Organization*, vol 21, pp 43-6.

Kupersmith, J., Holmes-Rovner, M., Hogan, A., Rovner, D. and Gardiner, J. (1995) 'Cost-effectiveness analysis in heart disease, part III: ischemia, congestive heart failure, and arrhythmias', *Progress in Cardiovascular Diseases*, vol 37, pp 307-46.

Land, K.C. (2000) 'Social trends in Australia: a 1999 Report', *Sinet* [Social Indicators Network News], August, no 63, pp 2-4.

Lovibond, S.H. and Lovibond, P.F. (1995) *Manual for the Depression Anxiety Stress Scales*, Sydney: Psychology Foundation.

McHorney, C.A., Ware, J.E. and Raczek, A.E. (1993) 'The MOS 36-item short-form health survey (SF-36): II. Psychometric and clinical tests of validity in measuring physical and mental health constructs', *Medical Care*, vol 31, pp 247-63.

McNair, R., Kavanagh, A., Agius, P. and Tong, B. (2005) 'The mental health status of young adult and mid-life non-heterosexual Australian women', *Australian and New Zealand Journal of Public Health*, vol 29, no 3, pp 265-71.

McNeil, H. and Segal, L. (1999) *Quality of Life and Obesity*, Research report 17, Melbourne: Centre for Health Program Evaluation, Monash University.

Mehrez, A. and Gafni, A. (1989) 'Quality adjusted life years, utility theory, and healthy years equivalents', *Medical Decision Making*, vol 9, pp 142-9.

Morris, D.M. (1979) *Measuring the Condition of the World's Poor: The Physical Quality of Life Index*, New York, NY: Pergamon.

Murphy, J.M., Monson, R.R., Olivier, D.C., Sobol, A.M. and Leighton, A.H. (1987) 'Affective disorders and mortality: a general population study', *Archives of General Psychiatry*, vol 44, no 473-80.

Murray, C.J. (1994) 'Quantifying the burden of disease: the technical basis for disability adjusted life years', *Bulletin of the World Health Organization*, vol 72, pp 429-45.

Neumayer, E. (2001) 'The human development index and sustainability: a constructive proposal', *Ecological Economics*, vol 39, no 1, pp 101-14.

Nord, E. (2001) 'Measuring population health: an organisation for economic cooperation and development survey of multi-attribute utility instruments', in J.L. Pinto, G. Lopezcasasnovas and V. Ortun (eds) *Economic Evaluation: From Theory to Practice*, Barcelona: Springer-Verlag, pp 72-84.

OECD (Organisation for Economic Co-operation and Development) (2002) 'OECD health data 2002' (www.oced.org/document/22/0,2340.en_2649_34631_1935190_1_1_1_1,00.html, accessed 16 March 2006).

Patrick, D.L. and Erickson, P. (eds) (1993) *Health Status and Health Policy: Quality of Life in Health Care Evaluation and Resource Allocation*, New York, NY: Oxford University Press.

Redefining Progress (1995) 'What's wrong with the GDP as a measure of progress? The Genuine Progress Indicator: summary of data and methodology (www.rprogress.org/projects/gpi/whatswrong.html).

Revicki, D.A. and Kaplan, R.M. (1993) 'Relationship between psychometric and utility-based approaches to the measurement of health-related quality of life', *Quality of Life Research*, vol 2, pp 477-87.

Richardson, J. (1991) 'What should we measure in health program evaluation?', in C.S. Smith (ed) *Economics and Health: 1990*, Melbourne: Monash University, pp 80-104.

Roberts, R.E., Roberts, C.R. and Chen, I.G. (2000) 'Fatalism and risk of adolescent depression', *Psychiatry*, vol 63, no 3, pp 239-52.

Rose, G. (1992) *The Strategy of Preventative Medicine*, Oxford: Oxford University Press.

Russell, J.A. (2003) 'Core affect and the psychological construction of emotion', *Psychological Review*, vol 110, no 1, pp 145-72.

Sarason, I.G., Sarason, B.R. and Pierce, G.R. (1990) 'Social support: the search for theory', *Journal of Social and Clinical Psychology*, vol 9, pp 137-47.

Sherbourne, C.D., Unutzer, J., Schoenbaum, M., Duan, N., Lenert, L.A., Sturm, R. and Wells, K.B. (2001) 'Can utility-weighted health-related quality-of-life estimates capture health effects of quality improvement for depression?', *Medical Care*, vol 39, pp 1246-59.

Subramanian, S., Belli, P. and Kawachi, I. (2002) 'The macroeconomic determinants of health', *Annual Review of Public Health*, vol 23, pp 287-302.

Suh, E. and Diener, E. (1996) 'Events and subjective well-being: only recent events matter', *Journal of Personality and Social Psychology*, vol 70, pp 1091-102.

Torrance, G.W. and Feeny, D. (1989) 'Utilities and quality-adjusted life years', *International Journal of Technology Assessment in Health Care*, vol 5, pp 559-75.

US DHEW (United States Department of Health, Education and Welfare (1969) *Toward a Social Report*, Washington, DC: Government Printing Office.

Voogt, E., van der Heide, A., van Leeuwen, A.F., Visser, A.P., Cleiren, M.P.H.D., Passchier, J. and van der Maas, P.J. (2005) 'Positive and negative affect after diagnosis of advanced cancer', *Psycho-Oncology*, vol 14, no 4, pp 262-73.

WHO (World Health Organization) (1948) *Constitution of the World Health Organization basic documents*, Geneva, Switzerland: WHO.

WHO (2001) *The World Health Report. Mental Health: New Understanding, 30*, Geneva: New Hope.

Williams, A. (1988) 'Economics and the rational use of medical technology', in F.F.H. Rutter and S.J. Reiser (eds) *The Economics of Medical Technology*, Berlin: Springer, pp 75-95.

Williams, A. (1996) 'QALYS and ethics: a health economist's perspective', *Social Science Medicine*, vol 43, no 12, pp 1795-804.

Wilson, J. (1972) 'The industrial process and the quality of life', in G.J. Stober and D. Schumacher *Technology assessment and quality of life*, Proceedings of the 4th General Conference of SAINT, Salzburg: Elsevier Scientific Publishing Company. pp 131-46.

Young, R.C. and MacCannell, D. (1977) 'Predicting the quality of life in the United States', *Social Indicators Research*, vol 6, pp 23-40.

TEN

Community well-being strategy and the legacies of new institutionalism and New Public Management in third way New Zealand

David Craig

Well-being, and the role of community, civil society and local government in achieving it, has a considerable profile in contemporary public policy (Nussbaum and Sen, 1993; The Treasury, 2001; DEFRA, 2005; Manderson, 2005). Internationally, this emergence has been supported by developments in the new public health, community health and primary healthcare, especially focused on addressing health inequalities (often conceived in terms of inequality between locations) (Marmot and Wilkinson, 1999, 2001; Baum, 2002; Kawachi and Berkman, 2003; Anand et al, 2004). At the same time, in countries including New Zealand and the UK, attention to the well-being of citizens has emerged as a part of a broader policy agenda focused on social investment and human capability, and supporting the supply side of labour markets (The Treasury, 2001; Bevir, 2005). In such contexts, addressing well-being is presented politically as a turn away from previous conservative neoliberal reforms, and towards a more inclusive liberal or social democratic social policy, concerned with building the capability of individuals, and reconstructing community relations alongside retained market reforms (Porter and Craig, 2004; Larner and Craig, 2005). These changes are also commonly presented as a shift from a 'welfare' orientation (focused on income security and equity) to a 'well-being' orientation, focused on individual opportunity and enablement (Ministry of Social Development, 2001; Kendall and Harker, 2002).

In both rich and more particularly poor country settings, such concerns have commonly been joined to other supply-side concerns over strengthening institutions (especially market-related institutions), building trust and social capital, providing a more efficient and effective allocation and delivery of basic services, and decentralising governance (Bevir, 2005; Clark and Gough, 2005; Craig and Porter, 2006). This institutional focus has predominantly centred on the 'hard' institutional aspects emphasised by the New Institutional Economics (NIE) and New Public Management (NPM) (public finance reform, strengthening juridical and budget frameworks, market contractualism, decentralisation and disaggregation) (North, 1990; Boston et al, 1991; Coase, 1998). More recently, however, the institutional focus has dilated to include the potential of 'soft' institutions such as partnerships, civil society and other networks for enhancing both governance and well-being (Powell et al, 2002; Stoker, 2002; Bevir, 2005; Tenbensel, 2005). In these, neocommunitarian emphasis on communities, inclusion, participation, partnerships and social capital (Baum, 2002; Fyfe, 2005) come together in local community health plans, well-being partnerships and community well-being strategies found on local government websites throughout the Anglo world (LGA, 1998).

In sum, this paradigm presents the promise of enhanced local well-being through partnership and joined-up strategy, with multiple actors drawn from government, civil society and the market, working in hybrid relations involving both competition and collaboration, and experimental agglomerations of hierarchical, network and market governance modes[1]. These approaches have not surprisingly generated a degree of scepticism, both from critics questioning their theoretical premises and coordinative efficacy (Gregory, 2003; Davies, 2005; Humpage, 2005; Craig and Porter, 2006), and from social epidemiologists who offer evidence that health inequalities are determined by inequalities in access to material resources (Pearce and Davey-Smith, 2003). On the other hand, public health activists interested in psychosocial determinants of health and well-being, and the role of community in promoting these, have warmly embraced them (Baum, 2002; Hunter and Killoran, 2004).

New Zealand is exemplary in many of these areas for the fact that since 1985 much of this has passed into policy, achieving quite radical reforms to the ways health and well-being, communities and local territories are governed. NIE and NPM reforms were achieved in the early 1990s, with, as this chapter will describe, significant positive (improved fiscal accountability) and negative (fragmentation, coordinative/strategic weakness) impacts. Subsequently, the late 1990s and early 2000s saw the emergence of decentralised health governance, and a wider social governance ethos in which 'all the king's horses and all the king's men' sought to put the Humpty Dumpty of fragmented governance back together again (Gregory, 2003), and where goals like well-being, inclusion and enhanced social capability were prominent in reform rhetoric and programming (The Treasury, 2001). Among key mandates for decentralised health governance was a series of coordinative activities involving community, local government, and district health boards, designed to address New Zealand's substantial health inequalities (Howden-Chapman and Tobias, 2000)[2].

Well-being per se was especially prominent in reforms to New Zealand's 2002 Local Government Act, with its core reference to the 'four well-beings' (social, economic, environmental, cultural), and in wider promotion of local partnerships for what are called community outcomes. The Local Government Act's wide-ranging but unfunded well-being mandate has been taken up with special enthusiasm in Waitakere City, a part of greater Auckland, where the 'Waitakere Way' of community–council–government partnership has become a model for building inclusion and tackling social well-being issues 'at the flax roots'[3] (Waitakere City, 2005). As this chapter will describe, Waitakere is arguably New Zealand's leading example of local government and community activism around well-being. But while, for example, Waitakere's Well-being Collaboration initiative has leveraged $1.1 million in new project funding, it, like other community initiatives around well-being, has also encountered significant obstacles, many arising as a direct legacy of previous governance reforms.

This chapter sets out to tell the story of Waitakere's community well-being strategies, but as part of a wider story of New Zealand's ongoing reforms and changing policy context. It is based on research conducted over four years (2001-05) by the Local Partnerships and Governance research project, involving the University of Auckland and Waitakere City Council. In this research, the author participated in parts of the Waitakere Community Well-being process, particularly in the governance group of its Well-being Collaboration Strategy. Operational and process aspects of the collaboration are considered elsewhere (Craig, 2003a; Craig and Courtney, 2004). What are offered here are key findings and summative reflection based on research conclusions, as presented to and discussed by government and community groups at a series of workshops and feedback events.

At the same time, this chapter seeks to engage an international and comparative audience by putting Waitakere's Well-being Collaboration in wider perspective. Here, New Zealand offers a unique opportunity to consider what can already be seen as the legacies of the kinds of new institutional governance, public choice and decentralisation reforms now being introduced elsewhere. The first part, then, charts New Zealand's shift from a Keynesian liberal welfare regime to NIE and NPM governance, and the reform flaws that became evident. The second part narrows the focus to Waitakere City, showing how Waitakere's innovations in well-being grew in the face of NIE disaggregation, to become a key referent for the post-1999 Labour government's social development approach, discussed in the third and final part. Here, the chapter also shows how constrained this locally focused approach has been in the face of NIE legacies, including rising complexity, voluntaristic institutional participation, strategic and coordinative weakness and high transaction costs. It adds perspectives from international experience of fiscal decentralisation to explain how the reforms have failed to generate shared accountabilities around clear, funded local mandates.

New Zealand's institutional reform revolution

This section describes New Zealand's welfare regime, and the changes wrought during the 1990s reform period. New Zealand's Keynesian welfare state was elaborated after the 1930s depression, and retained bipartisan political support into the 1980s. Yet despite 'cradle to grave' welfare, New Zealand remains a 'liberal welfare-capitalist regime' (Esping-Andersen, 1990). Thus social protection transfers ('benefits') are residual and sharply targeted, and welfare primarily dependent on workforce inclusion (Castles, 1994). By the 1950s, and on into the late 1980s, social governance and services were governed through a deconcentrated command economy, with some regional governance around district offices of social welfare, and regional boards of education and health (Gauld, 2001).

Neoliberal reform came under the 1984-90 Labour government, which entered office in the teeth of fiscal crisis, and gave political rein and rapid legislative effect to radical reform (Russell, 1996, p 109f). Under close guidance of central agencies, especially The Treasury and the State Services Commission, social sector management was subjected to NIE/NPM reforms shaped direct from theoretical principle (Russell, 1996). In New Zealand's Treasury, highly influential institutional economist Peter Gorringe (Grimes et al, 2001) was a personal acquaintance of international NIE gurus Ronald Coase and Douglass North. Gorringe, in his papers[4], considered at length the possibility of the executive being captured by a small cartel of decision makers. Ironically, especially in his contribution to The Treasury's seminal (1987) *Government Management* briefing, he and a small network of powerful central actors largely achieved precisely that.

Narratives of crisis and waste in the public service were used to sharpen vertical and managerial accountabilities according to NPM 'output-objective' principles, and to instigate NIE service delivery markets and disaggregation (Boston et al, 1996). Here, a series of institutional 'splits' was central. In the outcome-output split, ministers would set (and be nominally accountable for) outcomes, and various agencies would deliver the contributing outputs. Outputs, on the other hand, could be and were narrowly conceived, costed, and allocated within sharp regimes of downwards-managerial accountability (Boston et al, 1996). In theory, agents without territorial affinities to particular communities could deliver them. In the policy operations spilt, policy in, for example, social welfare, became a separate function, managed centrally by the Ministry of Social Policy, but its provision was opened to the competing perspectives of consultants. Separate from policy, operations (workforce inclusion, income support) were implemented by other agencies, government and/or private. Funder–provider splits separated fundholding from delivery, enabling multiple competing providers to deliver services within territories or sectors. The net effect was a radical disaggregation: area health boards were abolished, and individual hospitals set up as Crown Health Enterprises, imagined as competing within wider regions to provide services for profit (Gauld, 2001); regional education boards were abolished, and individual schools were bulk funded for recurrent costs, and set to compete for pupils (Waslander and Thrupp, 1995).

Under the NPM rubric of 'let managers manage', managers were given new flexibility in how and by whom outputs were produced (Schick, 1996; Scott, 2001). Management was moved closer to the delivery point, where, in theory, competition would incentivise a knowledge market involving information about price, what competing providers were doing, and local knowledge of client needs (Girishankar and de Silva, 1998). It was envisaged that bureaucratic capture and heavy transaction costs of inefficient centralised decision making would decline, and allocative efficiency improve. The direct nexus between the *citizen* and the state through elected regional health boards, would be replaced by privatised service deliverers in which *clients'* rights would become a key node for accountability (Gauld, 2001).

Uunraveling and reaction

The successes of these reforms have been widely discussed (Schick, 1996; Scott, 2001): in general, they centre on improved fiscal and financial accountability, and increasing managerial discretion. Criticisms have also been widely canvassed, especially in recent reconsiderations directed towards new reform. Under the reforms, the state was conceived as an internally de-territorialised domain (Craig and Porter, 2006), wherein markets would transparently allocate services to whichever providers offered best rates and minimum compliance. In practice, however, effective markets failed to emerge, while fragmentation, dominance of departmental 'silos', and managerial risk aversion were reinforced. Effective and strategic governance of outcomes was impeded, as within the singular vertical NPM output accountabilities dictated by agency theory, the prospect of promoting horizontally shared accountabilities was precluded (Kelsey, 1993; Wellington Health Action Group, 1993; Martin, 1995; Boston et al, 1991, 1996, 1999; State Services Commission, 1998, 2001; Petrie and Webber, 2001; Schick, 2001).

Such weaknesses were especially apparent in health and education. In health, a ministerial committee embarked on a costly, ultimately abandoned exercise to define and cost a set of 'core services' that might be contracted (Gauld, 2001). Markets for secondary and tertiary healthcare and education were not created (Petrie and Webber, 2001), and pro-market arrangements generated resistance. Surgery patients from the north of Auckland were by no means keen on travelling to a small town in the middle of the country for elective surgery, although their operation had been allocated there on a regional cost basis. Even among health services non-governmental organisations (NGOs), competition dissipated as the limits (and costs) of the quasi-market were realised, and relational aspects entered contractualism (Ashton et al, 2005). With operational focus limited to outputs, the overall population characteristics determining health outcomes were removed from local or regional policy reach. In education, schools could compete for students. But once an elite or, very quickly, a mid-range school had filled its roll, it would unilaterally re-territorialise its catchment zone and cherry-pick other elite students. The possibility of students voting with their feet and motivating educational improvement dissipated, especially among poorer schools (Waslander and Thrupp, 1995). The dominance of central hospitals and elite schools was reinforced, while powerful national NGOs secured contracts across multiple jurisdictions, but with few responsibilities to local social situations.

As recounted in interviews with Waitakere community sector agencies, the regime actively rewarded contractors for simply 'sticking to their knitting', delivering services to the letter of 'the beancounter's' contracted outputs, regardless of the complexity of client needs. Clients received fragmented services from multiple agencies, none of which was accountable for the client's overall well-being. A client with drug and alcohol dependency, and perhaps mental health issues, would have counselling sessions delivered by one agency, living arrangements overseen by another, and mental health assessments made by a third. Competitive contractualism damaged collegial trust and cooperation between agencies, greatly reducing the extent to which front-line workers and agencies communicated. Morale and job satisfaction declined rapidly, as social workers employed by competing agencies found themselves unable to respond to cross-cutting family issues, and bogged down in compliance reporting (see also Petrie and Webber, 2001, pp 20-5; State Services Commission, 2001, p 54f). Funding negotiations between government and private or NGO contractors became nitpicking exercises, focused on cost-cutting and compliance. As front-line staff resources were cut and cut again, strain on managers and front-line caseworkers' time and resources mounted, reducing their ability to transact costly coordination.

Quickly, then, a range of fragmentation, inequity and coordination issues became apparent. Ultimately, when in several sectors local coordination issues approached crisis, front-line staff, strategic brokers, contract managers and case managers were assigned coordination duties. But even here, the coordinating focus was rarely territorial, attending to the overall social profile of citizens within their territorial jurisdiction. Rather, the focus of coordination remained on the managerial and contractual risk to outputs. Initially, such difficulties were exacerbated by unprecedented rises in unemployment and inequality at both national and inter-local levels, again raising stresses on Waitakere's providers (Easton, 1997, ch 11; Howden-Chapman and Tobias, 2000; Ministry of Social Development, 2005).

A consumer-led political backlash occurred first in the health sector: the government had to back off 'user pays' in hospitals, framing hospitals as commercial enterprises, and the shuffling of surgical patients around regional markets (Gauld, 2001). Waitakere providers recall that while consumers (and citizens) had plenty to say about this new market for social services, their 'voice' was less able to cause service improvements from either contacted providers or government funding or regulating agencies. From health clients' viewpoint, raising accountability for outputs remained difficult, with responsibility diffused through multiple levels and agents responsible for policy, standard setting, contracting, contract monitoring, compliance audits and basic enforcement. In the end, it was raw political resistance, as measured at the ballot box, opinion polls and the media that enabled (citizen, not client) voice.

There remain considerable practical and theoretical ironies around New Zealand's NIE reforms. While, for example, Gorringe made frequent reference to the scarcity and perverse, gamed use of knowledge in, for example, the prisoner's dilemma (Gorringe, 1991), he failed to anticipate how The Treasury's reforms would destroy cooperation and the shared knowledge it generated; how the policy operations split would mean central policy making was starved of substantive local knowledge; how knowledge relations between services would be reduced to mere quantifications, shorn of qualitative sense and crucial context; how substantive local information gathering (related, say, to social outcomes like crime) was systemically disincentivised, in that it risked producing evidence of managerial failure; and how local competitors would obscure information from each other. In short, within government and social services, assumptions that linked a decentralised competitive environment to better information that in turn would result in better services proved naive; in crucial ways, markets and useful shared information proved inimical.

In public health, however, international developments in social epidemiology were beginning to be applied. Social epidemiology's 'social determinants' approaches demonstrated that health outcomes were determined by underlying 'social determinants' including (chiefly) income, and other resources (Marmot and Wilkinson, 1999). In New Zealand, researchers linked income, housing transport and other measures from the Census into a 1–10 'deprivation index' score where household scores were combined by small geographical areas ('mesh blocks') of some 80 persons, and which (as we will see in Waitakere) could be mapped against both local neighbourhoods and territorial jurisdictions such as Waitakere Council. Here, health outcomes (mortality, morbidity, violence, exposure to risk factors) were shown to be powerfully related to deprivation in all age groups and for most diseases, across a social gradient from rich to poor. Figure 10.1 is from *Social Inequalities in Health 1999: New Zealand* (Howden-Chapman and Tobias, 2000). When these mesh blocks are colour-coded and mapped, the territorial ensconcement of poverty-related health outcomes becomes apparent. While relative deprivation is not absolute deprivation, its implications for territorial population health outcomes are substantial, this not least because, as we will see in Waitakere, the ability of post-NIE social governance to respond to peripheralising shifts in distribution of poorer deciles across territories remains low.

Reform and reaction on the ground: towards community well-being in Waitakere City

Among the social sector in Waitakere, the 1990s are widely recalled as the 'nasty nineties' – a period when progress towards collaborative local focus on social issues took several steps backwards, and trust between agencies

Figure 10.1: All-cause mortality, males 45-64 years, by deprivation, area of residence and age group, New Zealand (1996-97)

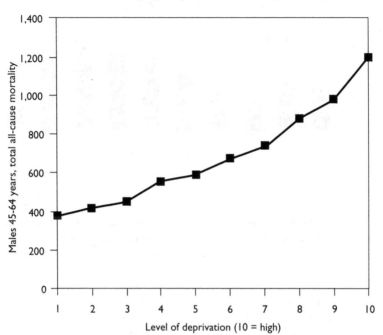

Source: Howden-Chapman and Tobias (2000, p 25)

was undermined. This section describes Waitakere's particular situation, its experience of and reaction to the reforms, and early moves to create coordination around well-being issues.

Waitakere City, with a population of 186,000, comprises Auckland's western quarter, a sprawling suburbia, set against regenerating rainforest hills. Waitakere's growing population has included a mix of working-class, indigenous and migrant people, with the middle classes occupying rainforest ranges and waterfront subdivisions. Auckland (population 1.25 million), consistently ranked among the world's most liveable cities, is nonetheless the New Zealand city where social disparities are most apparent. Waitakere, however, in terms of New Zealand's Deprivation Index (Crampton et al, 2004), as seen in Figure 10.2, until recently had relatively small populations in the richest (1) and most deprived (9-10) deciles, its population mesh blocks spread fairly evenly across the middle to lower deciles, peaking around deprivation decile 7 in the 1996 Census, but slipping to peak at decile 8 by 2000.

Figure 10.2: Deprivation in Waitakere (1996-2001)

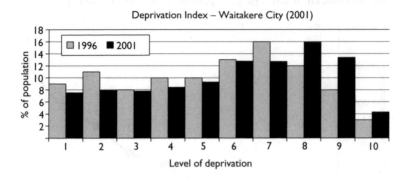

Deprivation Index – Waitakere City (2001)

Source: NZ Census data (1996, 2001)

The area's explosive growth during the 1960s and 1970s as greenfield suburbia saw an absence of services motivating a range of community innovators and service pioneers. In their words:

> The growth of community organizations in the West was quite organic.... In terms of working together it was key people that were the critical factor and made things happen, rather than dollars. We didn't really need much funding to get things happening initially. (Craig, 2003b)

Following its formation in a late 1980s round of council amalgamations, Waitakere City Council adopted a range of headline approaches to social and environmental activism, positioning Waitakere as an eco-city. Local government amalgamation in the 1980s left Waitakere City Council both policy rich and relatively asset and income poor. On the one hand, it has a thin base of own-sourced revenue (largely residential land tax income), and little industrial development. On the other, an activist, predominantly left-leaning council has attracted very able strategic policy leaders and activists, who would drive the eco-city and its well-being ambit. One consequence of the disjuncture between high policy ambition and tight budgets was the incremental accrual of programmes (injury, safety, children, the environment) by pilot project economy entrepreneurship. Here, as recounted by council and social sector staff, Waitakere City has earned a reputation as 'a safe pair of hands' for demonstration projects, under the motto 'if it can be done, it can be done in Waitakere'.

The eco-city vision hybridised local resource management regulatory arrangements together with commitments to sustainable, triple bottom line reporting. It grew to include pioneering commitments to the 1840 Treaty of Waitangi with the Indigenous Māori people, and effectively picked up the 1974 Local Government Act's very general scope to address citizen well-being. This statutory provision underpinned innovative activities in Waitakere from environmental activism to community strategy facilitation and advocacy, and even 'strategic real estate acquisition'. When the Local Government Act was redrawn in 2002, Waitakere's experience was influential in expanding this well-being mandate; although, as we will see, its functional content remained mired in conflicting jurisdictional overlaps, and lack of assignment of matching revenue.

Waitakere became known for other collaborative initiatives. In the 1980s, a remarkable inter-agency youth justice programme began in Waitakere, which was eventually scaled up into the 1989 Children Young People and their Families (CYPF) Act. Drafted just prior to the outcomes–output split, this Act conceived overall objectives in this area in broad outcome terms[5], enabling local agencies to coordinate around these. Initially exemplary for its collaborative approach, it soon became exemplary of how NPM/NIE could undermine intentions. The NPM outputs emphasis overlaid (and only rewarded) a narrow specification of process outputs (for example, mere convening and punctual attendance of meetings funded for a limited number and time), and failed to recognise the range of inter-agency commitments and underpinning coordinative activities (managing relationships, coordinating load sharing, going the extra mile) necessary to the outcomes envisaged by the CYPF Act. By 2000, both the youth justice system and its agency were in crisis, with a major critical review sheeting responsibility emphatically back to ineffective coordination, over-specification (but poor conception) of outputs, and chronic under-funding (Brown, 2000; Smith, 2002).

Outputs such as coordination, reaching enforceable agreements, and resolving jurisdictional conflicts ultimately became fundable as output classes in their own right. But underlying problems of diffused accountability, jurisdictional overlaps, discordant policy, planning, budget and expenditure management by vertically disaggregated agencies were pushed down to front-line service providers, as local problems requiring local solutions. Again, Waitakere innovators stepped into the breach, piloting an inter-agency case management modality later called Strengthening Families (Roelvink and Craig, 2005). This and similar goodwill-heavy solutions were quickly upscaled by a central government grateful for having local coordination to fill the gaps. But under-resourcing and narrow shared accountabilities undermined this too, with the programme plagued by unallocated cases, and lack of real compulsion for core agencies (police, justice, social development) to accountably contribute[6]. By 2004, poor outcomes here drove management of family and children's crises into media attention and critical review.

In Waitakere, the competitive orientation was widely recognised as destructive, and over time, locals managed to build non-competitive information swapping, networking, and informal collaborative arrangements. Perhaps the best success came in developing a strategic alliance initiative in community safety, called Safe Waitakere, which combined injury prevention, crime prevention, road safety and alcohol initiatives in a programme based on partnership, strategic planning and shared, devolved funding. As community safety policy (and now child safety and domestic violence) has started devolving funding to locally collaborating groups, the Waitakere model has been exported and upscaled, with Waitakere again attracting pilot funding.

Reforms 1999-2006: third way approaches to coordination impact on Waitakere's community well-being approach

This section describes key governance reforms of the fifth Labour government (1999-), with its third way markets-*and*-communities platform. Here, while a series of reforms variously drew on and enabled Waitakere's community well-being approach, the scope of these reforms, and the durable path dependencies of the previous NIE reforms, meant that the scope of community-oriented well-being strategies like Waitakere's remained strongly constrained.

The new government declared neoliberalism over (Larner and Craig, 2005), and set about implementing a social policy agenda based on active labour market policy, reinvestment in core services and re-engaging community (Porter and Craig, 2004). Much was made of the inequalities and fragmentation it inherited, and of the government's desire to fix these, especially through community partnerships. Underpinning these commitments were governance reforms, including the Key Government Goals to Guide Public Sector Policy and Performance; the Social Development orientation; the Review of the Centre process, which addressed overall state sector integration; a shift in the accountability regime from outputs to outcomes; a re-territorialisation of the health sector; and a review of the Local Government Act.

The core 1999 policy statement, Key Government Goals to Guide Public Sector Policy and Performance, required all departments to reconfigure programmes around cross-cutting goals. Most ambitious (and first dropped) was Goal Five, which sought to gain better outcomes for poor (particularly Māori and Pacific peoples) communities, 'through education, better health, housing and employment, and better coordination of policy across sectors, so that we may reduce the gaps that currently divide our society and offer a good future for all' (State Services Commission, 2001). Elsewhere, while some disaggregations including policy operations splits were reversed (merging, for example, the Ministry of Social Policy, and Work and Income New Zealand, to create the Ministry of Social Development), existing neoliberal public finance and accountability legislation was retained. However, new reforms blurred NIE separations with the language of partnership, inclusion and joined-up governance. Thus they embraced both the hard institutionalism of NIE, and the soft institutionalism of networks and partnership (Bevir, 2005). All these would operate together, within what were now the quasi-territories and relativised scales (Jessop, 2002) of 'community' and 'locality', and the Auckland 'region'.

Waitakere's leadership in such areas was underscored as the Prime Minister and the Chief Executive Officer of the newly merged Ministry of Social Development launched the government's *Social Development Strategy* in the city. The Social Development approach focused on getting people into work, through active labour market policies. However, it also highlighted that partnerships 'with the voluntary sector, with local government, and with business' would help communities 'find local solutions to local issues' (Ministry of Social Development, 2001, p 18). As a subsequent policy statement noted,

> This commitment to partnership also means that government agencies will need to be better co-ordinated in their dealings with others.... The government expects that others will recognize the partnership approach as our normal way of doing business. (DPMC, 2003)

With Waitakere's dextrous deployment of the 1974 well-being mandate explicitly in mind, the 2002 Local Government Act encouraged councils to do whatever might support citizens' well-being, introducing a statutory obligation to consider all activities against a 'four well-beings' rubric: social, cultural, environmental and economic. The Local Government Act also demanded a Long-term Council Community Plan from all councils, to be developed in extensive consultation with community and government agencies. But, in the absence of substantive devolved funding for these plans or mandatory government agency participation in well-being-related programmes, councils could only rely on own-source revenues and voluntaristic participation by government. Unable to make mandatory claims on government agencies' local budgets or demand their mandatory participation in shared planning processes, councils were left to go 'wish list in hand' to agencies operating in and around their territories. Relations were complicated by non-aligned territorial boundaries and scales of operations between different government agencies, some of which programmed in Auckland at regional level. Across the country, councils were left with long lists of unfunded priorities. These, as fiscal decentralisation literatures make clear, are the predictable outcomes of decentralisation processes that vaguely define mandates, and fail to align funding, function and mandate (Mullins, 2004; Craig and Porter, 2006).

More substantive in decentralisation terms was the establishment of district health boards (DHB) with devolved funding regimes, and population health mandates. Here, potentially, begins greater territorial accountability, via elected boards, and with social determinants of health issues surely clamouring in these territorially-based well-being regimes. Yet again, silo-ed vertical accountabilities and funding deficit regimens have characterised these hospital-dominated entities (Ashton, 2005). Substantive coordinated address to population health issues – where important gains seem possible – still seems a long way off. Even if the DHB devolution has for the time being stabilised some slippery scale assignments in health (Gauld, 2001; Craig, 2003a), it has not replaced the basic parameters of health governance, which remain focused on vertical cost restriction, effective contracting and service standards (Ashton, 2005). It has not resolved fraught subsidiarity issues around identifying levels of scale to address inter-agency well-being and poverty issues (housing, transport, ghettoising of low-income families and so on), nor has it devolved the means, mandates, discretion and shared responsibilities to achieve them. New primary health organisation arrangements for joined-up front-line services will add something to population-oriented well-being, while adding new layers of non-contiguous, autonomous organisation yet to be aligned.

More generally, substantive collaborative approaches remain hindered by the risk management legacy of NIE/NPM governance reforms (Petrie and Webber, 2001). Here, it seems increasingly likely that undoing fragmentation might require not just incrementalism, but radical re-engineering (Schick, 2001). Here, the Review of the Centre process recommended 'alignment improving innovations', including,

- establishing *networks of related agencies to better integrate policy, delivery, and capability* building;

- an *accountability and reporting system* that puts more emphasis on *outcomes* and high-level priorities, as well as output specification;
- changes to vote structures to facilitate a *greater outcome focus and better prioritisation across agencies*; and
- gradual *structural consolidation targeting*: small agencies, Crown entities required to give effect to government policy, policy/operations splits and sectors where there are ministerial concerns about agency performance or alignment. (State Services Commission, 2001; emphasis added)

The intentions were good: but the on-ground reality highlights the difficulties of rebuilding after NIE, especially in the absence of a clear sense of which regional and local alignments were required to produce which outcomes. As Gregory (2003) judges, the Review of the Centre process was both problematic and disappointing, having laboured mightily to produce minor change, and failed to address fundamental problems including responsibility assignment. While notionally referenced to regional strategy and local service delivery integration (Ministry of Social Development, 2003), it especially lacked substantive devolution and shared accountability parameters in this area. A related shift from an 'output' to an 'outcomes'-based accountability regime – or rather, retrieving outcomes from being something only ministers were concerned with, to something to be 'managed for' on a day-to-day basis – was also supposed to help inter-agency action prosper. However, practically, outcomes remain something for which managers in all contracting parties are accountable for only within departmental silos and particular contracted output classes, and links between them are often frail (Petrie and Webber, 2001). As a result, 'outcomes' to be managed for often resemble what one Waitakere official called 'hairy outputs', or risk-managed outputs framed in outcome terms[7]. Evidently, changing real social processes requires more than such reframings.

Building well-being from the locality up: the 'Waitakere Way' and the 'muffin economy'

In Waitakere, community-reactionary aspects of New Zealand's turn from hard neoliberalism were under way by the mid-1990s, as council-instigated forums, which gave local activists a platform for lobbying and information sharing, specifically oriented around well-being. 'Wellbeing', as the 1996 *Towards Wellbeing in Waitakere* report noted, 'is a far reaching concept.... The possible factors that affect individual, community and city wellbeing are divergent, wide ranging yet inextricably linked: housing, income, employment, mental health, crime, safety, leisure, recreation, the environment and family relationships are but a few' (Waitakere City, 1996, p 3). Activists drew on goodwill and expertise among Waitakere's long-standing networks and coordinators in trying to draw these sectors together. The iterative consultation, dialogue and strategic processes around the *Wellbeing* report became what was, by the Prime Minister's launch of the 2000 community well-being strategy, branded the 'Waitakere Way', a three-way (community, council, central government) partnership.

Sustaining the Waitakere Way has meant continual engaging, networking, collaborating, promoting of dialogue and exercising of both political and technical sensibility: what Waitakere people came to call 'strategic brokering'. In the words of one broker,

> There's no way you could do this sort of stuff on your own. It's around understanding how politics works, understanding how to actually get things done from within a bureaucratic organization. It's understanding your own community in the sense of the dynamics of that community – who can get things to happen, community wise. Process, process, process – absolutely critical. (Craig, 2003b)

No accounting was ever made of the 'people–process' costs incurred in networking, getting a strategic and tactical sense of local and national developments in other sectors, getting to know significant local others, and not least by providing good muffins, orange juice and coffee at meetings (thus producing what is called a 'muffin economy' of collaboration). But these processes enabled some participants to reaffirm their sense of collaborative agency.

> There's been a big investment of everyone's time upfront, over the years. But once you've been through the rounds a few times sitting round a table, in Wellbeing Network or inter-sector things, you know who people are and where they're coming from. Sometimes it's just a matter of one phone call, you can get straight to the person you know can make a decision. (Craig, 2003b)

On one level, this might be seen as the soft institutions of networks delivering the enhanced coordination institutionalism promised. Just as clearly, there were structural limitations. Many wondered whether all these meetings 'really achieved anything', or simply 'wasted a lot of people's time' (Craig and Courtney, 2004). As our research observed, over time the limits to the kinds of progress and accountability to be expected of this kind of community well-being process have become clearer. Often the intensity and complexity of the process (and the limited resources on the table) has seemed to crowd out focus on wider social outcomes (such as poverty). Directing substantive responsibility questions around such issues to senior bureaucrats merely ensured their withdrawal from forums, while collaboration niceties sometimes blunted advocacy and lobbying. In general, the accountability generated was largely voluntaristic, based in peer esteem and reputation, demonstrating capability, and hedged about with a need to let everyone save face in public forums.

The limits of voluntarism were also the limits of bottom-up strategy: accountability to outcomes was unlikely without links to substantive planning, budgeting and operations. While professionals evidently enjoyed and benefited from the networking, there were neither institutional nor fiscal incentives to engage with, for example, restructuring service delivery and other social governance to address poverty. While participation in local forums was sometimes made explicit in managers' employment and in NGO/private sector service delivery contracts, even high-level managers attending meetings would acknowledge that their budgets contained 'not one red cent' for collaboration activities, and that hard accountabilities to other key outputs dominated their priorities. This meant innovation was largely restricted to the edges: to micro-level partnerships around subcontractual service delivery, pilot projects or information sharing.

Nevertheless, important lessons were learnt, and new modes of coordination experimented with. Further iterations of the *Wellbeing* Strategy moved away from general, bottom-up coordination to focus on smaller areas of coordinative focus. In 2002-03, a committee of central and local government and community leaders prepared seven headline, outcome-oriented 'calls to action', for example, 'Families give their children a great start', 'Every student in Waitakere leaves school with a Plan', and 'Violence against children and women is reduced'. Voluntary groups of government and community agencies met regularly to instigate small to medium projects, pilot national initiatives and build networks. Popular, widely recognised, and able to umbrella pilots and new sectoral clusters[8], the Collaboration Strategy had by late 2005 leveraged $1.1 million in ongoing project monies, albeit spread unevenly over its clusters and over four years. But it has also suffered from familiar difficulties. It has been, for example, intensive on process and transaction costs. Its resourcing and accountabilities (to both collaborate and deliver) have been voluntary and (outside of particular projects) have been largely unenforceable, and have had little or no claim on core/higher budgets, which has meant that its ambit has been largely at the innovative and coordinative margins of Waitakere social services.

Nonetheless, by running ahead of central government and its resourcing, well-being collaboration agencies have been able to experiment, develop shared understandings, and in some cases to later capture money for pilots. Many remained aware of the need to progress to what they called the 'hard stuff' of aligning budgets and plans in strategic areas, and of the need to engage much more intensely if even the current well-being implications of Waitakere's changing deprivation profile (see Figure 10.2 above) were to be addressed. Some new realism and determination emerged, wherein activists were wielding critical terms like 'slippery subsidiarity' (wherein no one was sure which level of government should be doing what), and moving 'from the mess to the mesh' to address issues from poverty to local playground provision. By 2004, it became clearer that this meant both more substantive, core budget-linked local coordination, and more local discretion, incentivised and enabled, for example, via a devolved fund (Craig, 2004; Craig and Courtney, 2004). Here well-being activists are eyeing other sectors, including transport and regional economic development, that now have devolved, shared responsibilities and budgets, especially in Auckland.

But how far Labour's social development will succeed beyond soft communitarian and hard-work inclusionism will be tested by some new well-being-related inter-agency initiatives. These include priority areas in the 'opportunity for all' framework (Ministry of Social Development, 2004): education and workforce inclusion, obesity, diet and exercise, alcohol and drug abuse, and family violence. Here again, however, very little extra funding has so far been allocated, much less devolved. What there is to show for these reforms by the 2008 election will be a tough measure of the historical and political sustainability of third way networked governance approaches.

Conclusion

> The new system brought accountability at the expense of responsibility, contestability was more ideal than reality, strategic capacity was under-developed, managers had a narrow view of their work, transactions costs were high, and most contracts lacked means of enforcement. The model worked, but to what end? (Schick, 2001)

New Zealand's experience is a sharp reminder that the fragmentation legacy of NIE reforms runs deep. Under these circumstances, desire for inclusion and joined-up services cannot easily overcome fundamental governance barriers. Even in Waitakere, a strong civil society and an activist, high-capability local government can leverage little social outcome purchase around health, housing, poverty and well-being. Meanwhile, political representatives, the executive and citizens all face an extraordinary complexity of regional and local assignments and disaggregations: herding the cats of contractualised service delivery NGOs via voluntary meetings, into growing complexities of process, incoherent consultation and short-lived pilot projects. In the absence of higher coordinative planning, and budgeting and enforcement arrangements to support them, local strategic brokers struggle to improve service coordination. At the same time, they bear the brunt of a shifting of coordinative and outcome responsibilities down to front-line case managers and NGOs, without the requisite alignments for local success.

In this difficult context, Waitakere must struggle to put social governance back together. So far, however, for reasons beyond its control, it has not been able to achieve more than soft, quasi-territorial dimensions of local joining up: general consensus and innovation without substantive claim on budget or sustained, accountable reference to outcomes. While many territorial outcomes will remain beyond its ambit, it must seek smart territorial leverage in a number of areas (such as housing, transport and health outcomes), if it is not to be a mere receiver of wider market outcomes. This means making it clear across government that incremental joining up of 'hairy outputs' is not enough, and that in specific areas, substantive commitments to shared accountability, and clearer alignments and assignments, are needed. Here, despite obvious problems, collaborative population-oriented initiatives combining the territorial mandates and institutional power of health, local government and social development still look promising. Yet even health's best joined-up initiatives, in Healthy Housing and early childhood service access (Family Start) so far affect only the most marginal, and in a limited aspect.

In terms of real well-being outcomes in Waitakere, the dominant factor has been six years of high national economic growth and steep falls in unemployment. Here, in a commodity boom and property debt-fuelled economy, and with an OECD (Organisation for Economic Co-operation and Development)-low minimum wage and an expansive cheap service sector, active case management and retraining of unemployed people has resulted in rapid workforce reinsertions. Waitakere has seen unemployment fall by double-figure annual reductions to 20-year lows. In early 2006, New Zealand had the lowest unemployment in the OECD, at 3.4%. In this context, the government's communitarian and supply-side labour market approaches have tended to dominate, squeezing out other modes of population health and social outcome management. The Waitakere 'call to action' cluster gaining most traction is 'Every student in Waitakere leaves school with a Plan', which pre-secured six figure funding for its Waitakere Employment and Skills Project, and has fostered a range of smaller youth labour market educational programmes. On the other hand, child poverty, which is entrenched in sole-parent, welfare-recipient, often ethnic populations, has also been subordinated to workfare under the major 'Working for Families' initiative (St John and Craig, 2004).

Yet New Zealand's new inequality now appears ensconced at post-1990s heights (Giddens and Diamond, 2005). Unprecedented household debt and OECD-low savings are driven by housing loans and deregulated loan sharks at respective ends of the economy. With the housing boom, housing affordability for the poor has fallen, and real estate markets are more active than ever in sorting the poor into urban peripheries, mapping poverty onto places like Waitakere's margins. As Figure 10.2 above showed, it is now clear that all through the period of the Wellbeing Strategy, local coordinators and service providers have been fighting a rising tide of relative poverty among their population. But currently, even service delivery funding is not directly referenced to local social deprivation levels.

In such contexts, it is apparent that voluntary strategic approaches to well-being are frail. Under current policy ambits, despite goodwill and recognition, they remain a weakly re-territorialised mode of governance coordination and shared responsibility, undercut by risk aversion, high transaction costs, and a lack of substantive reassignments from the centre. Also apparent, however, is the realisation that the underlying NIE reforms are highly resistant to pragmatic realignment. As Alan Schick (2001) notes,

> In contrast to other countries in which reform meant adding peripheral elements to the pre-existing managerial system, in New Zealand, the reforms are the system. There is no other managerial system. This means that dismantling the reforms would require the government to divest itself of the ways in which it prepares and administers the budget, runs departments, links ministers and managers, and decides what to do. In other countries, an unsuccessful reform can be stripped away, leaving the core system intact. This would be more challenging in New Zealand.... It remains to be seen, however, what will be left if critical elements are stripped away.

Notes

[1] For example, Northern Ireland's Investing for Health policy urges local governments to 'identify opportunities for improving the health of the people in its area by addressing the social, cultural, economic and environmental determinants of health. They will develop long-term local cross-sectoral health improvement plans to address the identified health and well-being needs of their local populations to meet the strategic aims and objectives of "Investing for Health"' (DHSS&PS, 2002, p 145).

[2] For example, New Zealand's national Health Strategy provides that district health boards will:

- identify community-driven initiatives that are either achieving results for Māori and Pacific peoples or that have the potential to do so;
- identify ways they can respond to communities needs and interests;
- advise communities and provide them with information to help them meet their needs and fulfil their interests;
- help communities to access the optimum mix of resources to achieve their own goals;
- adapt policies, programmes and funding to support successful community initiatives;
- implement programmes identified in the intersectoral Closing the Gaps initiative as this develops, in order to address health inequalities;
- liaise with other government agencies on a national and local basis to build more coordinated policies and programmes.

[3] The term 'flax roots' is widely used especially in indigenous groups in New Zealand to refer to 'grassroots' or 'bottom-up' initiatives.

[4] A fuller sense of Gorringe's extraordinary eclecticism can be drawn from The Treasury's website 'The Gorringe Papers' (www.treasury.govt.nz/gorringe/).

[5] For example, its safety outcome – ensuring the safety of the child or young person and the safety of the community – includes physical, cultural and emotional/ psychological safety.

[6] According to a senior regional manager, the problem is that without strong, locally focused compulsion for, eg, the Waitakere Police to share accountability for outcomes with Waitakere CYFS, Ministry of Social Development and others, youth programmes struggle painfully to deliver outcomes.

[7] The Waitakere Collaboration Strategy's 'call to action' banners ('Every student in Waitakere leaves school with a Plan') are examples here, but any departmental statement of intent will furnish multiple cases of outcomes which barely go beyond outputs in scope.

[8] For a review of 'call to action' projects and outputs, see the Wellbeing Collaboration Project website (www.waitakere.govt.nz/OurPar/collabproj.asp).

References

Anand, S., Peter, F. and Sen, A. (2004) *Public Health, Ethics and Equity*, Oxford: Oxford University Press.

Ashton, T. (2005) 'Recent developments in the funding and organisation of the New Zealand health system', *Australia and New Zealand Health Policy*, vol 2, no 9.

Ashton, T., Mays, N. and Devlin, N. (2005) 'Continuity through change: the rhetoric and reality of health reform in New Zealand', *Social Science and Medicine*, vol 61, pp 253-62.

Baum, F. (2002) *The New Public Health* (2nd edn), Melbourne: Oxford University Press.

Bevir, M. (2005) *New Labour: A Critique*, London: Routledge.

Boston, J., Dalziel, P. and St. John, S. (eds) (1999) *Redesigning the Welfare State in New Zealand: Problems, Policies, Prospects*, Auckland: Oxford University Press, pp 134-53.

Boston, J., Martin, J., Pallot, J. and Walsh, P. (eds) (1991) *Re-shaping the State: New Zealand's Bureaucratic Revolution*, Auckland: Oxford University Press.

Boston, J., Martin, J., Pallot, J. and Walsh, P. (eds) (1996) *Public Management: The New Zealand Model*, Auckland: Oxford University Press.

Brown, M. (2000) *Care and Protection is about Adult Behaviour. The Ministerial Review of the Department of Child, Youth and Family Services*, Wellington: Child, Youth and Family Services (www.msd.govt.nz/documents/publications/sector-policy/care-and-protection-is-about-adult-behaviour.pdf).

Castles, F. (1994) 'The wage earners' welfare state revisited: refurbishing the established model of Australian social protection, 1883-1993', *Australian Journal of Social Issues*, vol 29, no 2, pp 120-45.

Clark, D. and Gough, I. (2005) 'Capabilities, needs and wellbeing: relating the universal and the local', in L. Manderson (ed) *Rethinking Wellbeing*, Perth: API Network, pp 45-68.

Coase, R. (1998) *The Firm, the Market and the Law*, Chicago, IL: University of Chicago Press.

Craig, D. (2003a) 'Re-territorialising health: inclusive partnerships, joined up governance, and common accountability platforms in Thirdway New Zealand', *Policy & Politics*, vol 31, no 3, pp 335-52.

Craig, D. (2003b) 'From the wild west to the Waitakere way', LPG Working paper no 8 (www.arts.auckland.ac.nz/lpg/paper8.pdf).

Craig, D. (2004) 'Building a better context for partnership: a review of core issues, with on-the-ground examples from the "Waitakere Way"', *NZ Journal of Social Policy*, vol 23, pp 45-64.

Craig, D. and Courtney, M. (2004) *The Potential of Partnerships: Key Learnings and Ways Forward based on Waitakere City Experiences*, Auckland: Local Partnerships and Governance Research Project (www.arts.auckland.ac.nz/lpg/plainenglishguide.cfm).

Craig, D. and Porter, D. (2006) *Development beyond Neoliberalism: Governance, Poverty Reduction and Political Economy*, London: Routledge.

Crampton, P., Salmond, C. and Kirkpatrick, R. (2004) *Degrees of Deprivation in New Zealand: An Atlas of Socioeconomic Difference* (2nd edn), Auckland: Bateman.

Davies, J. (2005) 'Local governance and the dialectics of hierarchy, market and network', *Policy Studies*, vol 26, nos 3-4, pp 311-35.

DEFRA (Department for Environment, Food, and Rural Affairs) (2005) *The UK Government Sustainable Development Strategy*, London: DEFRA.

DHSS&PS (Department of Health, Social Services and Public Safety) (2002) *Investing in Health*, Belfast: DHSS&PS.

DPMC (Department of Prime Minister and Cabinet) (2003) *Sustainable Development for New Zealand: Programme of Action*, Wellington: DPMC (www.mfe.govt.nz/publications/sus-dev/sus-dev-programme-of-action-jan03.html).

Easton, B. (1997) *Globalisation and a Welfare State* (book typescript incomplete; see www.eastonbh.ac.nz/article252.html).

Esping-Andersen, G. (1990) *The Three Worlds of Welfare Capitalism*, Cambridge: Polity Press.

Fyfe, N.R. (2005) 'Making space for neocommunitarianism: the third sector, state and civil society in the UK', in N. Laurie and L. Bondi (eds) (2005) *Working the Spaces of Neoliberalism*, Oxford: Blackwell, pp 143-63.

Gauld, R. (2001) *Revolving Doors: New Zealand's Health Reforms*, Wellington: Institute of Policy Studies and the Health Services Research Centre, Victoria University.

Giddens, A. and Diamond, P. (2005) *The New Egalitarianism*, Cambridge: Polity Press.

Girishankar, N. and de Silva, M. (1998) *Strategic Management for Government Agencies*, Washington, DC: World Bank.

Gregory, R. (2003) 'All the king's horses and all the king's men: putting New Zealand's public sector back together again', *International Public Management Review*, vol 4, no 2, pp 41-58.

Gorringe, P. (1991) 'A glossary of microeconomic jargon with special emphasis on the jargon of transaction costs and property rights', Wellington: The Treasury (www.treasury.govt.nz/gorringe/papers/gp-1986a.pdf).

Grimes, A., Jones, A., Procter, R. and Scobie, G. (eds) (2001) *Economics for Policy: Expanding the Boundaries. Essays by Peter Gorringe*, Wellington: Institute of Policy Studies.

Howden-Chapman, P. and Tobias, M. (eds) (2000) *Social Inequalities in Health: New Zealand 1999*, Wellington: Ministry of Health.

Humpage, L. (2005) 'Experimenting with a whole of government approach: indigenous capacity building in New Zealand and Australia', *Policy Studies*, vol 26, no 1, pp 30-47.

Hunter, D. and Killoran, A. (2004) *Tackling Health Inequalities: Turning Policy into Practice?*, London: Health Development Agency.

Jessop, B. (2002) *The Future of the Capitalist State*, Cambridge: Polity Press.

Kawachi, I. and Berkman, L. (eds) (2003) *Neighborhoods and Health*, New York, NY: Oxford University Press.

Kelsey, J. (1993) *Rolling Back the State Privatisation of Power in Aotearoa New Zealand*, Wellington: Bridget Williams Books.

Kendall, L. and Harker, L. (2002) *From Welfare to Wellbeing: The Future of Social Care*, London: Central Books.

Larner, W. and Craig, D. (2005) 'After neoliberalism? Community activism and local partnerships in Aotearoa New Zealand', in N. Laurie and L. Bondi (eds) *Working the Spaces of Neoliberalism*, Oxford: Blackwell, pp 9-31.

LGA (Local Government Association) (1998) *Community Leadership and Community Planning: Developing a Comprehensive Strategy to Promote the Wellbeing of the Area*, London: LGA.

Manderson, L. (ed) (2005) *Rethinking Wellbeing*, Perth: API Network.

Marmot, M. and Wilkinson, R. (eds) (1999) *Social Determinants of Health*, Oxford: Oxford University Press.

Marmot, M. and Wilkinson, R. (2001) 'Psychosocial and material pathways in the relation between income and health: a response to Lynch et al', *BMJ*, vol 322, pp 1233-6.

Martin, J. (1995) 'Contracting and accountability', in J. Boston (ed) *The State Under Contract*, Wellington: Bridget Williams, pp 36-55.

Ministry of Social Development (2001) *Pathways to Opportunity: From Social Welfare to Social Development*, Wellington: Ministry of Social Development.

Ministry of Social Development (2003) *Mosaics: Whakaahua Papariki. Key Findings and Good Practice Guide for Regional Co-ordination and Integrated Service Delivery*, Wellington: Ministry of Social Development.

Ministry of Social Development (2004) *Opportunity for all New Zealanders*, Wellington: Ministry of Social Development (www.msd.govt.nz/work-areas/cross-sectoral-work/opportunity-for-all.html).

Ministry of Social Development (2005) *The Social Report*, Wellington: Ministry of Social Development (www.socialreport.msd.govt.nz/).

Mullins, D. (2004) 'Accountability and coordination in a decentralized context: institutional, fiscal and governance issues', Mimeo (www1.worldbank.org/publicsector/decentralization/June21seminar/LiteratureReview.pdf).

North, D. (1990) *Institutional Change and Economic Performance*, Cambridge: Cambridge University Press.

Nussbaum, M. and Sen, A. (1993) *The Quality of Life*, Oxford: Clarendon Press.

Pearce, N. and Davey-Smith, G. (2003) 'Is social capital the key to inequalities in health?', *American Journal of Public Health*, vol 93, no 1, pp 122-9.

Petrie, M. and Webber, D. (2001) *Review of Evidence on Board Outcome of Public Sector Management Regime*, The Treasury Working Papers 01/6, Wellington: The Treasury.

Porter, D. and Craig, D. (2004) 'The third way and the third world: poverty reduction and social inclusion strategies in the rise of "inclusive" liberalism', *Review of International Political Economy*, vol 11, no 2, pp 387-423.

Powell, M., Glendinning, C. and Rummery, K. (eds) (2002) *Partnerships – A Third Way Approach to Delivering Welfare?*, Bristol: The Policy Press.

Roelvink, G. and Craig, D. (2005) 'The man in the partnering state: regendering the social through partnership', *Studies in Political Economy*, Spring, pp 103-26.

Russell, M. (1996) *Revolution: New Zealand from Fortress to Free Market*, Auckland: Hodder.

Schick, A. (1996) *The Spirit of Reform: Managing the New Zealand State Sector in a Time of Change*, Wellington: State Services Commission.

Schick, A. (2001) 'Reflections on the New Zealand Model', Paper based on a lecture at the New Zealand Treasury, August (www.treasury.govt.nz/academiclinkages/schick/paper.asp).

Scott, G. (2001) *Public Management in New Zealand: Lessons and Challenges*, Wellington: New Zealand Business Round Table.

Smith, C. (2002) 'Programme of change', Conference address, Department of Child, Youth and Family Services (www.conferenz.co.nz/2004/library/s/smith_craig.htm).

State Services Commission (1998) *Assessment of the State of the New Zealand Public Service*, Occasional paper 1, Wellington: State Services Commission.

State Services Commission (2001) *Report of the Advisory Group on the Review of the Centre*, Wellington: State Services Commission (www.executive.govt.nz/minister/mallard/ssc/summary.htm).

St John, S. and Craig, D. (2004) *Cut Price Kids: Does the 2004 'Working for Families Budget' Work for Children?*, Auckland: Child Poverty Action Group.

Stoker, G. (2002) 'Life is a lottery: New Labour's strategy for the reform of devolved governance', *Public Administration*, vol 80, no 3, pp 417-34.

Tenbensel, T. (2005) 'Multiple modes of governance: disentangling the alternatives to hierarchies and markets', *Public Management Review*, vol 7, no 2, pp 267-88.

The Treasury (1987) *Government Management: Brief to the Incoming government 1987* (2 vols), Wellington: The Treasury.

The Treasury (2001) *Towards an Inclusive Economy*, Working Paper 01/15, Wellington: The Treasury.

Waitakere City (1996) *Towards Wellbeing in Waitakere*, Waitakere: Waitakere City Council.

Waitakere City (2005) '"The Waitakere Way" tackles social wellbeing issue', Press release, 26 October (www.scoop.co.nz/stories/AK0510/S00175.htm).

Waslander, S. and Thrupp, M. (1995) 'Choice, competition and segregation: an empirical analysis of a New Zealand secondary school market 1990-93', *Journal of Education Policy*, vol 10, pp 1-26.

Wellington Health Action Group (1993) *The Health Reforms: A Second Opinion*, Wellington: Wellington Health Action Group.

Part Three:
Ageing and employment

ELEVEN

Extending working life: problems and prospects for social and public policy

Chris Phillipson

Introduction

Since 1997, issues relating to older workers and retirement have become major influences on the development of economic and social policy. In part this has reflected changes to the organisation of work and retirement during the 20th century. Donald Hirsch (2003) has observed that, throughout this time, the idea of a fixed point of leaving work – at age 60 or 65 – developed as one of the great certainties of life, particularly in the case of men. Modern retirement policy was itself a product of the late 19th century, as large private companies and branches of the civil service adopted pension policies of various kinds[1]. Following this, pension provision was extended to a wider range of groups, with recognition by government – especially in periods of economic depression – of the need to assist the retirement of older workers (Hannah, 1986; Phillipson, 1993). In consequence, modern states became responsible not only for the income maintenance of substantial sections of the older population but also for determining the rules governing access to different pathways into retirement (Kohli et al, 1991; Blanchet et al, 2005).

These 'pathways' or 'transitions' have become more diverse than once was the case, with trends towards earlier retirement ages, the development of 'bridging employment' between work and retirement, and greater diversity in the structure of pension provision (with the basic state pension joined by an array of means-tested credits, second state pensions, personal pensions and occupational pensions)[2].

Alongside these developments, however, governments across many Western countries have been highlighting the desirability of new approaches to the employment of older workers (Maltby et al, 2004; Reday-Mulvay, 2005). In the case of the UK, a variety of measures have been adopted to promote both re-entry into employment and to prevent premature exit, these including: Jobcentre back-to-work programmes, modifications to Incapacity Benefit eligibility criteria, reforms to pension access rules, and campaigns around age discrimination in the workplace (DWP, 2001, 2002a). These initiatives reflect a major change in the policy environment as regards older workers. While the 1970s and 1980s focused on the need to replace older with younger workers[3], the concern in the early 21st century is to encourage more people to work beyond state pension age.

To review this new turn in public policy, this chapter is divided into three parts: first, a consideration of the main elements driving current debates around work and retirement; second, an assessment of some of the key factors 'pushing' and 'pulling' older workers out of the labour force; and third, an outline of policy options for assisting the objective of extending working life.

Policy context

The ageing of the UK's population is one significant influence behind current debates on work and retirement. The First Report of the Pensions Commission (Pensions Commission, 2004) highlighted what it viewed as the dramatic change in the UK's demographic structure occurring over the first half of the 21st century, with only a negligible increase in the number of 20- to 64-year-olds, but a 78% increase in the number of those aged 65 and over. As a result the ratio of the 65+ group to those aged 20-64 will increase from 27% currently to 48% by 2050, with most of this increase concentrated in the next 30 years. In this context, the Pensions Commission took the view that encouraging a rise in average retirement ages would need to be a significant element in the policy response to demographic change (see Pensions Commission, 2005).

Ageing, along with changes in labour force participation, is already having a significant impact on the composition of the labour market (Dixon, 2003). The proportion of older people in the working-age population has been steadily increasing over the past decade since the 1990s. In 2004 the working-age population (defined as 16 to state pension age) stood at 35 million people, of whom 8.8 million (25%) were aged from 50 to state pension age. This proportion has increased steadily since 1992 when 21% of the population were aged between 50 and state pension age, a trend that is set to continue. Population projections suggest that

32% of the workforce will be aged 50 and over in 2021 (taking into account the increase in the retirement age for women to 65 between 2010 and 2020), with a slight fall to around 30% by 2031. Dixon (2003, p 74) concludes that one consequence of these changes will be that the '... experiences of older workers will have a growing influence on the performance of the labour force as a whole'. Hirsch (2005, p 3) suggests that an important policy issue stemming from this development will be the need to create more sustainable working lives, with the provision of improved support and assistance to older people within the workplace (see, also, Taylor, 2002; Whiting, 2005).

Encouraging older people to remain at work is closely linked with concerns about pensions and financial support to older people. The Green Paper *Simplicity, Security, and Choice: Working and Saving for Retirement* (DWP, 2002a) identified a number of policies aimed at people in their 50s to assist with expanding opportunities and choice for individuals to work and save longer. The 2004 Pensions Act, along with other supporting legislation, introduced reforms aimed at extending working life and giving individuals more generous and flexible options for how and when to retire. Changes to occupational pension rules mean that from April 2006 people will be able to carry on working for the same employer while drawing an occupational pension. In addition, the age from which a non-state pension can be taken will increase from 50 to 55 by 2010. These, along with other developments such as more generous state pension deferral options, provide the basis for incentives for people to remain at work up to and beyond state pension age[4].

Finally, questions have also been raised about the social desirability of early exit from the workplace. The Performance and Innovation Unit (PIU) (2000) report, *Winning the Generation Game*, identified what it viewed as the 'human costs' experienced by some of the 2.8 million people aged between 50 and state pension age outside the labour market. Some of the costs of premature exit were discussed in terms of disillusionment, depression and ill health, these compounded by sedentary lifestyles reflected in low rates of formal volunteering and lifelong learning among economically inactive 50-year-olds (PIU, 2000, pp 16-17). Whiting (2005, p 287) suggests that for many people, leaving the labour market can result in poverty, insecurity and social exclusion. Reday-Mulvey (2005) has pointed to the disadvantages associated with abrupt departures from work, arguing instead for greater flexibility in the transition from work to retirement. Again, the idea of flexibility is being promoted in different ways in many areas of social policy, with moves to extend rights to flexible working for workers undertaking care within domestic settings – an important issue for people in their 50s and early 60s where around one in four adults will have some caring responsibilities (DWP, 2005).

Changes in the employment of older workers

The policy of extending working life has been a significant outcome of the debate concerning the economic sustainability of ageing populations, and reflects in large measure pressures identified in the preceding section. In essence, the discussion has shifted from focusing on *early retirement/ early exit* to identifying *new routes back into employment*, combined with a focus on job retention and encouragement to working beyond state pension age. The aim is to reverse the trend – characteristic of the 1980s and 1990s – whereby older workers left work at earlier ages, and where early retirement came to be accepted as a normal event in the life course (Marshall et al, 2001; Taylor, 2004).

The extent of the decline in employment over this period is important to acknowledge given policy ambitions of removing barriers to employment. The dominant pattern, stretching over nearly three decades, has been characterised by the declining age of exit from the labour force – a trend that accelerated over the course of the 1970s and 1980s (Laczko and Phillipson, 1991; Pensions Commission, 2005). Even up to 1971, 93% of men in the UK aged 55-59 and 83% aged 60-64 were economically active, with around 19% of men working on after state pension age. The highest figure recorded was in 1961 when labour force participation rates reached 97% among men aged 55-59 and 91% for those aged 60-64. By 1989, however, the rate for men aged 55-59 had dropped to 79.8% and for those aged 60-64 to 54.6% (Phillipson, 1993). Put another way, while in 1950 the average age of exit (for men) from employment was 67.2 years, with life expectancy of 10.8 years at age of exit from the workforce, by 2004 estimates from the Pension Commission suggest that average age of exit from work had dropped to 63.8 years, with a near doubling of life expectancy after exit from employment to 20.1 years (Pensions Commission, 2004).

Over the course of the 1990s, with the move out of economic recession, the pattern of early withdrawal from work went into reverse with increases in economic activity for men and women in their 50s and 60s. The employment rate of men between 50 and state pension age was by 2005 higher than at any point since the mid-1980s. Since spring 1992, the level of employment has increased over the entire working-age population, with the greatest increase occurring in the 55-59 age group with a rise of seven percentage points in employment between 1992 and 2004. Over this period, the increase for men aged 55-59 was 4%, and for those aged 60-64 6%. Older women's employment showed a sharper rise over the period: 9% for those aged 50-54 and 55-59.

Disney and Hawkes (2003), Hotopp (2005) and the Pensions Commission (2004) have reviewed the reasons for these increases in economic activity. Disney and Hawkes (2003, p 67) make the general point that the aggregate increase for older workers conceals significant differences according to age, gender and educational qualifications (to which might be added ethnicity). Their analysis of data from the Labour Force Survey (LFS) and Family Expenditure Survey (FES) suggests that: 'Men close to [state pension age] with less educational qualifications have been less affected [by the rise in economic activity] than men closer to 50 with skills. Higher participation among later cohorts is driving up employment rates among women, especially those with more schooling'.

The Pensions Commission (2004, p 38) identified the upward move in employment rates among those aged between 50 and state pension age as the result of four main effects:

- *demand-side factors* such as the absence of major macroeconomic shocks comparable to the 1970s/1980s, this producing fewer redundancies and the possibility of re-entry into the labour market once unemployed;
- *supply-side factors* such as changes in pensions, in particular the move from *defined benefit* (DB) to *defined contribution* (DC) schemes – retirement behaviour in the latter tending towards later retirement given the context of a fall in equity markets and a reduction in annuities (Robinson et al, 2005);
- pressures arising from the substantial deficits that had developed in many company pension funds; and finally
- closure or restriction of pathways into early retirement (for example, changes in eligibility tests for disability benefits and initiatives to encourage those on benefits back into the workplace).

Phillipson (2004) noted additional factors in the encouragement of gradual pathways to retirement, such as part-time work and self-employment (18% of those aged between 50 and state pension age are self-employed compared with 12% of 25- to 49-year-olds and 4% of 16- to 24-year-olds). Such 'bridging' forms of employment have become increasingly significant for men as well as women in managing transitions from work to retirement (Phillipson, 2002; Platman, 2004a, 2004b; Loretto et al, 2005). The development of programmes such as New Deal 50 plus in encouraging training and returning to work may have had some influence

(Moss and Arrowsmith, 2003), although Disney and Hawkes (2003, p 67) argue that this may be '... through their symbolic importance and the association with relatively favourable demand conditions, rather than through the measures themselves'.

A demand-side factor put forward by Disney and Hawkes (2003) is the move from manufacturing to service-sector employment, with the hypothesis that work in the latter provides conditions more favourable to the retention and recruitment of older people. However, Hotopp's (2005) analysis using LFS data fails to support the view that the increase in the employment rate of older workers can be attributed to a structural shift away from manufacturing (although a longer-term perspective may still show this to be an influential variable). Of greater significance in Hotopp's (2005) study is the cohort effect of the increasing proportion in the population of economically active people from minority ethnic groups, this having a positive association with the employment rate.

Will employment rates for older workers continue to increase?

It remains unclear whether the trend of increased employment among older workers will continue for the foreseeable future. The Pensions Commission (2004, p 38) suggests that there are good grounds for believing that this is possible given: '(i) continuation of sound macroeconomic policy; (ii) the increasing shift from DB to DC pension provision; (iii) continued focus on Incapacity Benefit reform; (iv) active labour-market policies to encourage search for work at all ages; and (v) the forthcoming introduction of anti-discrimination legislation'.

On the other hand, large increases in the employment rate of older workers may, for a variety of reasons, be difficult to achieve. Despite the growth in employment rates among older workers, many still leave the labour force well ahead of state pension age. A number of explanations have been advanced for this, with a mixture of negative and positive reasons cited in the research literature. Poor health and disability are the most common negative factors cited for early withdrawal from work, although this may not be viewed at the time of leaving as a permanent move (McNair et al, 2004). Moreover, while problems with health may be cited as the main reason for leaving work, other factors – such as redundancy or pressures within the workplace – may also be present (Alcock et al, 2003).

Cappellari et al's (2005) analysis of LFS data found 45% of men and 41% of women aged between 50 and state pension age experiencing a health problem for a year or longer. The link between poor health and early retirement has been identified in both quantitative (for example, Humphrey et al, 2003; McNair et al, 2004; Cappellari et al, 2005) and qualitative (Barnes et al, 2002; Irving et al, 2005) studies. Humphrey et al (2003), in a survey examining factors behind labour market participation and withdrawal among those aged 50-69, noted a mixture of 'push' (mostly negative) and 'pull' (mostly positive) factors behind early retirement (defined in this study as all those retiring before state pension age). Among those respondents who had taken early retirement, 49% gave ill health as one of the reasons; this breaks down into 53% of men and 44% of women. The lower a person's retirement age, the more likely it was that they would have left because of an illness or disability of some kind; they were also less likely to have an income from a personal pension.

Another way of defining early retirement is to take a more selective population, focusing on those who have retired before the normal age in their pension scheme. This approach is adopted in the English Longitudinal Study on Ageing (ELSA), and the results again underline that for those leaving below the age of 55, early retirement appears as a phenomenon mostly related to health factors. Thereafter, financial factors appear as increasingly important as people get older, although ill health is a major element above as well as below age 55 (see Table 11.1).

ELSA data further suggest social class variations in reasons for early retirement. For men in higher social class groups, financial incentives appear as the biggest stimulus, in comparison with middle and lower social class groups, where reasons relating to ill-health are more often cited. Financial incentives and poor health are the reasons given by more than half of early retired men. The third most common reason stated by the ELSA respondents is redundancy (given by 15% of respondents). For women, ill health appears as the most common reason listed, although social class variations are important here: middle-class women are seemingly more likely to have taken early retirement for family reasons than those in higher and lower social class groups. Generally, family-associated reasons are more commonly cited for women in comparison with men (see Table 11.2).

General problems associated with work may also 'push' people out of the labour market. Green (2005) has reviewed a number of large data sets that suggest significant declines in job satisfaction over the course of the 1990s (see also, Crompton et al, 2003; Ginn and Arber, 2005). The programme of research on Transitions after 50 conducted by the Joseph Rowntree Foundation (for example, Barnes et al, 2002; Arthur, 2003) found that many people leaving work early disliked their jobs because

---

Table 11.1: Main reason for early retirement, by age

Men	50-55	Cell % Age 55-59	60-64	Total
Offered reasonable financial terms to retire early	21.6	30.6	31.3	30.1
Own ill health	48.6	23.5	24.2	26.6
Made redundant/dismissed/had no choice	5.4	15.3	15.2	14.2
To enjoy life while still young and fit enough	18.9	11.2	12.8	13.0
Fed up with job and wanted a change	0	8.2	8.1	7.2
Ill health of a relative/friend	2.7	5.1	3.8	4.0
To spend more time with partner/family	0	2.0	1.4	1.4
To retire at the same time as husband/wife/partner	0	0	0.5	0.3
Do not know	2.7	4.1	2.8	3.2
Total	100.0	100.0	100.0	100.0
n	32	104	209	345

Women	50-55	Cell % Age 55-59	Total
Own ill health	27.3	34.8	33.0
Offered reasonable financial terms to retire early	9.1	15.9	14.3
To spend more time with partner/family	4.5	14.5	12.1
Made redundant/dismissed/had no choice	9.1	8.7	8.8
Fed up with job and wanted a change	13.6	7.2	8.8
To enjoy life while still young and fit enough	13.6	4.3	6.6
Ill health of a relative/friend	4.5	5.8	5.5
To retire at the same time as husband/wife/partner	9.1	2.9	4.4
Could not find another job	0	1.4	1.1
Do not know	9.1	4.3	5.5
Total	100.0	100.0	100.0
n	26	84	110

Source: English Longitudinal Study of Ageing (ELSA), Wave 1 (2002) (own calculations)

they felt they were not leading anywhere, and they felt that they were undervalued by employers (Hirsch, 2005). In the survey by Humphrey et al (2003), 31% of men gave a work-related reason for their early retirement; 37% in the case of women. Eleven per cent of men and 16% of women reported that their work had become too 'physically demanding'; 8% of both that it had become too stressful.

Smeaton and McKay (2003, p 31) argue that the intensification of work within some organisations has become a considerable problem in the context of ageing populations and that there appeared limited scope for reducing pressures in the final years of employment. In this context, it is likely, they suggest, that a lack of opportunities to manipulate work tasks or hours may precipitate exits from full-time employment: 'Within

Table 11.2: Main reason for early retirement, by social class

Men	Cell %			
	Higher	Middle	Lower	Total
Offered reasonable financial terms to retire early	35.8	24.2	21.3	30.2
Own ill health	20.0	33.3	34.7	26.0
Made redundant/dismissed/had no choice	14.2	10.6	18.7	14.5
To enjoy life while still young and fit enough	12.6	15.2	10.7	12.7
Fed up with job and wanted a change	7.9	10.6	4.0	7.6
Ill health of a relative/friend	4.7	0	6.7	4.2
To spend more time with partner/family	1.6	1.5	1.3	1.5
To retire at the same time as husband/wife/partner	0	0	1.3	0.3
Could not find another job	0	0	0	0
Do not know	3.2	4.5	1.3	3.0
Total	100.0	100.0	100.0	100.0
n	192	63	74	329

Women	Cell %			
	Higher	Middle	Lower	Total
Own ill health	40.4	10.5	34.8	32.6
Offered reasonable financial terms to retire early	14.9	21.1	4.3	13.5
To spend more time with partner/family	6.4	31.6	8.7	12.4
Made redundant/dismissed/had no choice	4.3	0	21.7	7.9
Fed up with job and wanted a change	10.6	10.5	0	7.9
Ill health of a relative/friend	4.3	5.3	13.0	6.7
To enjoy life while still young and fit enough	6.4	5.3	8.7	6.7
To retire at the same time as husband/wife/partner	2.1	10.5	8.7	5.6
Do not know	10.6	0	0	5.6
Could not find another job	0	5.3	0	1.1
Total	100.0	100.0	100.0	100.0
n	58	23	24	105

Source: English Longitudinal Study of Ageing (ELSA), Wave 1 (2002) (own calculations)

this context it may prove difficult to encourage the older workforce to remain in employment beyond SPA [state pension age]'.

Informal care responsibilities may be a further 'push' factor for older workers. People aged 45-65 are a key group caring for sick, disabled or elderly relatives, as well as partners or children (Evandrou and Glaser, 2004). One in five people in the age group 50-59 are providing informal or unpaid care (cited in Loretto et al, 2005). Loretto et al (2005, p 42) suggest that: '... a significant minority of women in mid-life are unable to combine caring and work, or to modify their labour force participation effectively' (see, also, Arksey et al, 2005). They go on to argue that: 'Looking after the home and family accounts for nearly a quarter of female labour market activity in the age range 50-59.... Evandrou and Glaser found that one in five mid-life women who were faced with taking up caring responsibilities, either worked fewer hours or stopped work altogether' (Loretto et al, 2005, p 42; see, also, Phillips et al, 2002). Research by

Mooney and Statham (2002) found that hours of work were related both to the likelihood of being a carer and the amount of care given. People aged over 50 in full-time employment were less likely to provide care than part-time workers. Where full-time workers were caring, they were more likely to be providing five hours less caring on average than people working part time.

There are also 'pull' factors (mostly positive) encouraging people to leave work ahead of state pension age. Financial security is one highly significant element here, identified in research by, for example, Humphrey et al (2003), Smeaton and McKay (2003) and Lissenburgh and Smeaton (2003). Humphrey et al (2003, p 48) found that those retiring early reported higher incomes than those expecting to retire at state pension age. They comment that: 'This suggests that those expecting to retire early were more likely to have had the financial resources to enable them to do this'. Of those expecting to take early retirement, 45% said that this was because they could afford to do so. Smeaton and McKay's (2003) analysis of Family Resources Survey (FRS) data supported this finding. Their research confirmed the extent to which access to an occupational pension was associated – especially in the case of men – with more rapid exit out of the labour market.

Lissenburgh and Smeaton (2003) and Arthur (2003) link access to financial resources to the idea, following Titmuss (1958), of 'two nations' of early retirees (see, also, Mann, 2001). On the one hand, older workers from a disadvantaged background are more likely to leave employment *involuntarily* due to unemployment or ill health, while their more advantaged counterparts are more likely to leave *voluntarily* due to their acquired wealth or entitlement to a private pension (see, also, Whiting, 2005). Arthur (2003, p 41) links this dichotomy to issues of choice and control in the move from work to retirement, arguing that:

> The dimensions that appear to be central in framing people's experiences are first, the degree of choice and control they experience on moving out of work and towards retirement, and second, their financial circumstances during their working life (for example, their income from earnings, access to occupational pension, and accumulation of personal savings…). People who move out of work before [state pension age] range from either end of these two dimensions: total choice and control over circumstances to no choice and control, people in very high income brackets to people on low levels of state benefit. Perhaps not surprisingly, the findings suggest that on the whole, but not always, people in strong

financial and occupational situations have greater choice and control over leaving work and arranging their finances subsequently.

Alcock et al's (2003, p 159) study of men over 50 detached from the labour force also drew on the 'two nations' distinction, highlighting a 'middle-class' world embracing white-collar workers as well as professionals:

> Detachment [from work] for this group mostly takes the form of early retirement. On the whole they leave voluntarily from jobs which they have usually held for a very long time, and in so doing begin to draw on accumulated pension rights. They mostly own their home outright and they no longer have dependent children living with them. A sizeable minority maintain contact with the labour market though part-time working. Nearly all no longer want a full-time job, though a small minority do look initially for work before reconciling themselves to retirement. Overall, this group draws little if at all on the benefit system.

An important 'pull' factor for some individuals may be a desire to find a new direction to their lives. In the survey by Humphrey et al (2003) of those who had taken early retirement, close to one in four (23%) had done so to 'enjoy life while they were still fit and young'. Among those intending to retire early, 83% gave this response. The desire to spend more time with partners is also important in this context. In the Humphrey et al (2003) survey, this factor was mentioned by 16% of the early retired, and by 50% of those expecting to retire early (see, also, Barnes et al, 2004).

The idea of professional and managerial groups viewing the 50s as an appropriate point to take stock and possibly leave full-time employment was identified by Scales and Scase (2001, p 5) in their report *Fit and Fifty*, published by the Economic and Social Research Council. They make the point that among some groups an 'expectation of early retirement' had become entrenched by the end of the 1990s, with a desire for building a different life – notwithstanding potential financial pressures:

> Life after work is seen to offer a period of at least 30 years when personal talents and skills can be developed free from the demands of work. Those who are released from financial commitments – mortgages paid, children left home, and so on – are likely to exit the labour market in their 50s on either a full- or part-time basis, even in the face of a likelihood of a decline in living standards. The search for personal autonomy – a cultural

feature of the information age – will be seen to offer greater benefits than higher material living standards.

Whether this is a short-term (characteristic only of the first baby boom generation) or a longer-term development has important implications for policies such as extending working life. On the one hand, new attitudes to early retirement may encourage flexible working of different kinds; on the other hand, there may be resistance to closer involvement with types of work that fail to add to the quality of daily living in middle and older age (Ginn and Arber, 2005).

What prevents people returning to work?

Drawing those unemployed back into the labour market raises a number of complex issues. McNair et al (2004) observed that across the population as a whole, those who are economically inactive are much less likely to consider entering the workforce after retirement than those who are active. They further note that willingness to consider work is strongly influenced by the length of time which individuals have been retired. The Organisation for Economic Co-operation and Development (OECD) (2004) points out that with relatively low unemployment rates among older workers and relatively high hours of work per week (the exception being older women, most of whom work part time), one key to increasing labour force participation is in reducing the high levels of inactivity – 25.2% and 42.4% in 2003 among older men and women (50 to state pension age) respectively.

Analysis of LFS data by the OECD (2004, p 60) demonstrates that with increasing age, the share of the inactive population wanting to work decreases (see Table 11.3). For inactive men aged 60-64, only 18% would like to work and for inactive women aged 55-59, only 16% want to work. Some groups have, however, increased in the proportion wanting to work – notably men aged 55-59 with a rise of 4.5 percentage points over the period 1995-2002. The reasons behind inactive individuals wanting or not wanting to work are summarised in Tables 11.4 and 11.5. The importance of long-term illness in explaining why older men are not looking for work is confirmed in both tables. For women, long-term illness is also important but the family/home factors are also significant – affecting 25.4% of those aged 50-54 and 16.3% of those aged 55-59 who want to work but who are not looking, and 45.7% and 32.4% of those who do not want to work and who are not looking (Tables 11.4 and 11.5).

Table 11.3: Share of inactive population in the UK who want to work, by age and gender (1995-2002)

			Cell %			
	1995		2000		2002	
Age	Men	Women	Men	Women	Men	Women
25-49	41.1	31.2	45.4	32.2	46.3	30.8
50-54	36.1	23.3	39.0	24.2	38.0	20.9
55-59	26.6	13.8	27.5	15.8	31.1	16.0
60-64	17.2	6.4	20.2	7.2	17.8	6.0

Source: UK LFS (OECD, 2004)

Table 11.4: Reason why inactive individuals who want to work are not looking for work (2002)

				Cell %		
	Age	Family/ home	Temporary illness	Long -term illness	Believe no job available	Other
	25-49	0.6	4.9	11.3	2.8	80.3
	50-54	12.5	8.7	58.8	2.0	18.0
Men	55-59	7.1	5.7	74.4	2.3	10.5
	60-64	8.3	5.3	75.4	2.7	8.3
	65+	3.6	2.7	63.7	13.4	16.6
	25-49	58.4	4.1	22.0	0.9	14.6
	50-54	25.4	4.0	53.3	2.5	14.8
Women	55-59	16.3	3.8	59.3	3.4	17.3
	60-64	17.1	2.9	39.1	9.5	31.4
	65+	–	–	–	–	–

Source: UK LFS (OECD, 2004)

Table 11.5: Reason why inactive individuals who do not want to work are not looking for work (2002)

				Cell %			
	Age	Family/ home	Temporary illness	Long-term illness	No need	Retired	Other
	25-49	0.6	0.8	4.6	0.0	0.0	94.0
	50-54	14.5	4.3	55.6	1.2	0.6	23.7
Men	55-59	9.0	0.7	70.6	4.1	10.6	4.9
	60-64	4.5	0.7	52.2	6.2	33.2	3.1
	65+	3.0	0.6	41.9	2.9	49.0	2.6
	25-49	70.9	1.8	16.2	2.3	0.2	8.7
	50-54	45.7	1.1	34.3	9.6	5.3	4.0
Women	55-59	32.4	1.6	33.2	7.8	20.5	4.6
	60-64	13.5	0.3	15.1	3.0	66.2	1.9
	65+	–	–	–	–	–	–

Source: UK LFS (OECD, 2004)

Smeaton and McKay (2003, p 54) demonstrate in their analysis of secondary data from the LFS, FRS and British Household Panel Survey that working beyond state pension age is only a strong possibility for those working in the run-up to this stage. They go on to make the important observation that: 'It is difficult to re-enter the labour market having left it. Moreover, many of those leaving work may be doing so on health grounds, or because they have sufficient resources to live on in retirement. Rates of leaving work for those who do continue to work drop relatively quickly after 60/65. Even if more people can be encouraged to work after this age, on current trends they could not work for many more years'.

ELSA data confirm that expectations of being in work for those currently out of work are generally low and much more associated with health problems than for those individuals currently working. Table 11.6 shows that the majority of inactive individuals below state pension age do not expect to work in the future and this is even more exaggerated for those inactive individuals who consider themselves retired. Banks and Casanova (2003, p 140) comment here that: 'Looking across health groups, the average chances of working at age 60, reported by economically inactive men aged 50-59, vary from 21% for those who are in good

Table 11.6: Expected chances of returning to paid employment for economically inactive individuals below state pension age

	Sample size	Cell % Fraction reporting zero chance of working in future	Average % chance of returning to work
Men, 50-59			
All inactive	409	64.5	14.8
Inactive and retired	141	74.5	8.9
Men, 60-64			
All inactive	404	82.9	5.5
Inactive and retired	240	83.5	5.0
Women, 50-54			
All inactive	270	63.8	14.5
Inactive and retired	29	–	–
Women, 55-59			
All inactive	440	74.2	8.7
Inactive and retired	122	73.9	8.2

Note: Men below 60 are asked the chances of their being in paid employment at or after age 60; those between ages 60 and 64 are asked the same question with reference to age 65. Women below age 55 are asked the chances of their being in paid employment at or after age 55; those between ages 55 and 59 are asked the same question with reference to age 60.
Source: ELSA (Banks and Casanova, 2003)

health to 10% for those in fair or poor health. In the case of inactive women aged 50-54, the probability of being in work five years before the SPA [state pension age] goes from 19% to 8% across the broad health groups'.

Barham's (2002, p 307) analysis of the economically inactive in the LFS suggests, at least in the case of the older men, two different groups, both of whom may be resistant to returning to work: 'One group appears to consist of voluntarily retired professional workers, who may well have occupational pension schemes enabling them to have an income before state pension age. A second group includes skilled or semi-skilled workers who have been made redundant and are now unable to work due to long-term sickness'.

Alcock et al (2003, pp 150-1), in their survey of men detached from the labour market, found that the share of older (50+) detached men who would like a job declines with age, as does the share actually looking for work. Around 20% of the men in their early 50s are still looking for work. This falls away to only around 5% in their early 60s. The dominant reason given by 60- to 64-year-old men for not seeking full-time work is ill-health or injury – cited by 54% of men in the survey. The decision to retire was cited in only 30% of cases. The authors comment that: 'One in six men cited "little chance of a job due to my age"'. Given prevailing views about ageism in the labour market this proportion is perhaps surprisingly low but it may well reflect the importance of other factors, notably ill-health and retirement, in motivating men's decisions rather than the absence of widespread ageism'.

McNair et al (2004) grouped their sample of people aged 50-69 into 'choosers', 'jugglers' and 'survivors', with the first of these most amenable either to returning or staying in work. Mostly male, this was the most highly qualified group in the sample; fewer than one in 10 were unqualified. 'Jugglers' were mainly female and had been out of work the longest; they were much more likely to consider voluntary rather than paid work. 'Survivors' were the most resistant to returning to work: a high proportion had left the work for health reasons; most were men and three quarters were on low incomes. From their analysis of these groups, McNair et al (2004, p 61) draw the conclusion that:

> Economic inactivity is self reinforcing. Other studies have found that those who leave the labour market in their 50s stand a poor chance of successfully returning to it. This study shows clearly that those who are economically inactive are very much less motivated to work after retirement age, and that this effect increases with age. A policy approach

that increases participation at earlier ages might result in greater retention in later life. (see, also, Hirsch, 2005)

Developing policies to extend working life

The above review raises a number of important issues for interventions aimed at job retention along with the re-employment of older workers. To conclude this discussion, the chapter will highlight five areas for further development to assist the policy objective of extending working life: first, developing health interventions and improving the quality of work; second, improving the quality and availability of training and lifelong learning; third, improving support for older women in the workplace; fourth, extending the scope of flexible employment; finally, providing integrated public policies to support older workers.

On the first of these, data from the LFS, ELSA and related studies confirm the importance of ill health and disability as factors that can lead to premature withdrawal from the workplace. This is especially the case for those in routine or manual jobs, with one third of men in their 50s reporting a long-standing limiting illness. By comparison, similar rates for men from professional and managerial backgrounds are not reached until they are aged over 75: what Yeandle (2005, p 2) refers to as a '20 year "illness gap".' The OECD (2004, p 122) has emphasised the need for *preventative* measures in the area of health, arguing the need to make:'... jobs less arduous, staggered hours, shift swapping and job sharing. This could reduce the risk that all workers, notably older ones, exit the labour market for reasons of poor health'.

Awareness of the importance of this area is long-standing, both in the UK context (for example, HEA, 1994), and elsewhere in Europe, for example the Finnish Programme on Ageing Workers (1998-2002). McNair (2005) argues that the Finnish experience suggests that explicit health interventions, including job redesign for people in their 40s and early 50s, can significantly increase the employability of older workers. He concludes that:'Helping people to understand the ways in which work damages their health, and helping employers to design work to impose fewer physical stresses would help with this. So would strategies to encourage employers to review the balance of work across the life course, employing older people on less physically demanding jobs to conserve their skills and knowledge'.

Taylor (2002, p 40) confirms the importance of the above, arguing that:'A focus on the needs of older workers is almost certainly too late in some cases, although safety nets are essential'. He argues for preventive support coming through the provision of grants for ergonomic improvements in order to reduce the risk of disability among workers of all ages, and to make work more attractive to older workers. Hirsch (2003, p 17) summarises the issues in terms of developing policies that would '... change the character of work to take account of older people's characteristics as workers'. On the other hand, more research is needed about the kind of groups for whom health interventions are best suited, as well as the most effective way of encouraging groups such as employers and health advisers in the workplace to raise standards in occupational health and related services. The programme of work from the National Institute for Health and Clinical Excellence (2005), focusing on improving health in mid-life, is providing some illustrations of options in this area, with its focus on stimulating the work of those active in the field of health promotion at local and regional levels. The Pensions Commission (2005, p 343) also argues for a strategy '... focused on defining the best practices in middle-aged and older workers' occupational health which will tend to facilitate active labour market participation at older ages'.

It remains the case, however, that extending working life will prove difficult unless more general steps are taken to improve the quality of work. Research such as the Whitehall II Study confirms the role of stress in the workplace as a factor precipitating early retirement (Higgs et al, 2003). A range of studies over the 1990s highlighted the general decline in employee job satisfaction (Ginn and Arber, 2005; Green, 2005). Many of the studies in the Joseph Rowntree Foundation Transitions after 50 Programme confirmed how pressures at work motivated people to take early retirement (Barnes et al, 2002; Arthur, 2003). Further research is needed to identify specific policies aimed at improving quality of life in the workplace and their possible benefits for extending working life. More information is also required about the problems facing specific groups – notably those from routine and manual work occupations but also some white-collar groups.

Second, access to training and continuing education remains a crucial issue for older workers. Ford (2005a) makes the point that although many adults aged between 50 and state pension age have highly developed skills and experience currently lost to the economy, learning requirements are higher than for younger age groups. He notes that one in three in this age group have literacy or numeracy problems, compared with one in five of those aged 26-35. Current evidence suggests that the 50+ age group often misses out on courses provided by their employer. At the same time, evidence about what works in training older workers is lacking:

we need to know about what can best meet the diverse needs of this age group, and the range of benefits (for employer and employee) that training is likely to bring.

McNair (2005) argues that in addition to access to the mainstream of education and training, the distinctive learning needs of older people should also be recognised. Thus while it is possible that there are changes in ways of working and learning that relate directly to age, it is more likely that these reflect cohort effects or because the approaching end of employment reduces motivations for further training. On the other hand, cohort and attitudinal dimensions may be reinforced by experiences in the workplace, where long-serving employees may find themselves the least likely to be given the chance to learn new skills; or, for those who change jobs, to receive support in the form of additional training (McNair et al, 2004; McNair, 2005).

Regional and local initiatives directed at older workers may be especially relevant in terms of challenging prevailing attitudes – among employees as well as employers (Taylor, 2002). Encouraging Learning and Skills Councils (LSCs) to give greater priority to this group may be especially valuable in this respect. The National Audit Office (NAO, 2004, p 39) in its report, *Welfare to Work: Tackling the Barriers to the Employment of Older Workers*, noted the limited range of actions currently undertaken by the LSC:

> All 47 local Learning and Skills Councils have now produced Equality and Diversity Impact Measures. However, only seven Councils specifically address issues relating to older learners. These include targets to increase participation, retention and achievement in learning of people aged 50 plus, targets to improve further education data quality in terms of age, and identifying discriminatory practices within the local labour market. All seven have relatively high levels of inactivity among older people, but there are other Councils with higher inactivity rates that currently have no measures for older learners.

Mayhew and Rijkers (2004, p 2) stress the importance of 'continuous learning during the whole of working life as a means of reducing the dangers of labour market disadvantage in the older years'. The OECD (2004, p 116) has emphasised the importance of 'promoting a culture of lifelong learning', making the point that: 'Basic skill provision is just a starting point – individuals should have an incentive to invest in their human capital at all ages, so as to avoid their skills being eroded'. Ford (2005b, p 10) makes the case for an 'overall national third age guidance and learning strategy, one that would be linked to the national skills strategy and which would enable adults from mid-life onwards to maximise their skills and potential'. An important element of this might be closer involvement from higher education and further education institutions in responding to the needs of older learners, with the development of new programmes or the adaptation of existing ones to the needs of workers in the 40+ age group.

Third, programmes supporting women in the workplace are likely to be a major feature of measures to extend working life. The OECD has argued here that: 'In view of the impending rise of the State Pension age for women from 60 to 65, support programmes should be developed to help women remain in employment rather than using other pathways such as Incapacity Benefits to exit the labour market early. In this respect, early intervention and prevention should be the key approach used. This will require helping younger women as well, i.e. the age group 50-60. Otherwise it might be too late for intervention' (OECD, 2004, p 14).

Any support will need to take account of the informal care responsibilities of women, especially those in the 'pivot generation', of whom a significant proportion leave work as a result of family and domestic pressures. Maintaining a strong network of services, to assist women caring for parents and relatives in the community, is thus an important corollary of efforts to extend labour force participation among this group. Encouraging what Phillips et al (2002) refer to as 'family-friendly' employment policies is another dimension, with the need for flexible policies to assist line managers as well as carers in decision making about future work options. Arksey et al's (2005) research, however, suggests that access to care-friendly policies remains limited and that carers feel unable to take advantage of work-based schemes even when they do exist.

Fourth, despite interest and attention to promoting flexible pathways from work to retirement, the evidence at present suggests that these remain narrow in scope and limited to particular groups of workers and specific occupations. The lack of progress must be a concern given the extensive debate around encouraging gradual forms of retirement. Platman (2004a, p 3) makes the point that:

> Policy-makers and campaigning groups have been advocating a more flexible approach to later careers for many years. In 1980, the International Labour Organisation recommended that its member states introduce measures that ensured a gradual transition from work to retirement, by adopting voluntary, flexible ages for retirement and pension eligibility.... Since then, flexible employment as a solution to 'the problem' of older

workers has surfaced with increasing regularity in a broad range of international policy briefings, research reports, academic texts and good practice guides. (see, further, Hirsch, 2003; Platman, 2004a)

Loretto et al (2005) have highlighted some of the difficulties in this area, notably around problems of providing high-quality flexible employment and resolving difficulties presented by tax and occupational pension rules. Currently, the implication from the research evidence to date is that: (a) very few workers get access to high-quality flexible employment, and (b) options in this area remain limited. What can also be said is that flexible retirement is failing to fulfil its potential in contributing to policies that help people to delay their retirement. Further research examining some of the reasons for the present weaknesses and limitations in this policy would seem strongly justified if progress with extending working life is to be achieved. Much of this will need to focus on *organisational* (firm-specific) as well as *policy* (tax and pensions) issues limiting the development of flexible retirement. In relation to the former, examination of the role of human resources policies and line managers will be a significant dimension. In respect of the latter, the simplification of tax and pension rules will be especially significant.

Finally, an important issue to address will be embedding policies for older workers within the broad policy levers available to encourage labour market attachment. Taylor (2002, p 40) argues that: '... the current fragmentation of policy responses has often resulted in a range of similar initiatives targeting different so-called "disadvantaged" groups. This has been inefficient and may have weakened their effectiveness'. Taylor identifies a number of areas for development if this fragmentation is to be overcome, these including: linking policies on age and employment with other areas of public policy such as lifelong learning and equality more generally; recognition of the associated costs as well as benefits of extending working life policies, for example, training costs to help retain workers in the labour market; the importance of targeting particular groups in recognition of the diversity of the older workforce (see, also, Loretto et al, 2005); the importance of localised initiatives from regional, local government and trades union bodies; and the value of providing long-term support to older workers, given a context of increasing risk in respect of career and retirement planning (see, also, Admasachew et al, 2005; Vickerstaff and Cox, 2005).

Conclusion

This chapter has reviewed factors taking people out of or limiting the likelihood of their returning to paid employment ahead of state pension age. The areas identified, notably problems relating to poor health, responsibilities for informal care, stress in the workplace and changing attitudes to work, indicate potential obstacles to implementing policies for extending working life. Meeting this objective will require further progress on the policies discussed in the second half of the chapter, with major attention to areas such as health promotion in the workplace, improving the quality of employment and raising the profile of training for those aged 50 to state pension age.

A further requirement, however, will be managing the greater complexity of work and retirement transitions in the 21st century (Phillipson, 2004). A retirement where *everyone* finishes at 60, 65 or 67 (to take three possible ages) is no longer feasible (nor indeed desirable). This was characteristic (albeit only for men) of what might be termed the *traditional lifecourse* built around three clear stages of education, work and retirement (Marshall, et al, 2001). The reality now (itself partly a *consequence* of public policy) is for greater fluidity and flexibility in movement across the boundaries separating each life stage. Policies aimed at extending working life reflect this development. Schuller and Walker (1990) summarised this in terms of seeing the period of the 60s as a part of a 'decade of retirement', that is, 'the idea that when people reach 60 they should benefit from a number of years of transition between full-time work and complete retirement' (cited in Reday-Mulvey, 2005, p 37).

Central tasks for public policy arising from implementing this approach include, first, *ensuring that significant numbers of people are not excluded from the benefits of greater flexibility in moving from work to retirement*; and second, *helping people to secure greater control over transitions after 50*, for example, through measures aimed at improving financial security and alleviating poverty and social exclusion. By implementing the following types of policy, this might be achieved:

- those designed to create greater choice and flexibility about moves in and out of work, with the possibility of spreading work more evenly across the lifecourse;
- those that enhance the capacity of older workers as a group – through training, improvements to the work environment, lifelong learning and the development of anti-discrimination policies;

- those that encourage support towards the end of the working life, with the promotion of gradual retirement and preparation for retirement;
- those aimed at tackling the health problems that may cause or contribute to early exit from work, with the development of a range of preventive measures in the area of health.

Action on these points will be essential for tackling what has been termed the 'cycle of de-skilling' (Platman, 1999) affecting older workers, this arising from limited educational opportunities and restricted job-related training. The challenge for public policy is to create the conditions for greater choice within the various transitions experienced by those aged 50-69. Promoting extending working life as an inclusive policy, one that can meet the diversity of groups among older workers, will be a crucial test for the implementation of policy provision in this area.

Acknowledgements

This chapter draws on research commissioned by the Department for Work and Pensions (DWP) (see Phillipson and Smith, 2005). The author is grateful to David Johnson at the DWP for his assistance during that project. The author is also grateful to Tony Maltby, Kerry Platman, Philip Taylor and Stephen McNair for their suggestions about literature in the field of work and retirement. The author is also indebted to Jim Ogg for his assistance with statistical analysis of relevant sections in the ELSA and to Allison Smith for her help in collecting literature for the original DWP study.

Notes

[1] For excellent histories of retirement, see Graebner (1980) and Macnicol (1998).

[2] Phillipson (2002) discusses issues relating to transitions to retirement; see, also, Ekerdt (2004).

[3] The policy background here is reviewed in Laczko and Phillipson (1991).

[4] Detailed recommendations about incentives for continuing to work past statutory pension age can be found in the second report of the Pensions Commission (2005; see especially pp 334-8).

References

Admasachew, L., Ogilvie, M. and Maltby, T. (2005) *The Employability of Workers Over 50: Issues of Access, Retention and Progression*, Birmingham: University of Birmingham/Equal/European Social Fund/Forward.

Alcock, P., Beatty, C., Fothergill, S., MacMillan, R. and Yeandle, S. (2003) *Work to Welfare: How Men Become Detached from the Labour Market*, Cambridge: Cambridge University Press.

Arksey, H., Kemp, P., Glendinning, C., Kotchetkova, I. and Tozer, R. (2005) *Carers' Aspirations and Decisions Around Work and Retirement*, Research Report No 290, London: Department for Work and Pensions.

Arthur, S. (2003) *Money, Choice and Control*, Bristol/York: The Policy Press/Joseph Rowntree Foundation.

Banks, J. and Casanova, M. (2003) 'Work and retirement', in M. Marmot, J. Banks, R. Blundell, C. Lessof and J. Nazroo (2003) *Health, Wealth and Lifestyles of the Older Population in England: The 2002 English Longitudinal Study of Ageing*, London: Institute for Fiscal Studies, pp 127-66.

Barham, C. (2002) 'Patterns of economic inactivity among older men', *Labour Market Trends*, vol 110, no 2, pp 301-10.

Barnes, H., Parry, J. and Lakey, J. (2002) *Forging a New Future: The Experiences and Expectations of People Leaving Paid Work Over 50*, Bristol: The Policy Press.

Barnes, H., Parry, J. and Taylor, R. (2004) *Working After State Pension Age: Qualitative Research*, DWP Research Report No 208, London: DWP.

Blanchet, D., Brugivini, A. and Rainato, R. (2005) 'Pathways to retirement', in A. Börch-Supan, A. Brugiavini, H. Jürges, J. Mackenbach, J. Siegrist and G. Weber (eds) *Health, Ageing and Retirement in Europe: First Results from the Survey of Health, Ageing and Retirement in Europe*, Manheim: Manheim Research Institute for the Economics of Ageing.

Cappellari, L., Dorsett, R. and Haile, G. (2005) *Labour Market Transitions among the Over-50s*, London: DWP.

Crompton, R., Brockmann, M. and Wiggins, R. (2003) 'A woman's place ... employment and family life for men and women?', in A. Park, J. Curtice, K. Thomson, L. Jarvis and C. Bromley (eds) *British Social Attitudes: The 20th Report*, London: Sage Publications, pp 161-88.

Disney, R. and Hawkes, D. (2003) 'Why has employment recently risen among older workers in Britain?', in R. Dickens, P. Gregg and J. Wadsworth (eds) *The Labour Market Under New Labour: The State of Working Britain*, Basingstoke: Palgrave Macmillan, pp 53-69.

Dixon, S. (2003) 'Implications of population ageing for the labour market', *Labour Market Trends*, vol 111, no 2, pp 67-76.

DWP (Department for Work and Pensions) (2001) *Research Summary Evaluation of the Code of Practice on Age Diversity in Employment, Final Report*, Nottingham: DWP/Age Positive.

DWP (2002a) *Simplicity, Security and Choice: Working and Saving for Retirement*, Pensions Green Paper, Cm 5677, London: The Stationery Office.

DWP (2002b) *Pathways to Work: Helping People into Employment*, Incapacity Benefit Green Paper, Cm 5690, London: DWP.

DWP (2005) *Opportunity Age*, London: The Stationery Office.

Ekerdt, D.J. (2004) 'Born to retire: the foreshortened lifecourse', *The Gerontologist*, vol 44, pp 3-9.

Evandrou, M. and Glaser, K. (2004) 'Family, work and quality of life: changing economic and social roles through the life course', *Ageing and Society*, vol 24, pp 771-91.

Ford, G. (2005a) *Am I Still Needed? Guidance and Learning for Older Adults*, Derby, Centre for Guidance Studies, University of Derby.

Ford, G. (2005b) 'Am I still needed?: guidance and learning for older adults', Summary of report in D. Hirsch (ed) *Sustaining Working Lives: A Framework for Policy and Practice*, York: Joseph Rowntree Foundation.

Ginn, A. and Arber, S. (2005) 'Longer working: imposition or opportunity? Midlife attitudes to work across the 1990s', *Quality in Ageing*, vol 6, pp 26-35.

Graebner, W. (1980) *A History of Retirement: The Meaning and Function of an American Institution, 1885-1978*, New Haven, CT/London: Yale University Press.

Green, F. (2005) *Understanding Trends in Job Satisfaction: Final Report*, Report to the Economic and Social Research Council, Swindon: ESRC.

Hannah, L. (1986) *Inventing Retirement*, Cambridge: Cambridge University Press.

HEA (Health Education Authority) (1994) *Investing in Older People at Work*, London: HEA.

Higgs, P., Mein, G., Ferrie, J., Hyde, M. and Nazroo, J. (2003) 'Pathways to early retirement: structure and agency in decision-making among British civil servants', *Ageing and Society*, vol 23, pp 761-78.

Hirsch, D. (2003) 'Crossroads after 50: improving choices in work and retirement', *Foundations*, York: Joseph Rowntree Foundation.

Hirsch, D. (2005) *Sustaining Working Lives: A Framework for Policy and Practice*, York: Joseph Rowntree Foundation.

Hotopp, U. (2005) 'The employment rate of older workers', *Labour Market Trends*, vol 113, no 2, pp 73-86.

Humphrey, A., Costigan, P., Pickering, K., Stratford, N. and Barnes, M. (2003) *Factors Affecting the Labour Market Participation of Older Workers*, London: Department for Work and Pensions.

Irving, P., Steels, J. and Hall, N. (2005) *Factors Affecting the Labour Market Participation of Older Workers: Qualitative Research*, Research Report 281, London: Department for Work and Pensions.

Kohli, M., Rein, M., Guillemard, A.-M. and van Gunsteren, H. (1991) *Time for Retirement: Comparative Studies of Early Exit from the Labour Force*, Cambridge: Cambridge University Press.

Laczko, F. and Phillipson, C. (1991) *Changing Work and Retirement*, Milton Keynes: Open University Press.

Lissenburgh, S. and Smeaton, D. (2003) *Employment Transitions of Older Workers: The Role of Flexible Employment in Maintaining Labour Market Participation and Promoting Job Quality*, Bristol/York: The Policy Press/ Joseph Rowntree Foundation.

Loretto, W., Vickerstaff, S. and White, P. (2005) *Older Workers and Options for Flexible Work*, Working Paper Series No 31, Manchester: Equal Opportunities Commission.

Macnicol, J. (1998) *The Politics of Retirement in Britain, 1878-1948*, Cambridge: Cambridge University Press.

Maltby, T., de Vroom, B., Mirabile, M.-L. and Øverbye, E. (eds) (2004) *Ageing and the Transition to Retirement*, Aldershot: Ashgate.

Mann, K. (2001) *Approaching Retirement: Social Divisions, Welfare and Exclusion*, Bristol: The Policy Press.

Marshall, V.W., Heinz, W.R., Kuger, H. and Vermer, A. (eds) (2001) *Restructuring Work and the Life Course*, Toronto: University of Toronto Press.

Mayhew, K. and Rijkers, B. (2004) 'How to improve the human capital of older workers, or the sad tail of the magic bullet', Paper prepared for the joint EC–OECD Seminar on Human Capital and Labour Market Performance, Brussels, 8 December.

McNair, S., Flynn, M., Owen, L., Humphreys, C. and Woodfield, S. (2004) *Changing Work in Later Life: A Study of Job Transitions*, Guildford: Centre for Research into the Older Workforce, University of Surrey.

McNair, S. (2005) 'The age of choice: a new agenda for learning and work', in A. Tuckett and A. McAulay (eds) *Demography and Older Learners*, Leicester: National Institute of Adult and Continuing Education, pp 27-38.

Mooney, A. and Statham, J. with Simon, A. (2002) *The Pivot Generation: Informal care and work after fifty*, Bristol/York: The Policy Press/Joseph Rowntree Foundation.

Moss, N. and Arrowsmith, J. (2003) *A Review of 'What Works' for Clients Aged Over 50*, London: Department for Work and Pensions

NAO (National Audit Office) (2004) *Welfare to Work: Tackling the Barriers to the Employment of Older People*, Report by the Comptroller and Auditor General, HC 1026, Session 2003-04, London: The Stationery Office.

National Institute for Health and Clinical Excellence (2005) *Measuring Impact: Improving the Health and Well-being of People in Mid-life and Beyond*, London: NICE.

OECD (Organisation for Economic Co-operation and Development) (2004) *Ageing and Employment Policies: United Kingdom*, Paris: OECD.

Pensions Commission (2004) *Pensions: Challenges and Choices, First Report of the Pensions Commission*, Norwich: The Stationery Office.

Pensions Commission (2005) *A New Pension Settlement for the Twenty-First Century, Second Report of the Pensions Commission*, London: The Stationery Office.

Phillips, J., Bernard, M. and Chittenden, M. (2002) *The Experiences of Older Adults*, Bristol/York: The Policy Press/Joseph Rowntree Foundation.

Phillipson, C. (1993) 'The sociology of retirement', in J. Bond, P. Coleman and S. Peace (eds) *Ageing and Society: An Introduction to Social Gerontology*, London: Sage Publications, pp 180-200.

Phillipson, C. (2002) *Transitions from Work to Retirement: Developing a New Social Contract*, Bristol/York: The Policy Press/Joseph Rowntree Foundation.

Phillipson, C. (2004) 'Work and retirement transitions: changing sociological and social policy contexts', *Social Policy and Society*, vol 3, no 2, pp 155-62.

Phillipson, C. and Smith, A. (2005) *Extending Working Life: A Review of the Research Literature*, Research Report No 299, London: DWP.

PIU (Performance and Innovation Unit) (2000) *Winning the Generation Game*, London: The Stationery Office.

Platman, K. (1999) *The Glass Precipice: Employability for a Mixed Age Workforce*, London: Employers Forum on Ageing.

Platman, K. (2004a) 'Work–life balance and the ageing labour force: the need for a conceptual framework', Paper presented to the 'Work Life Balance Across the Lifecourse' Conference, Edinburgh, 30 June-2 July.

Platman, K. (2004b) 'Flexible employment in later life: public policy panaceas in the search for mechanisms to extend working lives', *Social Policy and Society*, vol 3, no 2, pp 181-8.

Reday-Mulvay, G. (2005) *Working Beyond 60: Key Policies and Practices in Europe*, London: Palgrave.

Robinson, P., Gosling, T. and Lewis, M. (2005) *Working Later: Raising the Effective Age of Retirement*, London: Institute for Public Policy Research.

Scales, J. and Scase, R. (2001) *Fit and Fifty*, Report prepared for the Economic and Social Research Council, Swindon: ESRC.

Schuller, T. and Walker, A. (1990) *The Time of Our Life: Education, Employment and Retirement in the Third Age*, London: Institute for Public Policy Research.

Smeaton, D. and McKay, S. (2003) *Working After State Pension Age: Quantitative Analysis*, Research Report No 182, London: Department for Work and Pensions.

Taylor, P. (2002) *New Policies for Older Workers*, Bristol/York: The Policy Press/Joseph Rowntree Foundation.

Taylor, P. (2004) 'A "New Deal" for older workers in the United Kingdom?', in T. Maltby, B. de Vroom, M.L. Mirabile and E. Øverbye (eds) *Ageing and the Transition to Retirement: A Comparative Analysis of European Welfare States*, Aldershot: Ashgate, pp 186-204.

Titmuss, R.M. (1958) *Essays on 'The Welfare State'*, London: Allen & Unwin.

Vickerstaff, S. and Cox, J. (2005) 'Retirement and risk: the individualisation of retirement and experiences?', *The Sociological Review*, vol 53, pp 77-95.

Whiting, E. (2005) 'The labour market participation of older people', *Labour Market Trends*, vol 113, no 7, pp 285-96.

Yeandle, S. (2005) 'Older workers and work-life balance', in D. Hirsch (ed) *Sustaining Working Lives: A Framework for Policy and Practice*, York: Joseph Rowntree Foundation.

TWELVE

Age discrimination in history

John Macnicol

Introduction

Age discrimination is once again back on the British political agenda. On 1 October 2006 there will come into force the new Age Regulations, which will outlaw age discrimination in key aspects of employment (principally recruitment, promotion and training) and extend full employment rights (for example, regarding unfair dismissal) to those aged 65+. All statutory retirement ages under 65 are to be banned (unless 'objectively justified') and employees will have a right to request to remain working past the age of 65. Both direct and indirect discrimination will be covered, and at any age. Much will be clarified in years to come: the 'objective justification' defence will be repeatedly tested and re-defined, as will those areas where age is a 'genuine occupational requirement', and it is likely that the proposed 'default age' for retirement of 65 will be abolished well before its review date (2011), in the face of a critical onslaught from many quarters. For example, the recent (November 2005) report of the Pensions Commission strongly urges its complete removal, hoping that this 'will be accompanied by changes in practice and culture towards older workers' (Pensions Commission, 2005, p 341). The future of mandatory retirement in Britain is thus uncertain. In addition, many other policies and initiatives have been introduced to encourage working later in life, such as the new financial incentives to defer claiming a state pension. As one recent commentator aptly puts it, the over-50s have become 'a key policy target group' (Whiting, 2005, p 286).

The immediate reasons behind this revival of interest are obvious. First, the economic activity rates of older men have fallen markedly since the 1970s, and those of older women have risen only slightly. One third of people aged between 50 and state pension age are now jobless. Their employment rates have risen by a few percentage points since the mid-1990s (from 62.5% in 1994 to 69.9% in 2004), in response to improved economic conditions, a tighter labour market and concerns over the erosion of private pensions. Their economic activity rates have risen less so, however, and there is continuing concern over the older 'discouraged worker'. Interestingly, the *number* who are economically inactive has actually risen since 1994, although this represents a proportionate fall (Whiting, 2005, pp 285-7). Projections suggest that no further decline in employment rates will take place (Armitage and Scott, 1998). It may be that future generations of older workers will be more 'flexible' in outlook and therefore willing to take the low-grade, entry-level and often part-time jobs that postindustrial labour markets increasingly offer. (Whether in human terms this would be desirable is another matter: forcing people to work later in life may be the ultimate form of ageism.) On the other hand, any future recession could restart the downward trend. Essentially, the average age of male retirement has slowly fallen over past decades. This is a phenomenon common to all advanced industrial societies (Auer and Fortuny, 2000), and it is – in Britain, at any rate – a long-run one, originating as far back as the 1880s and part of a slow contraction of job opportunities for older workers. There is a debate among social historians of old age over whether the slow spread of retirement over the past 120 years has been more caused by demand-side or by supply-side factors (Macnicol, 2003): if the former are more likely, the prospects of reversing the trend to male early retirement are not good. On the other hand, the 21st century may witness a remarkable change in the working patterns of older people, and average ages of retirement may rise.

Compounding this is a second reason: the prospect of an ageing population after circa 2020. In addition to the problem of rising state pension costs, population projections suggest that by 2022 there will be 3,000,000 more working-age people over the age of 50, and 1,000,000 fewer under the age of 50, making it imperative that everything possible be done to improve the job prospects of older workers (Whiting, 2005, p 287). Third is the concern over skills shortages, lost Gross Domestic Product, foregone tax revenue, and benefit expenditure consequent on this waste of human capital (Cabinet Office and PIU, 2000, pp 28-32). A more recent fourth concern is that life expectancy at age 65 has been increasing, implying that more people should work into their late 60s and that citizens can only expect, on average, a finite number of years in state-subsidised retirement. Between 1970 and 2004, life expectancy at age 65 in England and Wales increased by 4.5 years for men and 3.5 years for women. There is much uncertainty about future projections for life expectancy and, more importantly, disability-free life expectancy in old age: the likely effects of cohort-specific positive factors (such as reduced cigarette smoking) and negative factors (such as obesity) are hazardous to predict (Macnicol, 2006, ch 7). A final concern is the human tragedy of so many jobless 'fifty-something' men who will probably never be employed again, and who have been stripped of their work-based identities.

However, these impulses, powerful though they may be, are insufficient to explain the *timing* of this recent revival of interest. Concern over the problems of older workers has also been driven by all those labour market changes that have emerged in the past 30 years since the early 1970s – in particular, the growth of low-paid, part-time, casualised jobs. Excluding employers and the self-employed, in 1951 there were 19,600,000 full-time jobs in Britain, and 831,000 part-time; by 2004, the number of full-time jobs had actually declined, to 18,100,000, but the number of part-time jobs had expanded remarkably, to 6,400,000 (CSO, 1970, p 68; ONS, 2005, p 47). Associated with this has been the macroeconomic strategy of achieving non-inflationary economic growth by raising employment rates and re-enlisting into the labour market all those who have become marginalised from it – including economically inactive older workers.

The recent revival of interest in age discrimination in Britain

Since the early 1990s, there has been a crescendo of interest in age discrimination in employment and the labour market problems of older workers. New Labour's February 1996 promise of 'comprehensive legislation' against age discrimination in employment (McCartney, 1996) was temporarily abandoned, and once in office its suggested solutions tended to focus on little more than a 'cultural change' on the part of employers, plus workfarist policies to encourage economically inactive benefit claimants aged 50+ to seek jobs (the New Deal 50 plus, introduced in April 2000). However, the government's formal position changed in November 2000 with the publication of the European Union (EU) Employment Directive on Equal Treatment (2000/78/EC), under which all EU member states undertook to introduce legislation prohibiting direct and indirect discrimination at work on the grounds of age, sexual orientation, religion and disability.

Finally, therefore, Britain is to have legal protection against age discrimination in employment. For those who have long campaigned against the indignities of ageism, this will mark a partial and belated victory. Having achieved legislative action outlawing sex, 'race' and disability discrimination, this final discrimination – perhaps more insidious and covert than the others, since it is the least acknowledged and most likely to be accepted as 'normal' or 'inevitable' – appears to be being tackled. We may be witnessing the emergence of an 'ageless' society, fulfilling what Erdman Palmore has called the 'democratic ideal' that each person should be 'judged on the basis of individual merit rather than on the basis of group characteristics such as race, sex and age' (Palmore, 1990, p 7).

However, Palmore's use of the word 'merit' is interesting: as postindustrial societies become more Social Darwinist, so does there seem to be emerging a new form of meritocracy, based on competitive individualism, participation in waged labour (via 'recommodification' workfarist policies) (Holden, 2003) and the attendant erosion of state welfare. Legislative action against age discrimination is part of a wider enhancement of 'social justice' and 'equality' by the Blair government. This undoubtedly gives it a wide appeal, and discourages critical comment. For example, the Department of Trade and Industry disarmingly states that tackling age discrimination is 'good for business, good for individuals and good for society' (DTI, 2005, p 7). In other words, there will be no losers. However, it must be borne in mind that the emphasis on individual rights is inextricably linked to the Blair government's macroeconomic strategy of expanding labour supply – in both a quantitative and a qualitative sense – and meeting the target of an overall 80% employment rate among the working-age population. As the latest *Opportunity for All* (DWP, 2005a, p 9) states,

> Equality, opportunity, fairness and social justice are our cornerstones, designed to provide both routes out of poverty and wider economic prosperity, for individuals, communities and society as a whole. We are committed to helping people to help themselves, by offering a ladder to self-reliance and self-determination, with the right to financial or other support going hand in hand with an obligation to take steps to avoid long-term dependency.

New Labour's conception of equality is certainly not equality of outcome. It is, instead, 'equal treatment': that there should be established an equal opportunity to participate in a market economy which will then produce highly unequal outcomes.

There is, accordingly, an intriguing tension in the age discrimination debate. On the one hand are social justice arguments relating to the indignities of ageism and the denial of the 'right to work' in later life, enforced by mandatory retirement policies. The low economic activity rates of older people are often seen as the consequences of employers' ageism. On the other are labour-supply arguments, in which the removal of discrimination will benefit employers and be 'good for business' (Fredman, 2002, p 7). This tension is evident in many government pronouncements, such as that by Alan Johnson MP (then Secretary of State for Work and Pensions) in February 2005 (Age Positive, 2005):

> Our goal is genuine inclusion – stamping out the discrimination and disadvantage that prevents people from fulfilling their true potential. This could mean having a million more older workers in the labour force, including many who will choose to work beyond the traditional retirement age. The benefits to business are very clear: Retaining skilled and experienced employees and avoiding unnecessary recruitment and training costs.

Applying the principle of equal treatment more effectively will assist employers in differentiating between job applicants, without regard to 'irrelevant' characteristics such as 'race', sex or age. Age equality therefore 'opens up a wide pool of talent from which employers can draw, and yields a diverse workforce with a range of skills and experiences' (Fredman, 2003, p 48). Hence Sean Rickard, writing from the point of view of the Employers Forum on Age, has argued that age discrimination – for example, manifesting itself in early retirement policies – is damaging to business, since it 'increases the propensity towards wage inflation as the available pool of younger workers dwindles' (Rickard, 2000, p 10). The EU Employment Directive is part of a strategy to achieve a target employment rate of 70% across EU member states (as articulated in the March 2000 Lisbon Agreement) and, specifically, to increase the labour force participation rates of older people (EU, 2000). The abolition of mandatory retirement may, on the one hand, open up new work opportunities for some older workers; on the other, it may be replaced by more exacting individual performance appraisal to 'manage the exit of older workers who are underperforming when they would previously have been "retired"' (Employers Forum on Age, 2004). In this push to improve the quality of labour supply, less productive older workers may lose out: one form of discrimination may replace another.

Ageism and age discrimination in employment

'Ageism' (in social relations and attitudes) can be distinguished from 'age discrimination in employment' (manifesting itself in personnel policies relating to hiring, firing, promotion, retraining, employment rights and mandatory retirement). 'Ageism' refers to those attitudes, actions and vocabularies that serve to accord people a diminished social status solely by reference to their age. It is often seen as having recent origins (although 'prejudice' against older people has long been researched) (Tuckman and Lorge, 1953), deriving from the civil rights movement in the 1960s. The term 'ageism' was first coined in 1969 by Robert Butler, in a brief but effective comment on the interaction between class, 'race' and age discrimination (Butler, 1969). By contrast, age discrimination in employment has been discussed regularly since at least the 1930s – although many participants in the current debate are unaware of this.

The two concepts may, of course, overlap: for example, the personnel policies of employers may be subtly affected by their subconscious ageism (stemming from a dread of their own ageing, decrepitude and death); conversely, seemingly irrational prejudices against older people may derive from economic causes (the fact that, over the past 120 years, retirement has spread and pension costs have grown greatly). However, for analytical purposes it is useful to separate the two concepts. Intriguingly, it can be argued that the main victims of ageism are older women (who suffer a 'double' or 'triple' jeopardy of discrimination by age, sex and/or 'race') (Sontag, 1978). By contrast, the principal victims of age discrimination in employment would appear to be older men (for it is they who have experienced marked falls in their economic activity rates since the 1970s).

Ageism and age discrimination contain many inherent complexities and ambiguities, which can limit effective action. First, we all use age as part of our cognitive schema, and it is very difficult to decide where strongly internalised notions of 'age-appropriate' behaviours end and 'ageism' begins. Age-targeted policies are widely accepted and approved – for example, minimum ages that protect young people. Mandatory retirement at a set age is often viewed, in Lawrence Friedman's words, as '*the* form of age discrimination par excellence' (Friedman, 2003, p 192). Yet it has widespread support in the case of key public safety personnel, such as airline pilots or uniformed police officers, and may even be a necessity in order to free up channels of promotion and make jobs available for younger workers (Palmore, 1972). If state pension ages in Britain are raised (as has recently been suggested by the Pensions Commission), much will depend on whether or not the labour market can expand and absorb more older workers without worsening the job prospects of the young.

Second, there is the question of whether ageism is akin to sexism or racism (Palmore and Manton, 1973). Age is often defined as a relative characteristic, whereas the latter are immutable characteristics: we all grow old, but we cannot easily change our sex or 'race'. Defining the 'protected group' in law is much easier in the case of the latter than the former (especially if age discrimination were to be taken as applying at any age). This is more than just a debating point, since it can affect the transferability of antidiscrimination legislation from sex or 'race' to age.

Third, there is the problem of proving age discrimination. The operation of the 1967 Age Discrimination in Employment Act in the US over the past 40 years shows that the 'smoking gun' of proof is difficult to detect: tortuous legal wrangles have taken place over such questions as whether adverse impact can be applied in the case of age. The 'true' level of age discrimination in any society is impossible to determine. Even if we accept that what employees perceive as age discrimination really is that (and not something else), surveys in Britain of employees' experiences of age discrimination have thrown up rather contradictory results (Macnicol, 2006, pp 18-20). A recent survey by the Chartered Institute of Personnel Development even suggests that, although 59% of respondents reported having experienced age discrimination at some point in their careers, its incidence in job application, promotion, training, appraisal and redundancy has actually *declined* since 1995 (CIPD and CMI, 2005, pp 6-7). 'Direct' discrimination may be easily proved by citing, in a court of law, ageist remarks uttered in the workplace. But 'indirect', 'statistical' or 'institutional' discrimination (facially neutral, but having an adverse impact on one specified group) is much more problematic, since in most employing organisations seniority correlates with age and there is a natural tendency for older employees to be replaced by younger ones. Achieving an 'age-diverse' workforce is therefore difficult, since the age structure of a firm is the result of many factors other than discrimination – for example, how long it has been in existence (newly established sectors always tend to have youthful workforces). Again, were the new age discrimination legislation in Britain to cover the distribution of goods and services (as many campaigners wish), there would be immense difficulty in deciding what would be a 'just' distribution in areas such as healthcare, and what indicators would demonstrate this. For example, it would be hard to infer age discrimination from hospital admissions data.

A fourth difficulty is that there exists substantial positive discrimination in favour of older people – bus passes, subsidised public transport, free medical prescriptions, additional tax relief (via the 'age allowance'), special insurance policies, and so on. Indeed, the British welfare state is a complex balance of positive and negative age discriminations: for example, old people consume disproportionate amounts in pensions and healthcare costs, yet there are areas (such as age-based healthcare rationing) where substantial negative discrimination has operated (Roberts, 2002). While the most egregious forms of age-based healthcare rationing are now being eliminated by official directive (DH, 2001), there is no doubt that much informal, attitudinal and institutional discrimination still exists in this area. A final difficulty is absolutely central: are ageism and age discrimination in employment essentially rational (based on 'generalisations' regarding age-based declines in productivity, or other labour market factors, that have an approximate accuracy at the group level, even though there may be many cases of individual injustice) or are they irrational (prejudices based on 'false stereotypes')? Put another way, how *reasonable* are age proxies? Are they simply cheap, convenient and quick ways of making judgements about employee productivity – an acceptable alternative to the humiliation of individualised performance appraisal?

In addition to these intrinsic difficulties – arguably more acute in the case of age than in the case of sex, 'race' or disability discrimination – there are several issues relating to the recent revival of interest in age discrimination in employment. One is the intriguing paradox that 'postmodern' theories of ageing, which emphasise a 'blurring' of the life course, the extension of an (allegedly) consumption-rich middle age and the emergence of an 'ageless' society, have become popular in academic gerontology alongside calls to extend the working life, raise state pension ages and generally remove many of the welfare protections that have hitherto shielded older people. Action against age discrimination is coinciding with a new orthodoxy that citizens should work later in life and that pension funding should be individualised, with many final salary pension schemes being closed to new entrants. Indeed, it may be that age-based social programmes face a very uncertain future (Neugarten, 1996). Terms like 'unemployment', 'disability' and 'retirement' are essentially 20th-century constructs, arising from the categorisations introduced by welfare states and partly designed to regulate labour supply. As the 21st-century labour market becomes more like its 19th-century counterpart, so may these categories disappear. Again, the long-standing question of how far biological ageing interacts with 'social' ageing has once again come to the fore with the contentious issue of whether today's older people are healthier than any previous cohort, and therefore 'could' or 'should' work later in life.

A final question is central: are the low economic activity rates of older workers caused by 'discrimination' and perhaps the 'perverse incentives' offered by early retirement schemes in the 1980s, or are they caused by other factors – notably, older workers' concentration in long-established industrial sectors that experience greatest labour force shake-up, their displacement by new technology, or their lack of skills relevant to new expanding industries? The tendency in government publications is to emphasise the former, presenting the problem as caused by employers' 'myths and misconceptions' about older workers. Media reporting also tends to operate at this level: headlines like 'Game over for age discrimination?' (Miller, 2005) imply that all will be solved once legislation is introduced. The experience of the 1967 Age Discrimination in Employment Act in the US shows that legislation can have a mildly beneficial effect in enhancing the workplace rights of older workers, but it does not appear to have slowed the trend to male early retirement, and its impact on job retention may have been only modest (Adams, 2004). Of course, those who work with unemployed 'fifty-somethings' (such as the The Age and Employment Network in Britain, or employment lawyers in the US) (Gregory, 2001) are convinced that substantial age discrimination exists: the evidence may be anecdotal, but it is, nevertheless, powerful.

Much of the discussion on age discrimination views the problem as one of misguided personnel policies (based on 'false stereotypes') at the level of the individual firm: hence the only effective answer is 'by altering attitudes and behaviours in the workplace' (Worman and Cotton, 2005, p 1). However, the real problem is much more a supply–demand mismatch between different sectors of the economy. Modern labour markets are highly patterned by skill, region, gender and age: one sector can decline despite an overall expansion of employment and growth in other sectors. This is precisely what has happened in the case of jobs for older people. The litmus test of any policy initiative against age discrimination in employment is whether it will make a difference in those de-industrialised parts of Britain where job prospects for older people are poorest. In the spring of 2005, the employment rate among people aged between 50 and state pension age was 76.1% in the prosperous South East of England, but only 60.6% in the North East, 63.7% in Wales and 64.7% in the North West and Merseyside (DWP, 2005b, p 12). In such areas, there exists a massive 'job shortfall' (Beatty and Fothergill, 2004) which is not attributable to employers' 'myths and misconceptions'. In addition, the actual working patterns of older people need to be considered. Currently, only 9% of men aged 65+ are in employment. Of these, 63.5% work part time and 41.9% are self-employed (DWP, 2005b, p 9). There is substantial evidence that older workers want to downshift to less stressful, part-time work towards the end of their working lives: one recent survey shows 68% of respondents desiring this (CIPD and CMI, 2005, p 15). If the number of people working on past existing state pension ages is to be doubled to 2,000,000 (as the government wishes), radically new employment patterns will have to be adopted by those aged in their 60s; the present situation is not a secure basis for extending working lives and providing adequate remuneration (particularly if state pension ages are raised). It is difficult to see how this can be reconciled with the Blair government's repeated assertion that working later in life must be a matter of individual choice. The early retired are a diverse group, but research has consistently shown that those who are poorest, least skilled and of the lowest socioeconomic status tend to leave the labour force earliest (Whiting, 2005, pp 287-8). They do so involuntarily, and not through choice.

Having briefly considered some of the difficult issues in the current age discrimination debate, we now need to look backwards: how can history illuminate the present?

Labour market problems of older workers: historical background

If we look back into history, we can see that the labour market problems of older workers have always been the subject of debate. The tendency in 19th-century agricultural employment was for older men and women to work on as late as possible in life, scaling down the physical intensity of their work as they aged. Their diminishing earnings would often be supplemented by Poor Law outdoor relief: indeed, the Poor Law operated substantial *positive* discrimination towards older paupers, generally treating them better than other categories. To an extent, small employers adopted the same policy, retaining older, long-serving employees on light tasks at low wages that amounted to a quasi-pension (Macnicol, 1998, ch 2).

From the last quarter of the 19th century, however, new industrial methods and the growth of larger units of production began to impact adversely on older workers. The economic activity rates of British men aged 65+ fell, from 73.6% in 1881 to 61.4% in 1901, 47.9% in 1931 and 31.1% in 1951. Late 19th-century social commentators began to notice that older men were being displaced from the labour force by new technology and a general 'speeding-up' of production methods (exacerbated by the decline in agriculture, which had employed a high proportion of older men). Workers appeared to be 'worn out' at an earlier age, and their labour market position was becoming relatively worse. New machines in factories required younger men: as Charles Booth put it, a man aged in his early 60s had to do more than his father had done, 'in order to keep pace with the way the work is done now' (Booth, 1895). Effective working life appeared to be 10 years longer in rural areas than in towns and cities – 'as is seventy to sixty' (Booth, 1894, p 321). Booth even tried to investigate the varying rates at which workers 'aged' in relation to the demands of their jobs (Macnicol, 1998, pp 48-59). Interestingly, some medical commentators were also concluding that the more precise division of labour spreading through industry (involving more intense, specialised tasks) placed an excessive strain on a few parts of the body, wearing them out prematurely and condemning older workers to industrial obsolescence at progressively earlier ages (Crichton-Browne, 1891).

In the 1900s, the solution advocated most frequently was state old age pensions, which would enable older, 'worn-out' workers to withdraw from employment. But other suggestions were forthcoming, such as Beveridge's idea (which was to resurface periodically in subsequent decades) that a specially protected labour market niche be created for jobless older workers, just as certain firms (such as railway companies) kept 'light situations' for those 'who have grown grey or become injured in the company's service'. A labour exchange, backed by sympathetic public opinion, argued Beveridge (1909, p 211),

> might do much to get all the old men's places for the older men and leave to the younger generations the task of finding and forcing fresh openings for themselves.

By the 1900s, a pattern had been established that was to be a feature of the 20th century: older men did not experience dramatically higher unemployment rates than younger men, but once unemployed, they had greater difficulty regaining employment. Their spells of unemployment were, on average, longer, and likely to lead to personal discouragement. Hence among members of the Amalgamated Society of Engineers in 1895, the average duration of unemployment for those aged 25-34 was 53.9 days, but for those aged 55-64 it was 108.9 days (Riddle, 1984, p 518). This problem became particularly acute in the 1930s recession. For example, of applicants to the Unemployment Assistance Board aged 25-34 in 1937, 15.8% had been unemployed for three years or more, but of those aged 55-64 this proportion was more than double (34.1%) (Unemployment Assistance Board, 1937, pp 71-4). Older workers tended to be concentrated in old–established industrial sectors that were relatively labour-intensive and in slow decline; they were therefore much more likely to be rendered jobless by new technology, plant closures or workforce downsizings.

But was this the result of age discrimination? Some have suggested so (Riddle, 1984, pp 517-18). However, a more measured verdict has come from the social historian John Benson, who recognises that, while there is evidence of overt negative discrimination against older and middle-aged workers in the 1930s (for example, age stipulations in job advertisements), there was also some positive discrimination in their favour (Benson, 1997, pp 63-9). Interestingly, in 1930s America there seems to have been much more discussion of how far the worsening relative position of older workers was caused by age discrimination and how far economic restructuring was to blame (Palmer and Brownell, 1939).

To be sure, we can find some examples of adverse treatment of older people in the interwar years that might well be described as 'discrimination'. First, there undoubtedly was a deliberate policy of encouraging their labour market exit. It was probably not the intention of the 1908 Old Age Pensions Act to force older workers out of the labour market: since over 90% of state pensions were awarded at the full amount (indicating that the recipient had little or no income), and nearly two thirds of pensioners were women (who had very low labour force participation rates in old age), the effect of the Act on employment was minimal. A qualifying age of 70 and means testing meant that Britain's first pensioners tended to be old, poor, female and of marginal labour market value. However, the 1925 Widows', Orphans' and Old Age Contributory Pensions Act – which lowered the eligibility age to 65, partially shifted the funding to contributory insurance and abolished means testing for most pensioners – certainly had the encouragement of retirement as one of its aims. In a famous statement, the Act's author, Neville Chamberlain, commented that what was needed was a scheme that would 'make it worthwhile for the old men to come out of industry' (Chamberlain, 1924).

Schemes for reforming state pensions discussed within the labour movement and by the independent research body Political and Economic Planning were also directed at encouraging the permanent labour market exit of older workers, via a higher pension carrying a retirement condition (Bevin, 1933; Political and Economic Planning, 1935). At a time of mass unemployment, it was considered socially just that there should be a redistribution of jobs from old to young. However, a major objection raised at the time was the argument – relevant today – that each 'old' job vacated would not necessarily yield a replacement 'young' one, given the spatial, skills, age and sectoral mismatches that existed.

Another possible example of ageist attitudes was the tendency to associate older workers with the industrial recession: since, as noted, they were concentrated in the depressed areas that suffered the highest unemployment, the implication was that they were a contributory cause of it (Political and Economic Planning, 1935, p 5). (Significantly, the fall in unemployment in the late 1930s was slowest among men aged 55+.) Many trades unionists in the interwar years protested at the 'discriminatory' treatment meted out to older workers: most notoriously, on attaining the age of 65 they might be subjected to wage cuts equal in amount to the state pension (which then carried no retirement condition). In evidence to the 1941-42 Beveridge Committee, the Trades Union Congress delegation protested strongly that this was 'unfair' on older workers (Macnicol and Blaikie, 1989, p 30). The problem here, however, is that recessions tend to increase the vulnerability of *all* workers: there are many personal testimonies from workers of all ages of how workplace harassment, bullying and job insecurity increased in the shadow of the dole queues (Beales and Lambert, 1934). Again, the 'population panic' of the late 1930s, when there were fears of a future ageing population, arguably encouraged the growth of an ageist rhetoric and a tendency to view older people as an economically unproductive 'burden' on the rest of society. Finally, there is no doubt that older people suffered substantial discrimination in access to healthcare before the National Health Service. After 1928, National Health Insurance eligibility ceased at age 65, meaning that the majority of old people had no recourse other than the low-standard municipal hospitals. There are many chilling accounts of the appalling conditions endured by old people in such hospitals in the 1930s; before the development of geriatric medicine, their needs were neglected (Macnicol, 2006, pp 155-8).

From the 1940s to the 1970s

That age discrimination played a relatively minor role in the labour market problems of older workers was evidenced by the effect of the Second World War, when stimulation of heavy manufacturing and labour shortages caused by military call-up led to a sharp rise in the economic activity rates of older men and women. In the absence of a 1941 Census, estimates of this rise are conjectural, but evidence from National Insurance records suggests a doubling of the number of men aged 65+ in employment between 1939 and 1945 (Macnicol, 1998, pp 23-4). The 1947 Nuffield Survey calculated the increase (in the firms it surveyed) as even higher, and found that older workers in wartime did not manifest higher rates of absenteeism, nor did they need special welfare provision at work. Only very heavy or rapid work was beyond them. The survey concluded that further inducements should be offered to persuade people to work later in life, but those who chose to retire at state pension age should be allowed to do so, and employers should be able to retire those 'whose continued employment would be uneconomic'. In apocalyptic and rather ageist language, the survey warned that, unless this were done, 'the maintenance of the aged' would soon become 'a crushing burden on the young and middle-aged, thus forcing down the whole standard of living' (Nuffield Foundation, 1947, ch 6). The events of wartime, and other evidence of substantial latent working capacity in old age were one influence that led Beveridge, in his 1942 Report, to recommend measures to encourage delayed retirement.

The 1950s witnessed a thorough and lively debate on older workers. Then, as now, there were concerns over future pension costs and an ageing population – figuring strongly in the 1949 Report of the Royal Commission on Population and the 1954 Phillips Committee Report (Royal Commission on Population, 1949; Committee on the Economic and Financial Problems of the Provision for Old Age, 1954) – and there was a strong governmental push to maximise labour supply and encourage the postponement of retirement. In some ways, this was curious, since in retrospect we view the 1950s as a time of full employment and steady economic growth. The economic activity rates of women aged 50-64 actually rose, and those of men aged 50-64 stabilised. A tight labour market was also assisted by the raising of the school leaving age in 1947 and the removal of many young men into National Service. But economic growth and the transition from manual jobs to service jobs was creating labour shortages in key sectors of the economy. The labour market re-enlistment of so many older workers during the Second World War appeared to indicate that there existed a substantial reserve of labour which should be utilised via policies to extend working lives and encourage employers to drop their 'irrational' prejudices against older workers. In reasoning uncannily similar to the recent Pensions Commission report, it was argued that future extensions of life expectancy at later ages and improving health status would justify later working and a raising of the state pension age to 68 for men and 63 for women. There was, accordingly, much research (such as that conducted at the Nuffield Research Unit at Cambridge University) into flexible or phased retirement, the timing of labour market exit, the possible age discriminatory practices of employers, the health status and working capacity of men aged in their late 60s, and so on (Dex and Phillipson, 1986, p 46).

This research was complex, and only a very brief summary can be made here (for a full account, see Macnicol, 2006, ch 6). Essentially, researchers were able to conduct laboratory experiments on the declines in working capacity that accompanied ageing, but transferring the resultant hypotheses to an actual workplace was very difficult: as a concept, 'working capacity' included not only the functional abilities of the individual, but also the functional requirements of the job and the myriad of influences over a workplace (for example, new technology). Central to the government's strategy was the contention that retirement was inimical to the health and happiness of an individual, but this was impossible to demonstrate: since those who retired earliest tended to cite ill health as the reason, it followed that those who continued working into their late 60s were generally fitter – and this would have been the case whether or not they worked. They were also more productive: hence it could not be concluded that there was little loss of productivity with ageing. Then, as now, ill health was a broad category that could mask the disappearance of a job. The state pension appeared to have little effect as an inducement to retire: roughly two-thirds of men worked on past the age of 65, financial hardship forcing them to postpone retirement for as long as possible. Formal regulations enforcing mandatory retirement only applied in a minority of cases (generally white-collar occupations), but it is likely that informal pressures were put on workers to retire when their productivity fell – making the distinction between 'voluntary' and 'involuntary' retirement difficult to establish. Working lives could only be extended if physically undemanding 'light' jobs were readily available. However, these were scarce in those regions where the employment rates of older men were lowest, or they were part time and poorly remunerated, or they tended to be taken by younger women workers. Job growth was in those areas that employed younger workers, women and white-collar workers of all ages. The labour market sector occupied by older, blue-collar workers was contracting, such that, by the mid-1950s, only 2.7% of the male labour force was aged 65-9 (Shenfield, 1957, p 25).

Essentially, by the early 1960s most informed commentators had concluded that older people were working as late in life as possible, considering their physical capabilities and the availability of suitable jobs. For example, an investigation into a sample of workers aged 65-9 in Birmingham calculated that 86.0% of them were physically fit for some employment – and 64.8% were actually employed (Brown et al, 1958, p 561). As a result, interest in extending working life diminished. Indeed, for a time in the 1960s the view was even taken that automation would lead to a 'leisured society'. However, a more sanguine verdict was pronounced by Frederick le Gros Clark, who accurately warned that further technological innovations in industry and the growth of white-collar jobs would displace more older workers; average ages of male retirement would continue to fall slowly, creating great problems in the future (Clark, 1962, p 13).

By the mid-1970s, the OPEC-led 'oil shock' had triggered a contraction of Britain's manufacturing industries, a sharp rise in unemployment and the shedding of older workers. The 1965 Redundancy Payments Act had facilitated the exit of older workers in declining blue-collar sectors, and this was accelerated by the Job Release Scheme of 1977-88 (Taylor and Walker, 1996, pp 161-2). In the light of this, age discrimination was sporadically discussed – for example, by the Labour MP Eddie Milne, who unsuccessfully attempted to persuade the House of Commons to consider a bill protecting older workers (Milne, 1971). Once again, there was a debate on whether 'discrimination' or economic restructuring was the prime cause (Slater, 1973). It is important to remember that this early exit strategy had the support of governments, employers and trades unionists. As in the 1930s, it was seen as socially just and economically rational that, at a time of recession, major economic restructuring and workforce downsizing, available jobs should be redistributed to younger workers with family responsibilities. This did not really accord with reality, of course, because a young worker did not fill each 'old' job vacated: more was it the case that long-established, heavy industrial jobs were disappearing permanently. Between 1979 and 1999, manufacturing's share of total employment in Britain fell from 26% to 17%, and by the 1990s the economic activity rates of older men had plummeted.

Conclusion

From late 2006, Britain moves into uncharted territory regarding the politics of age discrimination. The new Age Regulations will undoubtedly confer improved and much-needed job protection on older workers, and may encourage employers to see the value of their older workers. They may also offer more work–life choices for those in the less stressful, middle-class professions for whom postponing retirement is a viable option. However, an examination of history reveals that, while age discrimination in employment is certainly a problem that needs to be combated, the real difficulty (often obscured in the current age discrimination debate) is one of long-run structural labour market changes that have de-industrialised older men. Their future employment prospects will therefore depend on many factors. Some (such as their skills and educational levels relative to job requirements) may be amenable to supply-side policies. But most (notably, the overall health of the British economy, or labour market expansion in those sectors that will employ older workers) are demand-side, and will require more than just a removal of employers' ageist 'prejudices'. If we really wish to 'make work pay' for older people, more radical policies will be needed.

References

Age Positive, 'News' (2005) 16 February, (www.agepositive.gov.uk).

Adams, S. (2004) 'Age discrimination legislation and the employment of older workers', *Labor Economics*, vol 11, no 2, pp 219-41.

Armitage, B. and Scott, M. (1998) 'British labour force projections: 1998-2011', *Labour Market Trends*, vol 106, no 6, pp 282-5.

Auer, P. and Fortuny, M. (2000) *Ageing of the Labour Force in OECD Countries: Economic and Social Consequences*, Geneva: International Labour Organisation.

Beales, H.L. and Lambert, R.S. (eds) (1934) *Memoirs of the Unemployed*, London: Victor Gollancz.

Beatty, C. and Fothergill, S. (2004) *Moving Older People into Jobs. Jobcentre Plus, New Deal and the Job Shortfall for the Over 50s*, Sheffield: Centre for Regional Economic and Social Research, Sheffield Hallam University.

Benson, J. (1997) *Prime Time. A History of the Middle Aged in Twentieth-century Britain*, London: Longman.

Beveridge, W.H. (1909) *Unemployment, a Problem of Industry*, London: Longmans, Green and Co.

Bevin, E. (1933) *My Plan for 2,000,000 Workless*, London: Clarion Press.

Booth, C. (1894) *The Aged Poor in England and Wales*, London: Macmillan.

Booth, C. (1895) Oral evidence, in *Royal Commission on the Aged Poor*, vol III, C-7684-II, *Minutes of Evidence*, pp 579-80.

Brown, R., McKeown, T. and Whitfield, A. (1958) 'Observations on the medical condition of men in the seventh decade', *British Medical Journal*, 8 March, pp 555-62.

Butler, R. (1969) 'Age-Ism: another form of bigotry', *The Gerontologist*, vol 9, no 4, pt 1, pp 243-6.

Cabinet Office and PIU (Performance and Innovation Unit) (2000) *Winning the Generation Game. Improving Opportunities for People Aged 50-65 in Work and Community Activity*, London: The Stationery Office.

Chamberlain, N. (1924) Letter to D. Fraser, 20 May, National Archives PRO PIN 1/4.

CIPD (Chartered Institute of Personnel Development) and CMI (Chartered Management Institute) (2005) *Tackling Age Discrimination in the Workplace. Creating a New Age for All*, London: CIPD and CMI.

Clark, F. le Gros (1962) *Woman, Work and Age*, London: Nuffield Foundation.

Committee on the Economic and Financial Problems of the Provision for Old Age (1954) *Report*, Cmd 9333, London: Her Majesty's Stationery Office.

Crichton-Browne, J. (1891) 'Old age', *British Medical Journal*, 3 October, pp 727-36.

CSO (Central Statistical Office) (1970) *Social Trends No 1 1970*, London: HMSO.

Dex, S. and Phillipson, C. (1986) 'Social policy and the older worker', in C. Phillipson and A. Walker (eds) *Ageing and Social Policy: A Critical Assessment*, Aldershot: Gower, ch 3.

DH (Department of Health) (2001) *National Service Framework for Older People*, London: DH.

DTI (Department of Trade and Industry) (2005) *Equality and Diversity: Coming of Age. Consultation on the Draft Employment Equality (Age) Regulations 2006*, London: DTI.

DWP (Department for Work and Pensions) (2005a) *Opportunity for All. A Summary of the Seventh Annual Report 2005*, London: DWP.

DWP (2005b) *Older Workers: Statistical Information Booklet. Spring 2005*, Sheffield: DWP.

Employers Forum on Age (2004) *Working Age*, issue 1 (www.efa.org.uk).

EU (European Union) (2000) *Council Directive 2000/78/EC of 27 November 2000*, Brussels: European Union.

Fredman, S. (2002) *The Future of Equality in Britain*, Working Paper Series No 5, London: Equal Opportunities Commission.

Fredman, S. (2003) 'The age of equality', in S. Fredman and S. Spencer (eds) *Age as an Equality Issue*, Oxford: Hart, ch 3.

Friedman, L. (2003) 'Age discrimination law: some remarks on the American experience', in S. Fredman and S. Spencer (eds) *Age as an Equality Issue*, Oxford: Hart, ch 8.

Gregory, R. (2001) *Age Discrimination in the American Workplace: Old at a Young Age*, New Brunswick, NJ: Rutgers University Press.

Holden, C. (2003) 'Decommodification and the workfare state', *Political Studies Review*, vol 1, no 3, pp 303-16.

McCartney, I. (1996) Speech, in *House of Commons Debates*, 6s, vol 271, 9 February, cols 618-19.

Macnicol, J. (1998) *The Politics of Retirement in Britain 1878-1948*, Cambridge: Cambridge University Press.

Macnicol, J. (2003) 'Retirement', in J. Mokyr (ed) *Oxford Encyclopedia of Economic History, vol 4*, Oxford: Oxford University Press, pp 371-5.

Macnicol, J. (2006) *Age Discrimination. An Historical and Contemporary Analysis*, Cambridge: Cambridge University Press.

Macnicol, J. and Blaikie, A. (1989) 'The politics of retirement, 1908-1948', in M. Jefferys (ed) *Growing Old in the Twentieth Century*, London: Routledge, ch 1.

Miller, S. (2005) 'Game over for age discrimination?', *Scotland on Sunday*, 7 August, p 5.

Milne, E. (1971) Speech, in *House of Commons Debates*, 5s, vol 816, 5 May, cols 1377-8.

Neugarten, B. (1996) 'The end of gerontology?', in D. Neugarten (ed) *The Meanings of Age: Selected Papers of Bernice L. Neugarten*, Chicago, IL: Chicago University Press.

Nuffield Foundation (1947) *Old People. Report of a Survey Committee on the Problems of Ageing and the Care of Old People under the Chairmanship of B. Seebohm Rowntree*, London: Oxford University Press.

ONS (Office for National Statistics) (2005) *Social Trends No 35. 2005 edition*, London: The Stationery Office.

Palmer, D. and Brownell, J. (1939) 'Influence of age on employment opportunities', *Monthly Labor Review*, vol 48, no 4, pp 765-80.

Palmore, E. (1972) 'Compulsory versus flexible retirement: issues and facts', *The Gerontologist*, vol 12, no 4, pp 343-8.

Palmore, E. (1990) *Ageism. Negative and Positive*, New York, NY: Springer.

Palmore, E. and Manton, K. (1973) 'Ageism compared to racism and sexism', *Journal of Gerontology*, vol 28, no 3, pp 363-9.

Pensions Commission (2005) *A New Pension Settlement for the Twenty-first Century, Second Report of the Pensions Commission*, London: The Stationery Office.

Political and Economic Planning (1935) *The Exit from Industry*, London: Political and Economic Planning.

Rickard, S. (2000) *A Profits Warning. Macroeconomic Costs of Ageism*, London: Employers Forum on Age.

Riddle, S. (1984) 'Age, obsolescence and unemployment: older men in the British industrial system, 1930-39: a research note', *Ageing and Society*, vol 4, pt 4, pp 517-24.

Roberts, E. (2002) 'Age discrimination in health', in Help the Aged, *Age Discrimination in Public Policy. A Review of Evidence*, London: Help the Aged, ch 3.

Royal Commission on Population (1949) *Report*, Cmd 7695, London: His Majesty's Stationery Office.

Shenfield, B. (1957) *Social Policies for Old Age. A Review of Social Provision for Old Age in Great Britain*, London: Routledge and Kegan Paul.

Slater, R. (1973) 'Age discrimination', *New Society*, 10 May, pp 301-2.

Sontag, S. (1978) 'The double standard of aging', in V. Carver and P. Liddiard (eds) *An Ageing Population. A Reader and Sourcebook*, Sevenoaks: Hodder and Stoughton, ch 10.

Taylor, P. and Walker, A. (1996) 'Intergenerational relations in the labour market: the attitudes of employers and older workers', in A. Walker (ed) *The New Generational Contract: Intergenerational Relations, Old Age and Welfare*, London: UCL Press.

Tuckman, J. and Lorge, I. (1953) 'Attitudes toward old people', *Journal of Social Psychology*, vol 37, May, pp 249-60.

Unemployment Assistance Board (1937) *Report for the Year Ended 31st December 1937*, Cmd 5752, London: His Majesty's Stationery Office.

Whiting, E. (2005) 'The labour market participation of older people', *Labour Market Trends*, vol 113, no 7, pp 285-95.

Worman, D. and Cotton, C. (2005) 'Equality and diversity: coming of age. CIPD response to the DTI consultation on the draft Employment Equality (Age) Regulations 2006' (www.cipd.co.uk).

THIRTEEN

Training and learning in the workplace: can we legislate against age discriminatory practices?

Kerry Platman and Philip Taylor

Introduction

> Lifelong learning is no longer just one aspect of education and training;
> it must become the guiding principle for provision and participation
> across the full continuum of learning contexts. The coming decade must
> see the implementation of this vision. (CEC, 2000, p 3)

The notion of a society based on the principles of lifelong learning has
achieved a remarkable consensus among policy makers and practitioners
across the European Union. Although the concept is not new, in recent
years it has been promoted with increasing urgency in government and
educational circles. The reasons are due to a complex interplay of economic,
technological and demographic pressures. Economic restructuring has
led to a reconfiguration of industries, sectors and workplaces, leaving
those with outdated or inadequate skills vulnerable to extended periods
of unemployment. The speed of technological change, coupled with the
rapid advances in technological know-how in less developed economies,
has put enormous pressures on employers and states to ensure that their
workers have the skills needed to compete in a global, information-led
economy. Meanwhile, the ageing of the European population has led to
predictions of major skills shortages and intolerable welfare burdens, leading
to a broad agreement over the need to increase employment rates for
older people and to extend their working lives.

The impact of these factors is an unprecedented refocus on learning in
the information-led economy, and in the way training is designed, delivered
and financed. There has been a proliferation of reports and policy

statements that examine the rhetoric of lifelong learning and its implementation. More specifically, there has been an increasing interest in the way training opportunities are accessed by different age groups. In an era of unrelenting change, it is a paradox that the more years we spend in the workplace, on average the fewer formal, paper-based qualifications we have, relative to younger cohorts. Equally, the older we are, the less likely we are to engage in a recent period of vocational training. Government and expert reports have recommended 'age-friendly' approaches to learning provision for many years, but these have been based on voluntary guidance and codes of best practice. The age discrimination in employment law, implemented in the UK in 2006, heralds a more punitive, regulatory approach to unfair, age-based employment decisions, including those relating to vocational training.

Yet, so far, there has been remarkably little discussion about the role of the age discrimination regulations in bringing about a more equal distribution of training participation across our working lives. Consultation documents issued in the years prior to legislation have contained few details or examples about how the legislation will tackle cases of unfair age bias in the provision of training. Where examples exist, they tend to focus on 'payback' times for training investments, providing employers with a justification to deny training if insufficient time is left before retirement.

It is timely, then, to examine the likely impact of the new law on access to and participation in training opportunities. To what extent will the legislation provide an instrument for change for younger and older learners in the workplace? Given the default retirement age, which allows employers to set a date of exit at 65 years for staff, will employers and workers have sufficient incentives to carry on up-skilling?

The focus of this chapter is on vocational training, rather than the much broader agenda of lifelong education and learning from cradle to grave. This somewhat narrow definition is due to the parameters of the age regulations, which cover only employment-centred training.

This chapter begins by setting the policy context for the age discrimination legislation. It then examines patterns of vocational training according to age and other factors, followed by a critical examination of a select number of recent government initiatives designed to translate lifelong learning policies into concrete actions. Voluntary and statutory approaches to age equality in training provision are then discussed. The final section focuses on policy dilemmas in the execution of lifelong learning, due to the limited parameters of the age discrimination regulations and the radical changes in learning delivery.

Lifelong learning: the policy agenda

In the UK, as elsewhere in Europe, the ageing of the population has led to a widespread concern over fiscal pressures on pension, health and welfare systems, and over labour shortages. Governments, although to varying degrees, are introducing incentives and penalties to encourage employers to implement more age-inclusive employment practices that maintain the health, well-being and productivity of their staff across their working lives (von Nordheim, 2004). In European policy circles, there is a view that it is no longer acceptable (or affordable) for employers to solve problems associated with low productivity and out-of-date competences with attractive early retirement packages, although individuals, employers and even governments continue to find it an attractive option. Specifically in the UK, a number of pension and tax incentives have been or are in the process of being introduced in order to prolong the working lives of citizens and end 'the cliff edge' to retirement (DWP, 2004).

Meanwhile, pressures to compete in the global marketplace have led to a restructuring of industries and jobs, with organisations undergoing business rationalisations, mergers, takeovers, cost-cutting exercises and the outsourcing of functions. In the 'ultra competitive world' described by White et al (2004), organisational change is intense and continuous. In addition, organisations have become increasingly reliant on advanced technologies to reach new markets and to develop products and services that satisfy the cost-conscious consumer. The shift to 'knowledge work', although disputed in some quarters (see, for instance, Rose, 2002), has placed a premium on the know-how of key employees, but this is being constantly undermined by a rapidly changing knowledge base. The move towards ever-faster and more complex technologies has challenged traditional notions of the lifetime job and the corporate college-to-retirement career (Herriot et al, 1998). In the space of one generation, the UK has changed from being a manufacturing nation to one where most employment is in services. Management and professional jobs have increased steadily so that they now provide almost 40% of current jobs (White et al, 2004). Even for workers in low-skilled occupations, there is an increasing need to display competencies in computers and other electronic devices, and to show a willingness to embrace (if not demonstrate a rapid mastery of) new ways of working and new systems, mechanisms and processes for carrying out day-to-day tasks.

More advanced economies have sought to compete with the less developed world by outsourcing and off-shoring functions and services, and moving their workers up the skills chain, to higher value-added areas of design, research, specialist production and marketing (Green, 2002). Indeed, the EU has set itself a strategic goal for the next decade: 'to become the most competitive and dynamic knowledge-based economy in the world, capable of sustainable economic growth with more and better jobs and greater social cohesion' (European Council, 2000, section I.5). Higher skills and valued-added knowledge are recognised as the key to global competitiveness, and to ensuring that Europe meets its ambition of becoming a world-leading, information-led economy.

Such demographic, technological and economic forces provide the backdrop for a remarkable consensus on the value of lifelong learning, and a belief that it can solve many of the economic, social and cultural dilemmas facing European societies (Papadopoulos, 2002). The concept is far from new (Schuller et al, 2002), but the urgency of the lifelong learning mission emerges clearly in the European Commission's *Memorandum on Lifelong Learning*:

> The prospect of a sharply ageing European population means that the need for up-to-date knowledge and skills cannot be met by relying mainly on new entrants to the labour market, as happened in the past – there will be too few young people and the pace of technological change is too fast, particularly the accelerating shift to the digital economy. (CEC, 2000, p 9)

The Cabinet Office's influential report *Winning the Generation Game* identified obsolete skills and barriers to learning as central issues for the 50+ age group (Cabinet Office, 2000). A number of its conclusions contained age-specific recommendations on training provision. For instance, Learning and Skills Councils were urged to develop a lifelong learning strategy that considered the particular needs of older people. Employers, meanwhile, should be motivated to offer older staff equal access to training opportunities. The benefits of worker learning at all ages should be promoted, and practical guidance should be provided on the learning styles of older learners. These recommendations were in response to striking patterns in workplace training across different age groups, as detailed in the next section.

Age-specific trends in training

A stark finding of Schuller and Bostyn's study of learning in later life in the early 1990s was the low number of older people involved in workplace training (Schuller and Bostyn, 1992). The authors estimated that roughly nine out of 10 people aged 50+ received no vocational training at all. These 'third agers' had minimal initial schooling, few formal qualifications and very limited opportunities for continuing education. Equally alarming were the relatively high numbers in this age group who were demotivated by the idea of further training.

Analysis of Labour Force Survey data by Taylor and Urwin (2001) found a range of other, highly significant factors that were determining access to vocational education and training in addition to age, such as gender, ethnicity, contractual status, occupational group, industrial sector and educational level. For instance, public sector employees were more likely to undergo or be offered training than manufacturing or construction workers. Managers, administrators and professionals benefited from better access to training than those in lower job grades. More than a third of female workers aged 50-59 had no qualifications, nearly double the proportion for men of the same age group. Meanwhile, men and women from minority ethnic groups were less likely to have undergone training in the previous 13 weeks, compared with white employees. Nevertheless, the authors concluded that age was an overriding factor in training participation, and was proving a substantial barrier for older people in the labour market.

More recent evidence supports this picture. In their detailed analysis of the 2004 Labour Force Survey, Newton et al (2005) found that employees between the ages of 20 and 49 had a more or less equal chance of being offered or receiving training. But there was a sharp decline in training participation for workers aged 50+. The authors concluded that there was 'a clear association between age and the amount of training offered to and received by workers' (Newton et al, 2005, p 4). The authors also examined the timing of training among those who had reported receiving some kind of training in the previous three months. Again, age was significant, with far higher proportions of younger workers saying their training had taken place in the past four weeks compared to the 50+ age group.

Urwin (2003) conducted a similar analysis of job-related training in the previous four weeks by age, but tracked this over a decade. He found that the take-up had grown marginally among those aged 50 to state pension age, but this appeared to be part of an overall improvement in recent job-related training provision across the working population aged 25+, as Table 13.1 shows. It appears that employer decision making is an

Table 13.1: Percentage of employees receiving job-related training in the previous four weeks (1992-2002)

Age	1992	1993	1995	1997	1999	2000	2002
16-24	24	24	20	23	24	25	25
25-39	15	15	16	16	17	17	17
40-49	12	13	13	14	15	15	15
50-59/64	7	7	8	9	10	10	10

Source: Analysis of Labour Force Survey, Spring 1992-Spring 2002, in Urwin (2003, Table 2.27, p 110)

influential factor in shaping these age-specific patterns in training participation. Taylor and Urwin (2001) concluded that the primary factor constraining older workers' training activities was a lack of opportunities provided by employers rather than disinterest among workers. In their survey of 4,650 people in work aged 50-69, Humphrey et al (2003) found that most had received some degree of encouragement to learn more job-related skills from their employers, but 27% said they had received no encouragement whatsoever. This became more pronounced with increasing age, as Table 13.2 shows.

Workers aged 50-54 tended to receive the most encouragement to upgrade their job-specific skills from their employers. But for those in their 60s, especially women, there is a pronounced increase in proportions

Table 13.2: Percentage of male and female workers aged 50-69 receiving any encouragement to learn more job-related skills

	Age			
	50-54	55-59	60-64	65-69
Men				
A great deal	24	11	17	(6)
A fair amount	34	31	24	(29)
A little	23	20	23	(18)
None	21	36	36	(47)
Women				
A great deal	26	23	16	(*)
A fair amount	37	32	24	(5)
A little	20	15	12	(34)
None	17	29	45	(61)
Bases: all employees				
Men	203	140	70	15
Women	244	199	56	9

Notes: Figures in brackets based on very small sample sizes. Column percentages represent proportions within gender in that age category. * signifies less than 0.5% of cases.
Source: Humphrey et al (2003, Table 3.23, p 41)

receiving no encouragement. The study also found that levels of encouragement varied between full- and part-time employment, with a third of part-time employees aged 50-69, compared with a quarter of full-timers, being offered no encouragement to learn more job-related skills. This is of concern, given the greater incidence of part-time working among the youngest and oldest workers (Felstead et al, 1999).

Evidence of overt age-based decision making in access to training is generally lacking, but studies clearly point to concerns about skill levels among older workers and reluctance on the part of employers to train them. One survey of large employers (Taylor and Walker, 1994), which asked about factors that might discourage them from recruiting and employing older people, found that by far the most important factor, cited by almost three quarters (72%) of respondents, was a perceived lack of appropriate skills among older workers. Other factors cited as being important barriers to older workers' employment were a lack of qualifications held (51%) and a truncated payback period on training (49%).

A later survey of employers by Hayward et al (1997) found that the greatest deterrent to employers recruiting older workers remained the low return on training investment, cited by two thirds (65%) of employers questioned. Employers also remained concerned about the perceived lack of appropriate skills (50%) and qualifications (46%) among older workers.

A government-commissioned study of employers in a cross-section of industrial sectors and enterprise sizes in Britain found that age hardly featured as a formal reason for deciding on who should be offered training opportunities (DWP, 2001). Yet, when the issue was explored in more detail, managers and human resource professionals appeared to hold different attitudes towards the training of older and younger employees. There was a reluctance to train older people for completely new roles, since they were seen as slow learners requiring a greater training investment, and because there may be insufficient time to recoup the costs because of retirement. They were also expected to be in less need of training, compared with their younger counterparts. But the study also found a reluctance on the part of older employees to engage in training. Those lacking in information technology (IT) skills were anxious about revealing their ignorance to bosses and younger co-workers. Likewise, Irving et al's study of attitudes to work and training among a sample of people aged 50-69 found evidence of negative attitudes to skills investment on the part of individuals (Irving et al, 2005). Training older people was seen as wasteful, since they would not have the chance to use their newly acquired skills. There was also a concern that retraining would involve having to start again at the bottom of a new career and involve a possible cut in wages and responsibilities. Other studies have identified the difficulties experienced by mature workers in accessing careers advice and support (DfES, 2003; Ford, 2005).

Other research points to factors other than employer behaviour that reduce older workers' training activity. A study of 1,798 manufacturing workers drawn from different plants of a motor vehicle manufacturing company explored employee development activities outside formal training (Warr and Birdi, 1998). Four types of activity were studied: a company-sponsored tuition refund scheme; a company-subsidised employee development programme; a company-provided employee development centre; and a personal development record made available for employees to plan and record their progress. Among the mainly (95%) male workforce questioned:

- older employees were substantially less active in all of the schemes;
- education level, learning motivation and learning confidence, as well as lower age, were found to be predictive of participation in each type of activity;
- of the environmental factors, support from managers, co-workers and non-work sources were positively correlated with activity, while time constraints were found to have a negative association;
- controlling for other factors, age was found to have a negative impact on activity.

Research into individual-initiated vocational training among middle-aged workers indicates that it is primarily those with skills already who participate. Those with lower levels of education, who arguably have most to gain, are least likely to self-initiate learning activities (Elman and O'Rand, 1998).

Urwin (2003) explains the complex challenges involved in identifying and tackling issues of discrimination in training by giving the hypothetical example of two job applicants identical in all respects except for their ages. In the case of age, however, it would be perfectly reasonable, he argues, for the employer to assume that the older individual will have more years of experiences, and the younger individual a greater number of qualifications.

> Simply put, older and younger workers are not expected to apply for the same jobs and, furthermore, even in cases where they do, it is impossible

to isolate a 'pure' age effect as it is so closely linked to a range of other characteristics. (Urwin, 2003, p 28)

Urwin argues that the past three decades have seen a growing divergence between the educational profiles of older and younger individuals in the workforce, as the average age at which people leave full-time education has risen. Citing Labour Force Survey data, he says that around a half of men and women aged between 25 and 39 left full-time education before the age of 17, but the figure for those aged 50 to state pension age is just under three quarters. The growth in formal qualifications reflects the rise in formal accreditation in many sectors. Although formal academic qualifications and on-the-job experience are unlikely to be close substitutes, he says that rapid changes to the working environment may have reduced the value employers place on this experience. Taking this further, older workers' experience may be viewed with suspicion or even as a positive disadvantage by managers who associate this with ideologies and allegiances at odds with new systems of values they are trying to establish (Taylor, 2001).

Translating lifelong learning policies into concrete action

The UK government has signalled its commitment to lifelong learning in its recent White Paper on skills (HM Government, 2005a). The document contains an impressive list of initiatives to address the low level of skills and qualifications among certain sections of the labour force and to encourage employers to instil a learning culture among all employees. This section focuses on a select number of these initiatives and examines their potential for addressing age inequalities in training participation.

The government's National Employer Training Programme – designed to change the locus of control over the demand and supply of training – has been piloted in England and is being implemented nationally over 2006–08. Employers will be encouraged to identify their skills requirements – including the need for basic skills, qualifications and informal development among staff – through training assessments. These will then be turned into single, integrated training packages, sourced by the employer. Where skills are needed in literacy, numeracy and languages, the training will be free up to Level 2 standard, but employers will be expected to allow their employees time off work to complete the training.

The evaluation of the pilots suggests encouraging results, particularly for older learners (Hillage et al, 2004). The oldest learners (aged 56+)

were more likely to complete their training than younger age groups, particularly compared with those aged between 19 and 25. Those working part time were also more likely to complete, possibly reflecting a time advantage over full-timers. However, the interim evaluation report also noted that older workers were less keen than younger workers to take part in training in the first place, suggesting that such initiatives will have a limited impact on harder-to-reach groups unless employers find ways to motivate these staff. An additional obstacle is likely to be the cost of these programmes. The government has announced its intention of recouping more of the costs of such training from employers and individuals. While high levels of subsidy will still apply to staff needing to gain the basics, more provision will be delivered at full cost (Learning and Skills Council, 2005). Yet research has demonstrated the reluctance of many employers to bear such costs, and the financial burdens faced by many older people of mortgages, children and accumulated debts (DfES, 2003).

In 2001, the government launched Skills for Life, a national strategy for improving basic adult skills in literacy and numeracy. This was designed to improve the demand for learning through promotional campaigns and by encouraging employers and parts of government to identify and address the learning needs of employees and clients. It was also intended to help reduce barriers to learning and to raise the standards of literacy and numeracy provision. Targets have been met, according to an evaluation by the National Audit Office (NAO, 2004), although the Adult Learning Inspectorate (2005) was recently highly critical of the scheme, concluding that it was not achieving its aim of helping people from the most disadvantaged backgrounds. The government is now committed to strengthening its Skills for Life programme on adult basic skills, setting a national target to help 2.25 million adults achieve recognised literacy and numeracy skills by 2010. Better IT skills are seen as critical, and the learndirect initiative, run by the University for Industry (Ufi), is seen as pivotal to its delivery. Ufi manages a network of 6,000 online centres in the UK, including 3,000 in public libraries, offering access to Internet services. It also manages 1,500 learning venues. The intention is to use the Ufi and online centre network as a flexible, responsive system to help individuals decide on job options and training needs. This will include working with other partners to provide a new nationwide service offering intensive, personal guidance services using the web and telephone helplines. In addition, plans under the New Deal for Skills initiative will include skills coaching for priority groups of welfare claimants.

However, the effectiveness of online-based services will depend on individual mastery and confidence in IT. Although the majority of working people in older age groups (50-69 years) report that they find it fairly or very easy to learn a new technology, 13% report finding it fairly or very difficult (Humphrey et al, 2003, Table 3.21, p 40). Other research, for instance by the National Institute of Adult and Continuing Education (NIACE), has drawn attention to the digital divide among people in the 'third age', with significant differences between individuals over computing skills and access to facilities. While learndirect courses are both easy to access and relatively low cost, they are less likely to involve the presence of a personal tutor or face-to-face discussion with peers.

New Deal 50 plus was introduced nationally in 2000 to help people aged 50+ in receipt of benefits for the previous six months or more to return to work. The scheme's combination of one-to-one advice, tax-free wage top-ups and targeted job placement support has been seen as successful in helping at least 120,000 older people into work (NAO, 2004). However, doubts have been raised on a number of fronts, including value for money (the cost to date is estimated at £270 million), effectiveness in reaching the oldest age groups, and the waiting period of six months before eligibility (Admasachew et al, 2005; Ford, 2005). The scheme also makes a training grant available to clients, but initial evaluation found the take-up to be low. An evaluation of the longer-term outcomes of the scheme examined the extent to which clients had taken part in training provided by their placement employer (Atkinson et al, 2003). Around three quarters of the respondents had received no training at all from their employer, other than a small amount of workplace-related induction. The reasons given for this were the unskilled nature of their work or their existing competences. Training was seen as unnecessary or irrelevant to the immediate demands of the job, or too basic to be worthwhile. The authors of the evaluation expressed concern that this focus on the short term and the immediate job in hand was failing to provide a foundation for the development of further skills or expertise, and a progression to more advanced or challenging roles. Just over half the respondents appeared to hold negative views about the value of training, believing that they were either too old to train or happy to remain in their current role until retirement. Other factors limiting participation may be that clients have no experience of buying training for themselves, and therefore have little knowledge concerning what they need or where to access training.

The government has also committed itself to extending apprenticeships to a broader spectrum of employers and individuals. Although a priority group for the scheme has been those aged 14-19, the scheme recently widened its remit to people aged up to 26. In the skills White Paper, the government confirmed it was backing trials of adult apprenticeships for people beyond this age in three sectors – health and social care, construction and engineering (HM Government, 2005a). Initial promotional material suggests the scheme could be attractive to employers, due to the training subsidies involved. But it is unclear how predisposed employers will be to apprentices who are outside of the traditional apprenticeship mould, in other words beyond their late 20s and already seasoned in other skills or roles.

Finally, there is a growing recognition of the sensitivities around the existence of set age thresholds for eligibility to educational and training grants. The government has announced that from 2006, it is relaxing the age limit on higher education fee loans and will be examining ways to raise the age limit on maintenance loans to match the state pension age (HM Government, 2005b). However, this still leaves in place other age ceilings for eligibility to grants and has led to organisations such as the The Age and Employment Network calling for a fairer distribution of educational subsidies, and an end to the arbitrary cut-off points that divert funds to certain (younger) age groups (Grattan, 2005). Schuller (2003) writes of the 'huge *implicit and systemic bias* in favour of youth in education' (p 121; emphasis in original), with the needs and preferences of older people being commonly marginalised, and only a tiny fraction of the budget devoted to them.

Given the lifelong learning policy agenda, and efforts to turn this into concrete, effective opportunities for learning, the question arises as to what role the age discrimination legislation will play. The next section begins by examining voluntary approaches towards training and age issues, followed by the broad remit of the age regulations.

Voluntary and statutory approaches to age-specific training inequalities

Voluntary guidance on age diversity in the UK workplace has, for many years, recognised the importance of intervention in the provision of training and development opportunities, particularly for the oldest sections of the labour force. Fifteen years ago, the government-funded Training and Enterprise Councils (TEC, 1991) produced comprehensive guidelines on training provision for older workers. These stressed the need to encourage mature learners, by respecting their individual learning styles, the pace at which they needed to learn and their life experiences.

Guidance issued by the government some years later spelt out the components of best practice: managers needed to take account of individual differences, learning styles and educational experiences in order to get the best value out of training investments (DfEE, 1999). The guidance also noted that training and development should be monitored to ensure that these were reaching employees of all ages.

> It is important to ensure that development opportunities are provided regardless of age. The longer skills are left without updating, the more effort will eventually be needed to bring them up to a required level. On the other hand, the more that training and development is seen as an integral part of the work situation, the more willing to learn people of all ages become and the more adaptable the workforce becomes. (DfEE, 1999, p 16)

The government's Age Positive campaign went further in its business guide on age diversity, calling on employers to use employees who have successfully completed training as role models to encourage their less willing colleagues (DWP, 2002). In its most recent voluntary guidance, published under the umbrella Age Partnership Group, employers are presented with a range of 'top tips' on training and development provision (Age Partnership Group, 2005). The guidelines stress the need for equal access, age-neutral selection, active encouragement for learners irrespective of age, and the monitoring and evaluation of learning and development opportunities and take-up.

Yet, despite the increasingly prescriptive nature of these voluntary guidelines since the 1990s, there are doubts about the extent to which individuals will be able to exercise their rights over access to training and development opportunities under the new age discrimination law. In fact, one of the examples given for objective, justifiable age discrimination in the government's 2003 Age Consultation document is where an employer can demonstrate that there is insufficient training 'payback' time before retirement (DTI, 2003a, p 16).

The final part of this section turns to the broad remit of the legislation, focusing in particular on training. The 2006 Employment Equality (Age) Regulations cover acts of direct and indirect discrimination in employment and vocational training against people of all working ages (defined as post-school to 65 years). The regulations specify that it will be unlawful for any employer, training provider, qualifications body, employment agency or institution of further or higher education to discriminate solely on the grounds of age against someone seeking or undergoing training . Training is defined in the draft statutory instrument as 'all types and all levels of training which would help fit a person for any employment', including vocational guidance and practical work experience provided by an employer, even to someone s/he does not yet employ (DTI, 2006, p 16).

It will be unlawful for one person to be treated less favourably on the grounds of age than another person in a comparable situation, unless there is a clear and justifiable reason for doing so. It will also be an offence to harass someone because of their age, causing a violation to their dignity and creating an intimidating, hostile, degrading, humiliating or offensive environment. The legislation, in line with most other equality provision, will allow for discrimination where there are genuine occupational requirements and where positive action is needed. Two examples given in the final consultation document demonstrate how the regulations might apply (DTI, 2005, p 31).

The first example of permissible direct age discrimination is in the setting of age requirements in order to protect or promote the vocational integration of people in a particular age group. Using this clause, it may be possible to justify age thresholds for the eligibility of training grants, educational awards or the targeting of certain (younger or older) age groups for special initiatives.

The second example is the fixing of a maximum age for recruitment or promotion that is based on the training requirements of the post, or the need 'for a reasonable period of employment before retirement' (DTI, 2005b, p 31). In the first consultation exercise, the government gave the example of an air traffic controller needing 18 months of theoretical and practical training at the College of Air Traffic Controllers, followed by further on-the-job training (DTI, 2003a, para 3.15c, p 16). The legitimacy of this kind of opt-out is likely to be tested in the courts. But there appears to be some support for this pragmatic approach. In the first consultation exercise on age, 68% of respondents said they felt it reasonable for employers to deny a person training in certain circumstances, for example when there was little time left between the end of the training and the start of retirement (DTI, 2003b, p 6). Others, however, thought a fairer system was for employees to pay back the costs of training if they left the company before a specific length of time after training, a measure that would apply across all ages and ensure that employers were able to secure a return of their training investment.

Yet the default retirement age, where employers are able to retire staff at 65 without justification, is likely to hamper efforts to improve skills levels and training participation for older people. This age cut-off would appear to provide a convenient threshold for justifying age-based decisions on access to grants and lengthy training investments.

Policy dilemmas in workplace training

This final section examines the part that the age regulations are likely to play in furthering the lifelong learning agenda, and equipping an ageing workforce with the required skills and qualifications to compete in a global economy. This section also considers the impact of the radical shift in the way workplace learning is delivered.

Age laws and training access

At this stage in the legislative process, when the regulations have yet to be ratified by Parliament (set for October 2006), the impact of the new law on working practices is far from clear. A direct comparison with other countries where similar age legislation already exists is difficult, due to the different legal frameworks and exemptions permitted under the respective laws. However, it is instructive to see how, or whether at all, training considerations feature in age equality cases abroad.

A recent overview of international case law in Australia, Canada, the United States and Ireland found that age discrimination cases were relatively few in number as a proportion of total equal opportunity cases, and the majority were dismissed as having no reasonable cause (Leeson and Harper, 2005). Cases were primarily about dismissal (including retirement), promotion and recruitment, and age was often only one of a number of factors cited by the complainant (gender, disability and so on being others).

Insight into the difficulties of pursuing age discrimination cases generally, and on grounds of training in particular, is provided by a recent unsuccessful case in the Republic of Ireland (Equality Tribunal, 2006). A 52-year-old man had been accepted as a trainee vehicle inspector but had failed the three-week intensive training course. He alleged to the Equality Tribunal that he had been subjected to ageist remarks by training staff and that the decision to end his contract prematurely amounted to age discrimination. National Car Testing Service Limited denied the charge, and said his dismissal was because of his overall attitude to training and his lack of progress during the training course. In quoting case law, the final judgment (against the complainant) acknowledged the underlying problems in proving age discrimination:

> A case of age discrimination presents particular difficulties. Where there
> is no direct evidence on age grounds for the alleged discriminatory actions
> and decisions, the complainant is often faced with a great difficulty in

discharging the burden of proof placed upon him. The complainant faces special difficulties in a case of alleged institutional discrimination, which, if it exists, may be inadvertent and unintentional. (Equality Tribunal, 2006, point 5.6)

This same burden of proof will also apply to people pursuing cases under the UK age legislation law. The onus will be on the individual to prove that the employer, training provider or professional organisation acted unlawfully, by denying opportunities on age grounds without justification.

Maurer and Rafuse (2001) explore in detail the potential for pursuing cases of discrimination in vocational training and career development. They argue that although the 1967 US federal Age Discrimination in Employment Act does not specifically mention training, this can be implied under a more general clause covering 'compensation, terms, conditions, or privileges of employment' and practices that 'limit, segregate or classify employees in any way which would tend to deprive any individual of employment opportunities or otherwise adversely affect status as an employee because of an individual's age' (Maurer and Rafuse, 2001, p 111). The authors suggest that the denial of learning and development opportunities because of age, whether overtly or subtly, covers a diverse number of activities, from workshops, seminars and college courses to e-learning, job rotation, special work assignments, coaching and peer support. It might be possible, suggest the authors, for employees to argue that their careers have been blighted due to the lack of challenging job assignments, since these can be an important means of growth and development.

In practice, however, cases based on the denial of training opportunities on their own are likely to be rare in the UK, for two main reasons. Firstly, the complainant will have to prove that they were treated less favourably than another person in a comparable situation on grounds of age. The complainant may be able to find a hypothetical comparator but this still leaves unclear the question of how old the comparable person should be. People of the same age may have very different career histories, qualifications, skills sets, roles and expectations. A recent European Commission report highlights the complexities of the 'the comparator problem':

If a court or tribunal is hearing a claim of direct age discrimination brought by a 63-year old nearing retirement, should the appropriate comparator be 61, 55, 21, or any other age? A 63-year-old employee nearing retirement may be in a wholly different position to a 61-year-old in many key respects, and both may be in a different position to a 55-year old. (O'Cinneide, 2005, p 20)

Secondly, it is likely that the denial of training will have to be supported by evidence of a more endemic ageist culture, where individuals are subject to harassment and a hostile working environment. Being refused training by itself is likely to be regarded as insufficient unless there are other examples of age bias.

A further reason, mentioned earlier, is that employers can argue that there is insufficient 'payback' time between the training and the age of retirement. The legal position on this point is far from clear, however. In Australia, the airline Qantas argued that it recruited its pilots under a certain age because of the heavy investment involved in their training and the need for recouping the cost before retirement (Encel, 2001). The tribunal ruled against this, and awarded costs against Qantas, arguing that equal opportunity considerations overrode such economic justifications.

Learning and training in the knowledge economy

The rapid evolution of technology and its widespread implementation is changing the way training is designed, implemented, managed and financed. Increasingly, knowledge acquisition is seen as a process for individuals to manage, and as requiring mastery of an ever-changing set of competencies. The timing, location and delivery of learning are becoming increasingly fluid as online learning options become more sophisticated and acceptable. The Internet has allowed instant access to vast amounts of information, and allowed for new ways to communicate with colleagues and experts over geographical and time zones. As Caspar (2002) notes, we are now able to access all knowledge from any discipline or specialism, at any time. This will lead, he predicts, to 'the resurgence of less formal, less visible and less structured types of training' (p 108). This is borne out by the findings of an international study of workforce ageing among highly educated IT professionals[1]. The pressures to maintain cutting-edge knowledge have led to a relentless pursuit of private, self-organised learning (Platman, 2005). These intense learners (largely men, partly reflecting the gendered nature of the IT labour force) were able to create protected learning environments in their own homes. These self-funded investments were seen as critical to their future careers in a highly competitive and global labour market.

Such private, self-regulated learning spaces will create challenges for policy makers wishing to create a more equitable learning society in the coming decades. Less visible learning regimes create difficulties for governments and agencies needing to demonstrate a fair distribution of public spending, one that is well managed, fully evaluated and properly targeted at the most deserving. Extending learning opportunities to those already on the margins of the labour market, and thus excluded from the perpetual learning environments operating in the model (generally larger) organisations, will remain a challenge. A number of studies have documented the exemplar approaches taken by certain organisations towards 'age positive' training practices (for example, Hirsh and Jackson, 2004; Newton et al, 2005). However, Hirsh and Jackson conclude that the careers of older people present both the biggest challenges and the biggest opportunities for large organisations:

> The unspoken career deal for senior people in many large organisations is that you work unreasonably hard, but get out in your 50s with a good pension, and then 'get a life'. Demographics, skill shortages and the state of pension funds will see this deal dying away for all but the highest-paid. Large organisations have a huge opportunity to pace careers better, redesign jobs and offer flexible working options to older workers as a means of both retaining and developing their skills. (p 33)

Such opportunities are likely to be costly in the short term for many employers, due to the considerable management time involved, and the disruption to established people management policies and practices (Warnes and John, 2005).

Conclusion

Government policies based on the principles of lifelong learning have been gathering momentum in recent years. There is evidence that participation in vocational training has widened and that qualification levels are rising. The government has demonstrated its commitment towards encouraging and supporting adult learning beyond the early and teenage years, and is investing in a number of innovative and potentially far-reaching initiatives to improve basic and intermediate skills. Yet the changing contours of employment, global markets and technology are posing a number of profound dilemmas for policy makers. Ageing societies need to ensure that their oldest workers have the skills and training necessary for them to participate in employment. Inadequate savings, pension and retirement provision are forcing individuals to consider working beyond state pension age, or at least beyond the once common early retirement threshold of 50-55 years. Yet the speed of workplace change and technological innovation means that employers and individuals must engage in perpetual learning. At the same time, there is broad agreement that a good educational foundation at the start of life is likely to improve our appetite for and consumption of learning later on. There are tensions, then, over any major redistribution of resources, especially one that would favour adults over youth.

As a result, it is difficult to see how the pronounced inequalities in access to and take-up of vocational learning will be eradicated in the foreseeable future. This is partly to do with self-selection, where demotivated groups of largely older learners avoid training opportunities or see them as poorly designed for or irrelevant to their needs. It is also due to the limited parameters of the new age discrimination laws, where people nearing retirement age can be denied training investments if the 'payback' period is seen as insufficiently long. The existence of a default retirement age, where workers can be forced to retire at age 65 without employers needing to justify this objectively, is likely to preserve the long-standing trends in declining training participation for the 50+ age group.

However, the proliferation of technologically driven platforms for learning is making it possible to reach previously remote or inaccessible learners. Individuals are able, in theory at least, to engage in learning and knowledge that transcends discipline boundaries, narrow fields of expertise, time zones and geographical limits. But the danger is that this brave new world of virtual and remote learning may exacerbate even further the educational fissures that are already apparent between generations. This is not to deny that many people in later life are highly proficient and sophisticated learners, capable of absorbing and taking advantage of the latest technological advance. It is also important to acknowledge the early learning experiences of our current generations of children and young adults, weaned as they are (in the Western world at least) on computer screens, keyboards and consoles. For those people educated before the digital era, however, there is inevitably a degree of reliance on paper-based and oral sources of knowledge, namely in books, on radio and in face-to-face learning. The switch to new forms of delivery entails a change in 'our very intelligence ... not just our physical capacities and skills' (Caspar, 2002, p 112). Such profound transformations represent unprecedented opportunities as well as challenges for policy making.

Note

[1] Workforce Aging in the New Economy is an international study of working practices and individual careers in the information technology sector. It is funded by the Social Sciences and Humanities Research Council of Canada. Details of the study can be found at www.wane.ca.

References

Admasachew, L., Ogilvie, M. and Maltby, T. (2005) *The Employability of Workers over 50: Issues of Access, Retention and Progression. Final report of the EQUAL 'Older Worker' Research*, Birmingham: University of Birmingham.

Adult Learning Inspectorate (2005) 'Annual Report of the Chief Inspector 2004-05' (www.ali.gov.uk/News/Press+releases/Press+releases/December05/CIAR.htm).

Age Partnership Group (2005) *Be Ready Personnel Organiser*, Sheffield: DWP.

Atkinson, J., Evans, C., Willison, R., Lain, D. and van Gent, M. (2003) *New Deal 50plus: Sustainability of Employment*, Sheffield: DWP.

Cabinet Office (2000) *Winning the Generation Game*, Norwich: The Stationery Office.

Caspar, P. (2002) 'Training networks and the changing organization of professional learning', in D. Istance, H.G. Schuetze and T. Schuller (eds) *International Perspectives on Lifelong Learning: From Recurrent Education to the Knowledge Society*, Buckingham: Society for Research into Higher Education and Open University Press, pp 105-14.

CEC (Commission of the European Communities) (2000) *A Memorandum on Lifelong Learning*, Brussels: CEC.

DfEE (Department for Education and Employment) (1999) *Age Diversity in Employment. Guidance and Case Studies*, Nottingham: DfEE Publications.

DfES (Department for Education and Skills) (2003) *Challenging Age: Information, Advice and Guidance for Older Age Groups*, London: DfES.

DTI (Department of Trade and Industry) (2003a) *Equality and Diversity: Age Matters. Age Consultation 2003*, London: DTI.

DTI (2003b) *Towards Equality and Diversity: Report of Responses on Age*, London: DTI.

DTI (2005) *Equality and Diversity: Coming of Age. Consultation on the Draft Employment Equality (Age) Regulations 2006*, London: DTI.

DTI (2006) *The Employment Equality (Age) Regulations 2006. Draft Statutory Instruments*, London: DTI.

DWP (Department for Work and Pensions) (2001) *Evaluation of the Code of Practice on Age Diversity: Report of Research Findings*, Sheffield: DWP.

DWP (2002) *Age Diversity at Work: A Practical Guide for Business*, Sheffield: DWP.

DWP (2004) *Simplicity, Security and Choice: Informed Choices for Working and Saving*, Norwich: The Stationery Office.

Elman, C. and O'Rand, A. (1998) 'Midlife entry in vocational training: a mobility model', *Social Science Research*, vol 27, pp 128-58.

Encel, S. (2001) 'Age discrimination in Australia: law and practice', in Z. Hornstein, S. Encel, M. Gunderson and D. Neumark (eds) *Outlawing Age Discrimination: Foreign Lessons, UK Choices*, Bristol/York: The Policy Press/Joseph Rowntree Foundation, pp 12-30.

Equality Tribunal (2006) 'DEC-E2005/021 Full case report: Healy -v- National Car Testing Service Limited' (www.equalitytribunal.ie/ index.asp?locID=29&docID=108).

European Council (2000) 'Presidency Conclusions: Lisbon European Council', No 200/1/100, Brussels (http://ue.eu.int/ueDocs/cms_Data/ docs/pressData/en/ec/00100-r1.en0.htm).

Felstead, A., Krahn, H. and Powell, M. (1999) 'Young and old at risk. Comparative trends in "non-standard" patterns of employment in Canada and the United Kingdom', *International Journal of Manpower*, vol 20, no 5, pp 277-96.

Ford, G. (2005) *Am I Still Needed? Guidance and Learning for Older Adults*, Derby: Centre for Guidance Studies.

Grattan, P. (2005) *Age Legislation 2006 and Training. A Briefing Note*, London: Third Age Employment Network.

Green, A. (2002) 'The many faces of lifelong learning: recent education policy trends in Europe', *Journal of Education Policy*, vol 17, no 6, pp 611-26.

Hayward, B., Taylor, S., Smith, N. and Davies, G. (1997) *Evaluation of the Campaign for Older Workers*, London: The Stationery Office.

Herriot, P., Hirsh, W. and Reilly, P. (1998) *Trust and Transition. Managing Today's Employment Relationship*, Chichester: John Wiley & Sons.

Hillage, J., Loukas, G., Newton, B. and Tamkin, P. (2004) *Platform for Progression: Employer Training Pilots: Year 2 Evaluation Report*, Brighton: Institute for Employment Studies.

Hirsh, W. and Jackson, C. (2004) *Managing Careers in Large Organisations*, London, The Work Foundation.

HM Government (2005a) *Skills: Getting on in Business, Getting on at Work*, Norwich: The Stationery Office.

HM Government (2005b) *Opportunity Age: Meeting the Challenges of Ageing in the 21st Century*, London: DWP.

Humphrey, A., Costigan, P., Pickering, K., Stratford, N. and Barnes, M. (2003) *Factors Affecting the Labour Market Participation of Older Workers*, Leeds: Corporate Document Services.

Irving, P., Steels, J. and Hall, N. (2005) *Factors Affecting the Labour Market Participation of Older Workers: Qualitative Research*, Leeds: Corporate Document Services.

Learning and Skills Council (2005) *Priorities for Success: Funding for Learning and Skills 2006-2008*, Coventry: Learning and Skills Council.

Leeson, G.W. and Harper, S.H. (2005) *Examples of International Case Law on Age Discrimination in Employment*, Sheffield: DWP/Age Partnership Group.

Maurer, T.J. and Rafuse, N.E. (2001) 'Learning, not litigating: managing employee development and avoiding claims of age discrimination', *Academy of Management Executive*, vol 15, no 4, pp 110-21.

NAO (National Audit Office) (2004) *Report by the Comptroller and Auditor-General*, London: The Stationery Office.

Newton, B., Hurstfield, J., Miller, L. and Bates, P. (2005) *Training a Mixed-Age Workforce: Practical Tips and Guidance*, Sheffield: Age Partnership Group/DWP.

NIACE (National Institute of Adult and Continuing Education), *Older and Bolder Initiative* (www.niace.org.uk/research/older_bolder/default.htm).

O'Cinneide, C. (2005) *Age Discrimination and European Law*, Luxembourg: Office for Official Publications of the European Communities.

Papadopoulos, G. (2002) 'Lifelong learning – expectations and risks', in D. Istance, H.G. Schuetze and T. Schuller (eds) *International Perspectives on Lifelong Learning: From Recurrent Education to the Knowledge Society*, Buckingham: Society for Research into Higher Education/Open University Press, pp 39-46.

Platman, K. (2005) 'Extensions to working lives: the case of information technology professionals', Symposium paper, British Society of Gerontology 34th Annual Scientific Meeting, 14-16 July, University of Keele.

Rose, M. (2002) 'IT professionals and organisational ascendancy: theory and empirical critique', *New Technology, Work and Employment*, vol 17, no 3, pp 154-69.

Schuller, T. (2003) 'Age equality in access to education', in S. Fredman and S. Spencer (eds) *Age as an Equality Issue: Legal and Policy Perspectives*, Oxford: Hart, pp 117-43.

Schuller, T. and Bostyn, A.M. (1992) *Learning: Education, Training and Information in the Third Age*, The Carnegie Inquiry into the Third Age Research Paper No 3, London: Centurion Press Limited.

Schuller, T., Schuetze, H.G. and Istance, D. (2002) 'From recurrent education to the knowledge society: an introduction', in D. Istance, H.G. Schuetze and T. Schuller (eds) *International Perspectives on Lifelong Learning: From Recurrent Education to the Knowledge Society*, Buckingham: Society for Research into Higher Education/Open University Press, pp 1-21.

Taylor, P. (2001) 'Analysis of ways to improve employment opportunities for older workers', Report to the European Commission (http://europa.eu.int/comm/employment_social/international_cooperation/docs/eu_japan_symposium9/doc_taylor_en.pdf).

Taylor, P. and Urwin, P. (2001) 'Age and participation in vocational education and training', *Work, Employment and Society*, vol 15, no 4, pp 763-79.

Taylor, P. and Walker, A. (1994) 'The ageing workforce: employers' attitudes towards older workers', *Work, Employment and Society*, vol 8, no 4, pp 569-91.

TEC (Training and Enterprise Councils) (1991) *Training for Older Workers*, Sheffield: Employment Department.

Urwin, P. (2003) *Age Matters: A Review of Existing Survey Evidence*, London: DTI.

von Nordheim, F. (2004) 'Responding well to the challenge of an ageing and shrinking workforce. European Union policies in support of member state efforts to retain, reinforce and re-integrate older workers in employment', *Social Policy and Society*, vol 3, no 2, pp 145-53.

Warnes, T. and John, A. (2005) *Facts and Misunderstandings about Demography and the Workforce*, Sheffield: DWP/Age Partnership Group.

Warr, P. and Birdi, K. (1998) 'Employee age and voluntary development activity', *International Journal of Training and Development*, vol 2, no 3, pp 190-204.

White, M., Hill, S., Mills, C. and Smeaton, D. (2004) *Managing to Change: British Workplaces and the Future of Work*, Basingstoke: Palgrave Macmillan.

FOURTEEN

Ageing and employment: looking back, looking forward

Patrick Grattan

Introduction

This contribution is based on my experience of setting up and running TAEN, The Age and Employment Network, formerly known as the Third Age Employment Network. It was founded in 1998 as a not-for-profit enterprise and registered charity to find ways of making the labour market operate more effectively for people in mid- and later life. It is sponsored by and co-located with Help the Aged. Its members now include over 250 organisations, made up of employers, training providers, colleges, recruitment and employment agencies, voluntary and community organisations, public agencies at national, regional and local level, individuals, unions, employment lawyers, think tanks and others. Drawing on their experience, TAEN is able to play an influential part in all relevant public policy work.

In this chapter I look first of all back over the changes that have taken place in the eight years that TAEN has been operating. I then look at some of the major themes that must underpin plans for extending working life and for changing the pattern of retirement.

1998-2006: the changing perspective

The momentum for the foundation of TAEN was the feeling of deep frustration felt by many people who found themselves cast on the shelf well before they thought they were ready to be put there. Nobody else seemed to be interested in their fate. We were still in an era that Adair Turner and his colleagues on the Pensions Commission were subsequently to describe as a 'fool's paradise' (Pensions Commission, 2004).

Unlike the previous Conservative government, after coming to power in 1997 the Labour government started to take an interest in age and employment. New Deal 50 plus was in preparation to add to the New Deal for Young People. A Code of Good Practice on age and employment was issued. However, all this hardly registered on the Richter scale of political and business interest. Youth was a leitmotif of New Labour and ending youth unemployment an understandable central objective.

Now, at the time of writing in 2006, there is a very different perspective. There is widespread recognition that age and demographics is an important dimension of the labour market, that patterns and stages of life and work are changing.

Strong employment record

In 1998 the 30-year decline in employment of over-50s men had halted. The extent to which the employment rate had actually started to improve from the mid-1990s was so small that it had not registered widely.

Since then there has been an impressive record of steady growth in employment for all ages and in particular of the over-50s. Two out of three people contributing to the increase in the labour force to its current all-time high are over 50, including the fastest recorded growth among those over state pension age. The population in the 50-64 age cohort has been rising since 1998. This means that of the 1.2 million increase in workers over 50, some 800,000 represent absorption of the increased population of people over the age of 50, while the additional 400,000 represent an increase in the employment rate of people over the age of 50 from 64% to almost 71%.

Meanwhile, there has been a continuing change in the gender balance of the workforce. There was a massive drop in the employment rate of men over the age of 50 from the 1970s to the mid-1990s. Employment of women of all ages was increasing. The rate of increase of over-50s women was slower – if the growth had been as rapid as the growth among under-50s, there would be 250,000 more women over 50 in work by now. An interesting future issue will be to see how patterns of work among women now reaching their 50s and 60s are influenced by their career experience as younger women, which is quite different from their mothers' generation.

However, because of the increasing population in this age group, the improved employment position does not mean that the numbers of people over 50 who are 'economically inactive' (to use the jargon) have fallen. They have risen slightly. Second, most of the improvement has been in sectors such as retailing and financial services in low-skilled or routine employment. This has not met the need for quality work using the wide range of skills and experience of people who have 25+ years' career behind them and do not want 'any old job' (see below).

Nevertheless, the employment trends do create a different context from the late 1990s. Progress has been made – age and employment is a significant rather than a hidden issue.

Employer action

Action by employers has clearly contributed to the improvement in the unemployment rate of the over-50s. By definition, more people are being retained or recruited in their 50s and 60s than was the case in the 1990s. The cost of early voluntary redundancy (one of the main drivers for earlier retirement ages in the 1980s and 1990s) has become prohibitive for over-stretched pension funds, although exception is still made for a minority of senior executives as an aid to succession management.

A considerable body of good practice in all age recruitment and retention has built up (see the government's Age Positive website for some examples from employers large and small – www.agepositive.gov.uk). The Employers Forum on Age (EFA) members have set one such example (see www.efa.org.uk), although the EFA itself has avoided any suggestion that its members subscribe to certain employment standards or represent a more open door for older jobseekers. None of this existed in the 1990s.

The change should not, however, be exaggerated. The gap between statements of intent and day-to-day practice remains great. In large businesses the good intentions of corporate human resource departments do not translate overnight into operational practice by line management. Awareness of demographic change is limited. Senior management remains convinced that older workers cost more, are less productive and are sick more often. No amount of direct factual evidence to the contrary makes much dent in entrenched stereotypical thinking.

The views of the Confederation of British Industry (CBI) on retirement ages and legislation carry an implicit assumption that older workers are more problematic to manage than younger workers. Yet there is a body of positive qualitative and quantitative evidence on the commercial benefit to companies that have deliberately broadened the age profile of their workforce. No company has yet reported disastrous consequences of employing more people over 50; rather they have reported a win–win situation for employees and employer.

The position of the majority of UK businesses that have less than 50 employees is paradoxical. There is considerable evidence that they are less 'ageist' than large businesses and public sector employers where grade-equals-status-equals-age rules. They will normally employ the best person for the job without a thought for age. At the same time, they may be happily unconscious of age legislation and such matters as fixed retirement ages.

Life expectancy, health and wealth

Another change in the past few years is that we have become aware of the increased speed in the growth of life expectancy. With the benefit of hindsight we were all (including the actuarial profession), sleep walking for a few decades. The Pensions Commission administered a reality check in its first report in October 2004. Admittedly, the pace of improvement in mortality rates has recently accelerated. But forecasts of future life expectancy have been accelerating even faster in 2005. It is now hard to disentangle what is real change and what is speed of revision of forecasts.

Policy issues on age and employment are ill served by the evidence base and confusion surrounding life expectancy forecasts. Average life expectancy at birth and average life expectancy at age 65 are misunderstood and frequently confused (average life expectancy at birth factors in the one in 10 who people die by the age of 65). Even broadsheet newsprint, not to mention the tabloid scare headlines, reports hopelessly misleading messages about life expectancy. Life expectancy among middle-aged people is widely underestimated by most people and is not factored into their decision making. Official statements about average life expectancy are not believed, in part on the understandable grounds that none of us knows where we fall relative to the average. A separate discussion is needed on how to generate a more realistic view of potential life expectancy, and on how to relate data on average life expectancies to individual mortality risk, which is what matters for each of us.

Meanwhile health is improving. It is regularly observed that today's 70-year-olds are yesterday's 60-year-olds and are behaving accordingly. The scope for more years of working life, whether paid or unpaid, is enhanced compared with previous generations. The duration of healthy old age is increasing roughly in parallel with actual life expectancy, although the experts cannot agree how close the parallel is. In part, this is because health is a self-defined and reported condition, unlike death.

One important area that has remained unchanged over the past eight years is that of inequality of life and old age in British society. Despite nine years of Labour government, most social and economic indices do not show any narrowing of gaps, whether in educational attainment, income and asset accumulation, health or life expectancy. The poor, including lone parents and older people, have become less poor and have been aided in this by the tax credit system, but the better-off have continued to become better off at a faster rate, thus widening the gap. This is very significant for policy on age and employment because the circumstances of those with resources and choice and those without are so important.

It continues to be the case that those who retire earliest (because of good final salary pension schemes) are the best off in retirement, while those who retire latest (manual and unqualified workers with no savings who carry on until state pension age) are least well off in retirement. A total of 36% of all current occupational pension payments are made to those who have not yet reached state pension age. It seems perverse that those who retire earliest are rewarded for that. It would make better economic and social sense if those who worked longer were rewarded more for their efforts in retirement.

Retirement incomes

There is also a new reality of the economics of retirement income. Rightly or wrongly, it is now accepted that we cannot expect to see again the rates of return on investment in the stock and bond markets that prevailed for most of the last 30 years of the 20th century.

Whether we call it a 'pension crisis' or not, the world has changed since 1998, despite the partial recovery from the stock market drop of 2000-02. It is widely expected that the era of final salary pensions schemes is ending and will not be rebuilt, unless it is for a small elite of directors and public sector workers. The most common alternative is defined contribution schemes. On current calculations they yield a retirement income half what they would have done five years ago because of lower returns and increased life expectancy. It changes one's perspective to be told at the age of 60 that a pension scheme that you thought would give you £12,000 a year will now only give you £6,000.

In addition, there is a whole new perspective on pension risks. Most people with employer pensions genuinely thought that they were risk-free. It is only in the past few years that we have discovered that there is no such thing as a risk-free pension scheme.

This leads to a new and understandable doubt about how to plan for retirement. The high rates of return up to 2000 shielded us all from the reality of pension economics – they allowed the pensions industry to take a handsome cut for running our pensions while still giving most of us on such schemes a good deal. Lower returns have brought home that around half the total value of a private pension scheme will be used up on remunerating the pension manager, leaving insufficient to pay an acceptable level of pension. The economics of small or average-sized pension schemes run by the private sector, as opposed to the government, no longer make sense. This is what the Pensions Commission has had to grapple with, leading to its proposal of a National Pensions Savings Scheme.

State pensions

In the early days of the Labour administration, there was widespread support for the move to a means-tested state pension system. Concentrating public funds on those who most needed support made sense. The system of a standard state pension, more or less adequate to support a simple life in retirement, had operated since Beveridge and the 1940s (Beveridge, 1942), and was reckoned to have run its course. The 1996 Commission for Social Justice set out an agenda for New Labour for what was originally known as negative income tax but became tax or pension credits.

The new selective benefits and pension route has proved a classic example of a good policy purpose undermined by delivery problems such as:

- administrative machinery that could not cope;
- incomprehensibility to the general public and specifically to those who most need it;
- the spread of means testing on a massive scale that had not been envisaged;
- the decline of the basic pension to a risible level relative to average earnings.

The options are to stand by the New Labour means-tested model or to revert to the universal model of state safety net for those who do not have their own resources. This is at the heart of how the government responds to the recommendations of the Pensions Commission, with Chancellor of the Exchequer Gordon Brown maintaining the validity of the means-tested selective model and Prime Minister Tony Blair advocating a return to the universal model, albeit adjusted to suit women as well as men. Both have difficulties incentivising personal savings for retirement. One way or the other there is a transitional period from dependence on help to self-reliance. Savers are either penalised for saving by having a universal benefit taxed away, or the means-tested pension recipient is penalised for saving through the phasing out of means-tested benefit for those who do not need it.

Welfare reform

In the late 1990s, there was little realisation just what a massive move there had been in the pattern of welfare payments with a ten-fold growth in sickness benefit recipients. TAEN and Steve Fothergill of Sheffield Hallam University started to talk about the 'hidden unemployed'. The government, media and business seemed unable to realise (and are still unable to realise to a great extent) that the unemployment rate is no longer a good guide to the labour market or the state of the economy. There were eight people over the age of 50 dependent on Incapacity Benefit for every one registered unemployed. There were (and are) more over-50s on Incapacity Benefit than on the entire unemployment register.

It is symptomatic that when New Deal 50 plus was introduced David Blunkett, then responsible for education and employment, decided not to impose any form of compulsion to participate beyond an initial interview. Was there any reason to treat the over-50s differently from the under-50s? Many over-50s jobseekers would argue so, given their experience of trying to find work appropriate to their skills and experience.

Now, in 2006, the flow of people onto Incapacity Benefit is declining. There have been good results from pilots to provide in-depth help to people on Incapacity Benefit to get back to work, with the response being equally strong among those in their 50s as those in their 30s. The Department of Work and Pensions believes that a million of the 2.7 million people on Incapacity Benefit would like to be working. There is recognition that the focus of policy should be on what people can do rather than what they cannot do, and that only a modest proportion of people are unable to do any kind of work.

Mental illness is the largest single cause for being on Incapacity Benefit. This is probably the hardest area to tackle, most prone to prejudice and fear on the part of employers, and most hard to assess for sustained work capability over time.

One consequence of the increased role of Incapacity Benefit is that the distinction in the welfare system between pre- and post-state pension age is not very significant. There are differences in the regime, in particular in some sense of obligation to try to find work (which may strengthen in future). But many, especially men in locations where up to 50% of over-50s are 'on the sick', slide fairly seamlessly over to the pension system from the welfare system. The greater significance of state pension age is for those who are healthy, in work but without savings or potential retirement income, who have no option but to work until they can claim a pension.

Age legislation

In 1998 there was little or no prospect of age legislation comparable to existing legislation on gender, 'race' and disability discrimination, despite evidence that age was the most commonly experienced barrier to opportunity in work and learning. Labour figures made some commitments to legislation prior to 1990, but age legislation did not make it into the election manifesto and the government subsequently vigorously defended a voluntarist approach, with a code of conduct for employers.

By one of those quirks of circumstance, we owe it to Jorge Haider of Austria that for the past six years we have had age discrimination legislation on our agenda. The emergence of power sharing in government with his right-wing party sent a shiver through the European Union (EU). There was a sudden willingness to agree an Anti-Discrimination Directive in autumn 2000 on 'race', disability, age, religion/belief and sexual orientation. The vastly different attitudes to these subjects among member states were put aside in the interests of being seen to take action. Whether the UK government agreed to this against its better judgement or because it could see that the voluntarist approach to age was having little impact is not known. It did take the lead in arguing that age legislation had all sorts of difficult consequences and that member states should therefore have six years in which to transpose it to national law, unlike the other topics that had to be actioned within a three-year period.

Bodies like TAEN roundly criticised this delay, which meant that for a further six years people would have no redress against direct age barriers in work as the great majority of employers would not change age-based practices until the 11th hour or until after the legislation came into force.

There has, however, been an upside. While any issue remains unresolved, it remains to a degree in the limelight; once settled, everyone loses interest. So we have had six years, three rounds of government consultation, a flow of academic and other studies and debate on age discrimination legislation. The extreme contrast to this approach is that of France, where a one-line announcement in the *Official Journal* added age legislation to French law without anyone taking a jot of notice. The result in the UK has been to put a spotlight on many of the issues of the interaction of age and employment/training. It has been instructive because thinking has moved on since 2000. The terms of the Directive, in particular Article 6 on potential age-based employment decisions that might be justifiable, look very dated and no longer relevant.

Some may criticise this as an example of the UK 'gold plating' EU legislation and making everything more complicated than it need be. It has certainly consumed a good deal of time of the leading organisations involved. TAEN's view is that it has been a constructive part of the culture change, although so far one limited to a small group of experts.

It is often asked whether age is different from the other forms of discrimination on which we have legislation. This question will be relevant when we have a new Commission on Equality and Human Rights in 2007, replacing the existing Equal Opportunities Commission, Commission for Racial Equality and Disability Rights Commission, and taking on responsibility for the three new equality strands including age. An obvious observation is that age changes with time while other characteristics do not.

What the work on legislation in recent years has shown is that, despite widespread experience of age-based barriers and their impact on people's lives, there is less public involvement than in issues of 'race', gender or disability. Response to government consultations has been limited. There is nothing like the broad front of disability organisations that worked so hard in the 1990s to achieve disability legislation and that continue to work on its improvement. Many of those whose prospects are curtailed by age-based decisions accept it as their lot or conclude that they have 'had their turn'. There is no major head of steam from those excluded. As much as anything, the case for legislation comes from the economic imperative for change. It is not so much an equality issue as a business and economic change that legislation will help drive forward. In this the balance is different from the existing equalities legislation.

2006-12: what next?

The government has set out an 'aspiration' (not a target) to raise the employment rate of people of working age from the current 75% to 80% by an unspecified date. Given that the employment rate of 25- to 49-year-olds is on average already over 80%, this means raising the participation rate of those currently under-represented. That includes neighbourhoods of high social and economic deprivation, minority ethnic groups, disabled people and the over-50s. There will be more people in the population aged over 50 and fewer under 50. Achieving the government's aspiration requires at least another one million people over

50 in work on top of the 1.2 million already added. This appears to us eminently achievable, subject to the overall state of the economy and avoidance of a major recession. The 2006 government forecasts of the workforce show the majority of the growth in the next 15 years being workers in their 50s and 60s.

The big issue is whether it is going to be achieved in a way that brings satisfaction and reward to workers, employers and the economy. Most of the issues addressed in the second half of this chapter relate to that. TAEN believes that there are a series of preconditions that have to be met if longer working lives are to be fruitful and a positive contribution to adequate retirement quality of life. If not, the tabloid headline 'forced to work till you drop' may be nearer the mark.

In the discourse of labour markets and public policy, the participants, including the present author, are almost entirely people with degree level qualifications. They may not think themselves rich, but they have mostly experienced variety in their working lives, they know how to seek out opportunity and change and they often have some form of occupational pension to look forward to. Life may not be a bed of roses and for some health, family and financial problems will be major worries. But collectively they cannot put themselves in the shoes of those whose working lives have been largely repetitive, boring, unrewarding personally and financially, and outside their own control. Often those without choice or personal autonomy live in a dysfunctional personal environment and there is little or no tradition of seeking out help and advice from unknown sources.

TAEN is acutely conscious that policies and ideas about work and its place in life imply moral judgements about what is good for other people and generalisations about wide segments of society. The rest of this chapter discusses some of the tricky issues about making the job market a better place for people in mid- and later working life. Cultural and attitudinal change will have to take place among individuals, companies and government to achieve this. Discussion of these changes necessarily takes place at a high level of generality. We should not forget that each individual's set of circumstances is different, and it is the diversity of people, not age cohort stereotypes, that matter.

Personal barriers: does age confer any special status?

There is plenty of evidence of age barriers in recruitment or advancement in work resulting from employer attitudes. But there is also evidence that employers find it hard to recruit people in their 50s or 60s. They say that it is the attitude of the jobseeker that is the main barrier.

This touches on one of the dilemmas in making a success of the job market in mid-life. What should jobseekers be prepared to accept? What should be expected of them, whether their background is manual and elementary occupations or professional and managerial grades?

It is easier with 20-year-olds. Go out and do temporary work, gain any kind of experience (it's all good for you), don't do nothing – (although there is a separate issue about the scope of the labour market to provide jobs that challenge the ever-increasing number of graduate-level entrants). Get a foot in the door and work on the principle that one thing can lead to another.

Should we expect the over-50s to do the same? How should we judge what they should be prepared to do? It is clear that those who are most flexible about what they are prepared to do are most likely to get back into work. Those who start by defining all the things they are not prepared to do are least likely to ever work again. Those who approach Jobcentres convinced that they cannot help them with jobs to match their qualifications and experience will find it hard to get help.

If we take equality of treatment regardless of age to its logical conclusion, there is no reason why employers should treat someone with 30 years of work and life experience behind them differently just because they are 50. Age does not confer any special status. Employers like enthusiasm and commitment to turn a hand to whatever needs to be done, not an outlook based on what the world owes us because of who we are. Should we admire, as I have, the ex-army officer packing frozen chicken legs in a food plant ('sheer hell') in the West Country because that's all that was going and he needed to work?

However, common sense says that people deserve to have jobs that use their skills and experience. It is wrong that so many immigrant workers, women and disabled people are under-employed in jobs far below their qualification level. The same is true of older people who should not have to accept under-employment just because of their age. They are not the same as school leavers. They have a different financial threshold of how much they need to be paid to make work worthwhile, as compared with a 20-year-old. After decades of working life they have earned a right to be considered. They have a different risk profile as retirement approaches compared with 20-year-olds.

Many of the most frustrated non-workers in their 50s and 60s are indeed the most qualified. They know that lack of management and professional skills is always cited as one of the key constraints on British business. Yet their chances of getting back into a management job comparable to their last job are close to zero. They know that, despite the progress in the employment rate described above, putting their date of birth on the CV is fatal.

Added to that, duration out of work becomes a self-fulfilling and self-reinforcing barrier with the passage of time. In theory, a few years' break in employment could be seen as a stimulus to a new career with a new and fresh perspective. Instead, a period away from the workforce means not getting an interview.

These are issues throughout the workforce, whether at a highly skilled or relatively elementary level. The initial training and work experience of each of us has a formative influence on our perception of ourselves, even if we later go on to do different things. Once an assembly line fitter, always an assembly line fitter. This may go some way to explain the impact of self-identity and self-esteem in limiting imagination about career change. The majority of non-working men over 50 would not consider working in the sectors where job growth is currently strong – retailing, personal services and call centres.

These are not easy issues to resolve but progress is needed to free up the labour market so that those who have been formed by their initial training 30 years ago can respond to today's labour market. In summary, the way forward has to be a subtle mix on the part of the jobseeker, aiming for jobs that make good use of skills and experience but not ruling too much out, at least as a stepping-stone. An important contribution can come from career advice and reskilling (see below).

Today nearly 100% of those in temporary work are under the age of 30. We would like to see the growth of a tradition of 'temping' at all ages. Interim management and consulting are both a kind of temping and are common among professional people in later careers. More widespread temping would create flexibility for employer and employee to test new work environments, to act as a stepping-stone to longer-term employment, and to bridge the gulf between the economically inactive and the workplace.

Personal barriers: the role of career advice

When older people seek advice about what to do next in their life it is usually done informally, among friends and colleagues. Few people have heard of the government provision of adult career advice. As already mentioned, many people, especially those who most need it, are unwilling, not to say incapable, of a making a cold call contact with an unknown person or agency. Again, this is more true of men than women. A regular experience on the TAEN information line is talking to a woman ringing on behalf of her husband who cannot face calling.

Those who extend their working life are most commonly people who continue in the same line of work. The majority of those working after state pension age are in the same kind of job as they did earlier. This seems paradoxical when what so many people want is change, a move away from work they have done for long enough or for too long. When people say they want to retire, they more commonly mean they want to do something different. Career advice should come into play for those who do not want to go on doing the same thing and instead seek change. Given the limited numbers of people who manage to launch a new career in mid-life, there is much scope for improvement.

TAEN's belief is that individual choice rather than force of circumstance should play the main part in making a success of longer and varied working lives. This demands a change in the world of career advice. It should be as natural for a 40- or 50-year-old to seek career advice as for an 18-year-old. It is already considered natural for people coming out of the armed forces because the natural span of a military career is shorter and there are well-established agencies to help the transition to a second career. It should be equally natural for us all, but this will take time to achieve.

How much this should depend on government-run services is a matter for debate. Perhaps the natural growth of informal systems in work and social settings will be the main way forward. The problem with the work setting is that life and work options beyond dedication to the current employer are often a taboo subject. Work-based career planning seldom focuses on the potential to work and develop elsewhere. The irony is that workplaces that do this achieve a higher retention and satisfaction rating, contrary to expectation.

The Jobcentre is the largest single career advice service in the country. It is inevitably a formula-, rule- and target-driven organisation, but full of committed front-line workers who operate in difficult circumstances, often with individual cases that go way beyond their remit (or pay). It runs a range of courses for jobseekers. The fear is that too many jobseekers are cycled through programmes that presume that they are open to fresh fields of work when in fact they are not. Is there a need for a programme that seeks to move those with a fixed mindset on what they can do on to a fresh starting point – admittedly easier said than done. This is territory fraught with the dangers of telling people what is good for them.

Quality of work and work environment

An important employer contribution of this changing career scene must relate to the quality of work offered. This covers:

- the basic truths of good operational management that make all the difference to job satisfaction, whatever the job (the largest single reason for quitting or not returning, especially in the public sector, is dissatisfaction with management and frequent reorganisations and initiatives);
- the potential to advance, as a quid pro quo, for accepting an entry-level job at a modest level;
- proactive occupational health policies, job design and work environments to promote good health in mid- and later life, rather than damage it;
- terms and conditions of work that match business need with the desires and priorities of people in the middle stages of life.

There is huge potential for development in this area. Ill health is the most common cause of early retirement. Yet work in appropriate circumstances is also one of the strongest promoters of good health. Those who extend their working life tend to live longer.

The great majority of jobs taken up by over-50s are low-skilled and modestly paid. Supermarket work is the obvious example. There may be nothing wrong with that and it is the reality of the job market. Given creative employment practices, it can meet the needs of people who are not looking for jobs at the same level of pressure and responsibility as in the past, as well as offer flexible working hours. But it leaves unresolved the issue of all those who aspire to use higher-level skills and experience. It also plays to the conventional image of low-paid female employment rather than catering for women who need to build a stronger financial position for themselves in mid-life in preparation for retirement.

Retraining, reskilling for a fresh start

Demographic change and longer working lives present a new challenge to the pattern of lifelong learning. It is a challenge that has not yet been widely understood. If working lives last longer, then the need for change and variety through their course grows. Not many people will want to be a postman or postwoman, teacher, plumber, welder or manager for 40 years or more at a stretch. At the same time, the life span of many skills is foreshortening as technological change accelerates. What people want out of working life also changes over time.

From this it is evident that the model of foundation learning and training up to age 19 or the early 20s to last a lifetime is outdated. Encouragingly, there are more adults engaged in some form of learning, mainly part-time community-based learning that does not lead to qualifications, than in the mid-1990s. It is not known how many of these learners are motivated by employability rather than 'leisure' pursuits; it is not always easy to segment learners in this way.

Despite this, we still live with a model of government and employer-supported foundation learning to last a lifetime. The budget of adult learning funded by the government is fixed by what is left over after the needs of the under-19s have been met. There is a strong and rightful push to increase participation in learning up to age 19, but this is at the expense of adult learning. For every under-19 in government-funded learning there are 10 fewer adult learners because of the ratio of full-time to part-time costs.

Further education learners of all ages do benefit from some government subsidy. But adult learning grants are limited to those under 30 and funding of apprenticeships is limited to under-25s. The numbers of people in mid-career gaining new qualifications are insignificant. The amount of employer funding of training after 25, with the exception of statutory health and safety and job induction training, is minimal. The take-up of the training grant in New Deal 50 plus has been way below expectations, partly because it only applies once people have started a new job and no longer have the time to do it.

So, retraining for a new career in mid- and later life (including for women returners) is almost entirely limited to those who can afford to pay for it and have the wherewithal to live while they are doing it. There are a very few exceptions, such as the Department for Education and Skills' scheme to fund training of maths and science teachers because of the shortage of supply, and the Learning and Skills Council scheme to train welders to become gas fitters because of a dire shortage of the latter some years ago.

To undertake reskilling as a step to a new career also requires a reasonable assurance of a job at the end of it. It has been the experience of some that they dedicate the effort and resources to training only to find at the end that it is no easier to get a job because of their age and/or lack of prior experience.

Neither government nor employers can afford to pay for all the training that adults may want to do. Efforts to improve performance of schools and meet targets for school leavers, and to expand the higher education sector, have much higher political priority than adult learning. But unless we make a major shift in the balance of our efforts, the demographics of the workforce are going to catch us out. Ministerial talk of a globally competitive workforce will be whistling in the wind.

Making this change also means rethinking the relevance of courses and qualification design for all ages. Learning undertaken by adults is most commonly based on courses and qualifications designed for under-19s. The whole skills agenda is based on a qualification system built up from foundation learning. There has been a lot of work on accreditation of prior learning and informal learning. But there is a massive mismatch between adults in mid-career and the scheme of full National Vocational Qualifications. The potential of many people in mid-life to take up a new occupation or return to a former one, for example, nursing, is impeded by a long, laborious gold-plated approach. The motive for this, quality assurance, is laudable but it is having major unintended consequences for the training of adults.

This has to be addressed in order to achieve a fruitful prolongation of working life. It is a familiar sensation that neither we nor our employer can imagine what job we could do, other than the one we are doing now. This is the familiar career dead end. Learning of almost any kind is one route out of the cul-de-sac.

The status syndrome in large organisations – the undulating career pattern

TAEN's aim is to replace the cliff-edge view of work and retirement with an undulating pattern. The cliff edge implies that we climb through a hierarchy until reaching the highest point when we fall off the edge into retirement. This was nurtured by final salary pension schemes, which are now fading away.

An intrinsic and healthy part of working life is the ambition to increase earnings, to compete and advance up a career and power ladder. It is hard to imagine that this could be entirely separated from status, grade and age. Most of us need to earn more; choice over work–life balance and lifestyle is the privilege of a small minority.

Yet implicit in demographic change and longer working life is a more fluid situation. Changing pension and tax rules will make it easier to mix and match work and leisure and downshift without ending working life. In the US about a third of all people take a bridging job between their main career and full retirement.

There is a great deal of talk about flexible working in the UK. The evidence so far shows that there has been limited movement. Those who engage in job shares, part-time working, career breaks or study leave are seen as less committed and ambitious, even though there are more examples showing that these are win–win arrangements for business and employees.

We have a long way to travel to diminish the importance of hierarchies and create undulating careers. These ideas are profoundly counter-cultural in large public and private sector businesses. But there are characteristics for some people (certainly not all) in the second half of their careers on which we can build, for example:

- a desire to get back to 'front-line work', doing something practical, making something, as opposed to the years spent in people management and organisational change;
- a greater interest in flexible working and a more balanced view of the role of work alongside the other dimensions of life;
- a more settled view of where we want to get to and what we want to get out of working life – perhaps a realistic acceptance of our potential;
- a strong attachment to the social role of working life;
- a reduction, for some, of the financial pressures of bringing up a family and paying a mortgage.

It was exactly some of these characteristics that DIY retailer B&Q tapped into with its scheme to man stores (it was very largely men) with over-50s. TAEN hopes that the next few years will see an increasing number of examples of businesses exploiting this kind of outlook and making inroads into current company hierarchical culture. But this should not be at the expense of opportunity for others who are ambitious to build a first or second career aged 50 and who will resent the idea that the model just described is the only one available.

The government's role

The main hazard in the next few years is that the government will take the lengthening of working life and later retirement for granted. Increased employment of over-50s has been happening very nicely over the past eight years with limited intervention by government, apart from the crucial element of macroeconomic stability and growth. Expenditure on New Deal 50 plus and adult learning in mid-life has been small change compared with programmes for young people, lone parents and minority ethnic groups. Health and education budgets are politically preponderant and public expenditure is tightening. The budget cuts in adult learning have already been described above. The Department for Work and Pensions received the worst budget settlement in 2005 of any government department. Plans for welfare to work programmes have been put back as a result. So all government programmes that can bolster rewarding longer working lives are low down the pecking order.

There will be a fundamental review of public expenditure in 2006-07. The Chancellor of the Exchequer, Gordon Brown, has set out five big themes for this. One of them is the impact of demographic change and an ageing population. One element of that will be to ask seriously what the consequences of demographic change are for spending priorities. It needs thinking through.

A total of 20% of the UK workforce work in the public sector. The decision reached in October 2005 with public sector unions to retain pension age of 60 for all existing employees, while understandable, creates an unsustainable gulf between the public and private sector. Public sector workers will continue to retire earlier than others because they can access a risk-free, final salary pension based on employer contributions, regardless of their increasing life expectancy. To the extent that central and local government cannot afford this, the tax-paying population will fund it. It would appear imperative that public and private sectors are more closely aligned and that incentives to extend working life and save more apply across the whole economy.

It will also be for government to make a success of the new legislation on age discrimination. This means backing it up with clear guidance and good dispute resolution procedures so that only essential cases end up in employment tribunals. There must be a high quality and resourced body to promote the legislation, provide advice to the general public and to employers, and to support redress for those who have suffered from unacceptable employment practices.

Conclusion

So, in summary, TAEN looks forward to 2012 when it hopes to see:

* at least a million more people over 50 in work, many of whom will be over state pension age;
* a decline in the use of fixed retirement ages by employers, so that in practice when we retire is a matter of mutual agreement between employer and employee (as it already is for many);
* a spread of flexible pathways from main career to full retirement with gradual transitions in ways that will benefit both employer and employee;
* the declining significance of state pension age as a single point defining the end of working life and beginning of retirement as choice about when people take the state pension becomes common;

- a secure and stable settlement of state and private pension systems that is comprehensible to the public and gives a clear incentive to save rather than spend everything now;
- many more businesses where the age profile of the workforce more closely matches the age profile of their customers;
- a modest flow of employment tribunal cases on age discrimination because the great majority of organisations will respond to the new legislative framework and legal action will be last resort;
- a sea change in the culture of advice, debate, and choice on mid-life career change;
- a great expansion of opportunities in the workplace and in government programmes to train in flexible ways, either to return to a former occupation or start a new one.

References

Beveridge, Sir W. (1942) *Social Insurance and Allied Services* ('the Beveridge Report'), Cmnd 6064, London, Her Majesty's Stationery Office.
Pensions Commission (2004) *Pensions: Challenges and Choices: The First Report of the Pensions Commission,* London, The Stationery Office.

Index

C

D

Also available from
The Policy Press

Social Policy Review 17
Analysis and debate in social policy, 2005
Edited by Martin Powell, Linda Bauld and Karen Clarke

Paperback £24.99 US$42.50

ISBN-10 1 86134 669 7

ISBN-13 978 1 86134 669 8

216 x 148mm 312 pages June 2005

Social Policy Review 16
Analysis and debate in social policy, 2004
Edited by Nick Ellison, Linda Bauld and Martin Powell

Paperback £24.99 US$42.50

ISBN-10 1 86134 581 X

ISBN-13 978 1 86134 581 3

216 x 148mm 304 pages July 2004

Social Policy Review 15
UK and international perspectives
*Edited by Catherine Bochel, Nick Ellison and
Martin Powell*

Paperback £19.99 US$36.95

ISBN-10 1 86134 469 4

ISBN-13 978 1 86134 469 4

216 x 148mm 288 pages July 2003

Social Policy Review 14
Developments and debates: 2001-2002
Edited by Rob Sykes, Catherine Bochel and Nick Ellison

Paperback £19.99 US$32.50

ISBN-10 1 86134 377 9

ISBN-13 978 1 86134 377 2

Hardback £50.00 US$75.00

ISBN-10 1 86134 378 7

ISBN-13 978 1 86134 378 9

216 x 148mm 312 pages July 2002

Social Policy Review 13
Developments and debates: 2000-2001
Edited by Rob Sykes, Catherine Bochel and Nick Ellison

Paperback £18.99 US$29.95

ISBN-10 1 86134 291 8

ISBN-13 978 1 86134 291 1

216 x 148mm 308 pages July 2001

To order copies of this publication or any other Policy Press titles please visit **www.policypress.org.uk** or contact:

In the UK and Europe:
Marston Book Services, PO Box 269,
Abingdon, Oxon, OX14 4YN, UK
Tel: +44 (0)1235 465500
Fax: +44 (0)1235 465556
Email: direct.orders@marston.co.uk

In Australia and New Zealand:
DA Information Services,
648 Whitehorse Road Mitcham,
Victoria 3132, Australia
Tel: +61 (3) 9210 7777
Fax: +61 (3) 9210 7788
E-mail: service@dadirect.com.au

In the USA and Canada:
ISBS, 920 NE 58th Street,
Suite 300, Portland, OR
97213-3786, USA
Tel: +1 800 944 6190
(toll free)
Fax: +1 503 280 8832
Email: info@isbs.com